D1443545

TAKING ON GIANTS

Taking on Giants

Fabián Chávez Jr.
and New Mexico Politics

DAVID ROYBAL

UNIVERSITY OF NEW MEXICO PRESS | ALBUQUERQUE

Library of Congress Cataloging-in-Publication Data

Roybal, David, 1952–

Taking on giants : Fabián Chávez, Jr. and New Mexico politics / David Roybal.

p. cm.

Includes bibliographical references.

ISBN 978-0-8263-4436-6 (cloth : alk. paper)

1. Chávez, Fabián, 1924–

2. Legislators—New Mexico—Biography.

3. New Mexico. Legislature. House of Representatives—Biography.

4. Politicians—New Mexico—Biography.

5. Democratic Party (N.M.)—Biography.

6. New Mexico—Politics and government—1951–

7. Chavez family.

8. Governors—New Mexico—History—20th century.

I. Title.

F801.4.C48.R69 2008

328.789092—dc22

[B]

2007049774

Book design and type composition by Melissa Tandysh

Composed in 10.4/13 Minion Pro   ❧   Display type is Caslon Open Face LT Std

It probably has been said more than a million times
but never with more conviction:
I would have been nothing without my darling wife.
Coral Jeanne, it was quite a lifelong dance!

—Fabián Chávez Jr.

CONTENTS

LIST OF ILLUSTRATIONS

PREFACE

Most February mornings in New Mexico are cold, or at least unpredictable. This one, February 24, 1964, at the state capitol in Santa Fe was both. It was a Monday, and the New Mexico Legislature was meeting in its last full day of a special session Democratic Gov. Jack Campbell had called. An opinion just issued by the state attorney general, Earl Hartley, said the body would have to adjourn by noon the following day to comply with the state constitution's thirty-day limit on special legislative sessions.

Lawmakers had thought they could work through midday Wednesday so now there was a rush throughout the building. The legislature had yet to adopt the state budget for the new fiscal year that would begin in June, its principal reason for meeting. Details—and deals—of the $148.7-million budget for days had been hammered out in the powerful Senate Finance Committee. With the session's deadline approaching, the committee chairman, Gordon Melody of San Miguel County, got his panel to vote on the budget so that it could be presented to the full senate for a vote. That done, the measure was passed on to the house of representatives for a hurried review and likely revisions. Any changes would have to be sent back to the senate for concurrence. Meanwhile, senators turned much of their attention to bills that would address needs left unattended the previous year in the 1963 junior college and vocational school acts.

It was not just legislators who were under the gun, reported the *Santa Fe New Mexican*, which was then the only daily newspaper based in the capital city. Campbell, it had been learned, was suffering from high blood pressure.

That might explain his "shows of temper that have offended some staunch supporters," the paper said. It saw fit to tell in the popular column of the period, At the Capitol, that Campbell "was known to take a few drinks when he [served] in the Legislature" to help ease tension. "He seldom drinks in public now" as governor, it was reported in the column, whose only byline was El Chivo, or the goat. Campbell, who represented Chaves County in the legislature before becoming governor, had just undergone an extensive examination at Lovelace Clinic in Albuquerque.

At around nine that Monday morning, the temperature was struggling to break into the thirties after dipping below twenty the night before. Cloudy skies were forecast for outdoors. Indoors, the young senate majority leader, Fabián Chávez Jr., a liberal Santa Fe Democrat, was guiding the legislature's upper chamber through the day's business. "The clock was ticking, and I wanted to make sure we got as much done as we could while the house worked on the budget," Chávez said.

Chávez, as usual, was neatly groomed and impeccably dressed that day even after a long, disappointing weekend just a few blocks down the road on the opposite side of the Santa Fe Plaza. State Democrats had held their preprimary nominating convention at Santa Fe High School's Sweeney Gym on Saturday and Sunday. Politically, Chávez had been on a bold, meteoric ride since he was first elected to the legislature at the age of twenty-six. At age thirty-seven, he became the youngest man ever elected senate majority leader in the state. To do so, he had to overcome years of dominance in the legislature the conservatives from southern and eastern New Mexico had enjoyed. He advanced sweeping legislation that secured major reform of a slow, even corrupt, court system. Forcing even more reform, he took on a rich, arrogant liquor industry that for years had grown accustomed to getting its way from legislators and other state officials. He, along with Campbell, was instrumental in passing legislation that ensured New Mexicans would not be left in the backwater of medical care. Chávez, too, had launched and led the fight in the legislature for civil rights in New Mexico at a time when such efforts were meeting violent opposition around the country. It was a record that later would have him described at once as gentlemanly, tenacious, and perhaps the most productive state legislator in New Mexico history.

Chávez had targeted that year's Democratic preprimary convention to put him on the road to his next major political goal: the U.S. House of Representatives. For years, Chávez had envisioned himself succeeding Democrat Joseph M. Montoya as one of New Mexico's two representatives in the U.S. House. Montoya, after eight years in the House of Representatives, decided in 1964 to run for the U.S. Senate.

That opened the gates for a hotly contested house race among Chávez, longtime legislator Calvin Horn of Albuquerque, and the state land commissioner, E. S. Johnny Walker of Santa Fe.

"The fight boiled for four hours before [Walker] was named convention nominee for the office," the *New Mexican* reported. "After the fifth ballot, Chavez released his delegates. Enough swung over to Walker to put him over the necessary number for a majority. It was slim—50.35 percent."

Chávez and Horn each collected at least the minimum number of delegates, 20 percent, on the convention's first vote so each was assured a spot on the Democrats' primary ballot, even if not as the convention's choice. There was plenty of behind-the-scenes maneuvering involving some of New Mexico's highest-ranking politicians.

Stung by his defeat at the convention, Chávez had not lost hope for convincing New Mexico's Democratic masses that he was best prepared to represent the state in Congress, and he would point to his record in the state legislature to make his case. First, though, there was the matter of guiding that year's legislative assembly through its business.

"As majority leader, I established the calendar every day," Chávez said. "I used to start them around nine in the morning. Early in the afternoon, I asked for the customary ten- or fifteen-minute recess for a break. I walked down the hall and was the first senator into the restroom. I was there alone with one of the reporters who was covering the session. He turned to me and said, 'Senator, I've been hearing a rumor from some of your opponents that you were at one time enrolled in the boys' reform school in Springer. Is it true?'

"I said, 'It's not a rumor.' And that's it. I didn't say any more than that before walking out of the restroom. I was a little bit hurt that the issue would come up but I wasn't mad. I collected my thoughts, and I told myself I might as well get up on the senate floor and address it head on the moment we reconvened. Mack Easley was lieutenant governor and presiding officer of the senate. Once we were all in, I turned to Mack and asked to speak on a point of personal privilege. Mack said, 'State your point.'"

No one in the small chamber knew yet of the extraordinary nature of the remarks that were about to be spoken. Some were still settling in following the brief recess. All of the thirty-two senators sat behind long, slightly curved U.N.-style desks facing Easley, who was at the front of the room. To Chávez's left was Gordon Melody who doubled as finance committee chairman and majority whip. To Chávez's right, across the aisle, was W. C. Wheatley of Union County who served as president pro tempore. The chamber was small enough that microphones were not used. With a baritone voice, Chávez did not need one.

"I said, 'First of all, I'm a candidate for the U.S. congressional seat.' Then I said that during the break I ran into a reporter who told me he had heard a rumor that I had been in the boys' school in Springer. 'Well,' I said, 'it's not a rumor.' I was in Springer for something less than a year as a young boy."

The *New Mexican* was still an afternoon paper then, and its deadlines for the day had past. Its front page the following morning reported on Chávez's surprising, extemporaneous remarks to the senate, calling it "a highly emotional scene." It said Chávez spoke in a halting voice as he explained circumstances that had him sent to the reform school.

"He said he had run away from home several times . . . In 1936, his father took him before the district court and told the judge he was having a hard time keeping the boy in school," the paper said. It said Chávez also told colleagues, "The only thing that hurts me about this whole thing is that politics is so vicious as to bring up a childhood mistake in order to see if I will bend." He also said he regretted that the issue arose, fearing how it might affect his elderly father.

"When I was finished," Chávez recalled later, "I said simply that we should turn to that order of business, reports from the house of representatives. I wanted to move on." Other senators jumped to Chávez's defense, though, invoking their own rights to speak on points of personal privilege.

"If this statement is true, then possibly the rest of us would have benefited by the same treatment," Senator I. M. "Ike" Smalley of Deming said of Chávez's disclosure. His comments were carried in the next day's papers.

Chávez said he would never forget words spoken by the minority leader, Joe Skeen of Picacho. "His words stick to my mind most," Chávez said. "He said if he had a son, he would send him to the same boys' school in order to get the same results that I got. It was all kind of strange. Here I was forty-two years old. I was running for the United States Congress, and someone would come up with something that happened when I was twelve years old as if it should disqualify me from moving forward with my dreams."

"I'll tell you, those early years helped make me what I am. As a boy, I was adventuresome, and a lot of what I did then probably strengthened my instinct for survival, which would see me through a world war and some very trying political situations that often had me going against leaders of my party and even members of my family."

Despite his charm, drive, and historic accomplishments, Chávez fell short of his two biggest goals in politics. *Envidias*, or jealousies, well rooted in New Mexico's politics, as well as strategically timed acts of retribution by state Democratic Party leaders, including some of the party's biggest stars of the time, blocked Chávez's paths. Still, the verve that took Chávez beyond heartbreaking defeats while winning admirers in both major political parties continued to command attention around the state, including from those who denied him his two long-held goals.

ACKNOWLEDGMENTS

Critical support for this work was provided by the McCune Charitable Foundation in Santa Fe, New Mexico, and New Mexico Highlands University and the New Mexico Highlands University Foundation in Las Vegas, New Mexico. Appreciation also is expressed to individual donors who contributed to a fund the NMHU Foundation administered for this project.

Appreciation is expressed to the following people who granted interviews to the author, often multiple times in person, by telephone, or by letter during the years cited:

David Abbey, 2005

Harold Agnew, 2006

Toney Anaya, 2006

Jerry Apodaca, 2006

Manny Aragón, 2005

Anselmo Arellano, 2005

Sterling Black, 2006

Jerome Block, 2006

Nan Bowers, 2007

Maralyn Budke, 2005, 2006, 2007

David Cargo, 2006, 2007

Garrey Carruthers, 2005

Antonio Chávez, 2006

Christine Chávez, 2005

Coral Jeanne Chávez, 2005, 2006

Fabián Chávez Jr., 2005, 2006, 2007

Martin Chávez, 2006

Thomas Chávez, 2005

Hoyt Clifton, 2005

David Cox, 2006

Floyd Darrow, 2006

Thomas Donnelly, 2006

Tobías Durán, 2006

Mack Easley, 2005

Jerry Fickes, 2006

Richard Folmar, 2005

Steve Fresquez, 2007
Bill García, 2006
Rebecca Vigil-Giron, 2006
Sarah Anderson-Gómez, 2005, 2006
Mary Herrera, 2007
Patricia Herrera, 2007
Tracey Kimball, 2005, 2006
Bruce King, 2006
Dick Knipfing, 2006
James Koch, 2006
Tim Kraft, 2006
Imogene Lindsay, 2005
Ben Luján, 2006
Edward Luján, 2006
Manuel Luján, 2007
Victor Marshall, 2006
Bobby Mayfield, 2005
Billy McKibben, 2006

S. Q. "Chano" Merino, 2006
Tom Morris, 2005, 2006
James Mulcock, 2006
Emilio Naranjo, 2007
David Norvell, 2006
Bob Quick, 2006
Ty Ransdell, 2005
Ed Romero, 2006, 2007
Eugene Romero, 2006
Thomas Rushton, 2007
Raymond Sánchez, 2006
Greg Solano, 2006
Stephen Stoddard, 2006
Paula Tackett, 2005
Maurice Trimmer, 2005
Don Francisco Trujillo, 2007
Martha Vigil, 2006

CHAPTER ONE

A Proud Chávez Family Settles in Santa Fe

I t did not daunt his spirits, but Fabián Chávez Jr. learned at an early age that even the best-laid plans of mere mortals can be crushed, or at least derailed. The Great Depression had a cruel way of imparting such lessons.

"It was 1930. I was six years old, and we were living at 712 Acequia Madre in Santa Fe. It was a house that my dad built with adobes in 1926, two years after I was born," Chávez said. "It was a good-sized house: four bedrooms, a large kitchen, a dining room, a living room. It had beautiful French windows that my dad was especially fond of. But dad lost the house around 1931, early in the Depression. He couldn't meet the payments on the materials he had used to build the house along with other expenses so the mortgage lender foreclosed on him."

It was more than a house; it was a home. And it was taken from a very proud man.

"Dad purchased the property in 1923 when he and my mother moved to Santa Fe from Wagon Mound," Fabián Jr. said. "It was about ten acres with a big alfalfa field, and it ran from Acequia Madre clear to the hills south of us. Dirt for the adobes came from that piece of land itself, and I know it must have really hurt my father to lose it. The debt that was owed, believe it or not, was five thousand dollars."

Fabián Chávez Sr. brought his young family to Santa Fe when New Mexico's statehood was in its infancy. New Mexico was one of the poorest states in the nation. Unemployment and illiteracy were high. Greater opportunities, greater promise were evident in Santa Fe, where the state Capitol fueled activity along with commerce that had its roots in the Camino Real and the Santa Fe Trail.

Fabián Jr. came into this world while his family lived in a small, rented house on Abeyta Street, an offshoot of Acequia Madre. By then the family included firstborn Manuel Ezequil; Marta; twins Romualdo and Nicanora; Adela; María Consuelo; and Francisco. All were born in Mora County. There was a time after the births of Manuel and Marta that the elder Fabián and his wife, Nicolasa, moved briefly to San Diego, California, in pursuit of employment opportunities. They returned to the Wagon Mound area after less than a year. "Both my father and mother had a deep affection for the state. Their families were from here. There's no way they would have stayed in California for very long," Fabián Jr. said.

In the early 1920s, again in pursuit of work, Fabián Sr. moved his growing family to the Barelas neighborhood of Albuquerque where he worked for several months as a carpenter before the family's eventual move to Santa Fe, where it planted its roots and developed a rich—and mostly distinguished—history. After Fabián Jr. was born in the capital city on August 31, 1924, the family grew to include Antonio and José.

"Our folks gave us beautiful Spanish names. Nicanora, for example, was Nora's full name," Fabián said. "Nora: of the older sisters, she's the one who pushed me most and seemed to be around during critical times of my early years. And it was Manuel who suggested to my mom that I be named after my dad, noting that none of the sons so far had been given my father's name. Manuel was fourteen and on his way to St. Francis Seraphic Seminary in Cincinnati. He became Father Angélico, of course, when he was ordained a priest. Romualdo became known as Cuate because he was a twin."

Losing his beloved home on Acequia Madre as he was raising a young family a blow to the family patriarch. Still, as suggested in one of the many popular Spanish proverbs of the time, "No hay mal que cien años dura." The ill wind that blew upon the family, indeed, did not last more than a few years.

"In 1932, dad went to work as state Capitol Building Superintendent in Santa Fe," Chávez said. "We had moved to 343 East Alameda Street when my father was approached by a fellow in the government. Apparently a federal law had been passed under Franklin Delano Roosevelt to give those who lost their homes as a result of the Depression the first option to buy them back. Dad had a good, steady job and was able to buy back the house on Acequia Madre in 1935.

"As a kid, losing the family home for a while wasn't all that unpleasant. I just remember that we had to move. For a young kid, that really didn't mean a heck of a lot."

Moving about seemed to be in young Fabián's blood despite his deep fondness for the historic city in which he was born. "My parents had been in Santa Fe for only a year when I was born in Marrion Hall, the old hospital on Palace Avenue right next to St. Francis Cathedral. It was 1924, and since then I've lived knowing that this often is an imperfect world and that we have to use what we have to make things work. See, I was delivered by a one-eyed doctor. Dr. Charles Ward was our family doctor, and he had a patch over one eye.

"I had an active imagination from the start. I was a free spirit as a kid, and it got me into trouble more than once. It also moved me to do things that I realized only years later must have caused a lot of pain for my parents, especially my mother."

Some of that trouble unfolded amid the Loretto nuns assigned to Santa Fe by the Archdiocese of Santa Fe. "I made my first holy communion at age six and was taught by the nuns at St. Francis Parochial School, which was located right across the street from the cathedral and hospital where I was born. It was hard to program me to study everything that was put before me because I had no interest in some things, like mathematics, for example. But the nuns never gave up on me. They gave me a good basic education in those first eight grades. They liked me despite my errant ways, and I liked them."

Fabián's father was a regular donor to the parish that supported the school, but donations were modest. "The nuns took an interest in me but it wasn't because of the money that dad gave to the school. Dad didn't have that kind of money. He paid whatever the school fees were, and he made a regular, small contribution to the parish. The local Catholic schools—St. Francis Parochial School, Loretto Academy, St. Michael's—were super-duper, as far as my folks were concerned.

"The special attention I got from the nuns was probably rooted in their confidence in me, but it might also have had something to do with the fact that my older brother, Father Angélico, was already working as an ordained priest. If I got a B or a C, the nuns would get after me because they knew I had the capacity to get an A, and they always knew that I was a kid brother to a priest," Chávez said.

Occasional mediocre grades were not all that made the Loretto nuns get after Chávez. He was known to ditch school, or as he put it, "miss class deliberately from time to time."

"Like I say, I was a free spirit. I was curious. Instead of going to school, I'd go around town. But I'd usually spend my time productively, even if it was just collecting cardboard boxes," he said. "There was a local bakery on De Vargas Street just above the river that used boxes to move their goods back and forth. I'd take boxes to the bakery and exchange them for bread and cinnamon rolls, which I would take home. It wasn't enough to keep me out of trouble if mom and dad found out that I had missed school. When they did, dad would punish me with a strap to the rear end. He'd pull down my pants, hold my hands, and paddle me with his belt."

None of it really kept the young Fabián from sticking his nose where his parents were convinced it did not belong. As a young volunteer dispatcher for the Capital City Cab Company, he took phone calls from people who asked for things that a boy from a proper family had no business knowing about. "In the 1930s there was a brothel on West San Francisco Street and one on West Alameda, both just off the Plaza. The Capital City Cab Company operated on West Alameda just across the street from the bus station. The company was owned by Elías Roybal, whose father, José Roybal, owned the little grocery store on Canyon Road where my father did a lot of bartering.

"I'd walk into the cab company and help answer the phones and things like that. A lot of the calls would come from area hotels, like La Fonda, El Fidel, and the De Vargas. They were men who would call for a cab to take them to the brothels. And then, of course, some of the cabbies would buy beer and wine for the Indians whenever they called for a ride. Indians at that time were prohibited from buying alcoholic beverages. Having a little beer or wine in the car when Indians called for a cab was just part of the cab service. It was the real world that was unfolding around us, but it would have driven my parents crazy if they had known what I was doing."

Despite the brothels and occasionally rowdy bars, Santa Fe for the most part was a quiet town as the Roaring Twenties faded across the country and Fabián Chávez Jr. increasingly began yearning to see what lay beyond his hometown. There was light automobile traffic on paved streets around the historic Plaza, which provided perpendicular parking at an angle for those stopping to visit shoe stores, clothing stores, a soda fountain, or the bank on the east side of the Plaza. Locals, young and old, milled on the Plaza daily, commonly sitting on a wall that encircled the square's outer rim. Indians from nearby pueblos already were a familiar sight under the portal of the Palace of the Governors, selling their wares of mostly silver and turquoise along with pottery fashioned from indigenous clay.

The first Capitol of the Spanish government in Santa Fe, the Palace of the Governors was renovated from 1909 to 1911 to look much as it still did the following century and had become a popular museum with relics of New Mexico's rich past on display.

"The portal of the palace wasn't as full of vendors as it is now. Nor was the tourist traffic anything like it is today, not even close," said Thomas

Chávez, who was director of the Palace of the Governors for twenty-one years through 2002. Thomas's father, Antonio, is a younger brother of Fabián Jr. "The Harvey tours were bringing people in, and La Fonda was a Harvey House hotel. It was brand new, smaller than it is today, but it served as a draw because it was at the end of the Santa Fe Trail. An older hotel had served people at the same site for years. A World War I tank was used to tear down the old building before La Fonda was built."

Visitors also arrived in Santa Fe on the narrow gauge train, the Denver and Rio Grande Western, which was popularly known in the area as the Chile Line. Passengers got off on Guadalupe Street alongside tracks that stretched northward through Española and into Colorado. The D&RGW depot later became popular Tomasita's Restaurant.

"People were still burning a lot of firewood in the colder months, and burros were still being led into town carrying loads of wood harvested in the hills east of town. There was even an occasional horse-drawn wagon," Thomas Chávez said.

"All the business was done downtown. Downtown was the center of Santa Fe, and there was very little beyond it."

For a while—a very brief while—young Fabián Jr. found Santa Fe's downtown to be plenty. "The downtown Plaza was the place," he said. "Ninety-five percent of Santa Fe's activity was scattered around the Plaza, say about an eight-block area. At St. Michael's High School during the summertime there was a semiprofessional baseball team called Santa Fe Stationers that would play teams from out of town. I never played organized sports. I just didn't find it attractive. But I was at the baseball field often. It was right about where the PERA Building is today off Paseo de Peralta. Boyles Nursery, which sold trees and plants on the Plaza, was in the area. And the cemetery that belonged to the archdiocese was there, too.

"The Christian Brothers used to have a candy store with all kinds of treats that were sold at the games. I'd go get one of their boxes and fill it with candy and popcorn to sell to people watching the games. I chose candy and popcorn over sodas because they were the lighter things to carry. It's not that I was afraid of work. I'd actually seek it out. But I guess I had a knack for making money with the minimum amount of hard labor."

The cemetery, more than the baseball field, was one of the landmarks off the Plaza. It was encircled in part by wire fencing and adobe walls. "I used to cut across the cemetery every day to sell the morning *Albuquerque Journal*," Chávez said. It was a cemetery used until 1865 when the new Rosario Cemetery was opened for use. The old cemetery was falling victim to neglect when Chávez came to know it. Perhaps because Santa Fe had its share of colorful characters, the cemetery shared in some of that color as the characters passed on. The notorious Doña Tules contributed to the cemetery's aura during the time that Archbishop Jean Baptiste Lamy administered the archdiocese. Both names—La Tules and Archbishop Lamy—peculiarly would follow Chávez intermittently during his life.

Lamy, of course, is no stranger to New Mexicans. Gertrudis Barcelo (La Tules, or Miss Trudy), too, had her own substantial cadre of admirers and detractors. She arrived in New Mexico as a child with her family from Sonora, Mexico, in 1815 and by the late 1830s had established a lavish gambling hall in Santa Fe. Thomas Chávez and Fabián's elder brother, Fray Angélico, together wrote of La Tules's work and reputation in their 2004 book, *Wake for a Fat Vicar*. Prominent American travelers on the Santa Fe Trail described La Tules in sharply contrasting terms, they wrote. Matthew Field referred to her as "the supreme queen of refinement and fashion,"[1] but Josiah Gregg described her as a roamer and prostitute.[2] At least one account mentioned her as the mistress of then-Gov. Manuel Armijo.[3] Another, which was printed in a St. Louis newspaper, described her as a wealthy woman with "a reputation for chastity as distinguished as her extraordinary successes."[4]

La Tules was buried in the Roman Catholic cemetery in 1852 in a funeral that was attended by ranking government officials, soldiers from Fort Marcy, the wealthy and the poor, Thomas Chávez and Fray Angélico Chávez wrote.[5] Bishop Lamy, wearing a white miter and black cape, led a long procession from the church to the cemetery.[6] Vicar Joseph Machebeuf, who was a close associate of Lamy, told later that a local priest, who supposedly had been La Tules's lover, wept at the end of the procession.[7]

"Doña Tules had contributed five thousand dollars to the pastor of the parish to pay for her own funeral," Fabián Chávez Jr. said. "She had become a very liberal contributor to the parish, and she and the local priest had become good friends. Lamy arrived later and, yes, led the funeral procession for Doña Tules. He also took the five thousand dollars from the parish and contributed it to the diocese. Fray Angélico implies in his book that if the priest was crying at the funeral, it was because he had lost a good friend or, with tongue in cheek, because of the loss of the five thousand dollars that had been contributed to the parish before Lamy came into the picture."

Even amid his great reverence for the church, Fabián Jr. grew up well aware of the schism that developed between Lamy and many of northern New Mexico's natives, including the sharp differences between Lamy and Padre Antonio José Martínez of Taos that ripped at the church. E. A. Mares, writing as professor emeritus of English at the University of New Mexico, addressed divisions between Lamy and longtime New Mexicans in the book, *New Mexican Lives*. "The bishop was patronizing to his primarily

Spanish-speaking faithful," Mares wrote.[8] "On one occasion, Lamy wrote a very self-damaging letter in which he said that Mexicans faced a sad future because they didn't have the intellectual liveliness of Americans and their morals were primitive. The nuevomexicano priests and their parishioners were no fools. They undoubtedly noticed and felt the disdain and contempt so implicit in Lamy's words."[9]

Lamy's very construction of the cathedral a block east of the Plaza drove a wedge between the French prelate and many longtime residents of the upper Rio Grande. American poet Winfield Townley Scott invoked the names of two other noted writers while referring to the cathedral. "Presumably aside from any jealousy she may have felt for Willa Cather's intrusive achievement in *Death Comes for the Archbishop*, Mary Austin regretted Miss Cather's implied admiration for the Archbishop's French cathedral," Scott wrote. "'It was a calamity to the local culture,' said Mrs. Austin. She was right. It does not belong here. But pioneers customarily hark back to their own building traditions before they go on to evolve or discover what is proper to their new country; and that precisely is what Archbishop Lamy did."[10]

Questions rooted in church operations followed young Fabián into the cathedral throughout his youth and beyond. "I developed a sort of reluctance to enlist as a parishioner," he said. "Back in the thirties, they had several front rows of pews in the cathedral that were rented by parishioners who had their names on the pews. If you sat on those pews and the family members who had paid for them came in, you had to move to another pew. My mom and dad didn't have one of those rented pews because they couldn't afford one.

"Whenever the church published lists of who contributed to the parish, my folks were down there, I guess, as minor contributors. I wouldn't use the term hierarchy in what developed, but it was sort of demeaning to publish those names. I couldn't help but wonder if it was embarrassing to see your name published on a list and to be among the lower monetary echelons. It didn't have an effect on my faith in the Roman Catholic Church or anything like that, but it did rub me wrong. When I was older and went to Mass, I'd always pay offerings in cash. The only time I wrote a check that left a record was when I made a major contribution for renovation of the cathedral or something like that. The irony is that after the latest renovation, they put up a plaque with names of major donors. I'll be darn if they didn't end up putting my name and my wife's name on it."

Immediately around Lamy's cathedral, with its distinctive unfinished towers, was a mostly sleepy community that came to know Fabián Jr.'s face well.

"St. Michael's School was on one side of the Plaza, and Santa Fe High was on the opposite side within that same eight-block radius. Santa Fe

High was where city hall is now on Marcy Street," Chávez said. "There was the art museum, the Palace of the Governors, and, of course, the state Capitol was just above the Santa Fe River, where dad worked and where I spent a lot of time. It was the Capitol that preceded what we know today as the Bataan Memorial Building. It was the Capitol that was used beginning in 1900, which means it served during New Mexico's territorial period as well as when we became a state in 1912. It had a big dome in the middle and a pitched portal with tall columns just below it.

"There was a budding artist community visible around the Plaza. On the Plaza, there was a recreation pool hall. The J. C. Penney store. F. W. Woolworth. Two drug stores: Zook's Pharmacy and Capital Pharmacy. The first national bank with big Corinthian columns on the east side. La Fonda as we know it now was built in the early twenties. Around Christmastime, the St. Francis School choir seemed to be everywhere. The choir had about fifteen members, boys and girls. They'd dress us up real neat in white shirts, and we'd go around singing Christmas carols. La Fonda was one of the big stops."

Santa Fe, then as now, was a community reluctant to let go of the past even as some of its residents embraced society's shiny new entrants. "I remember the occasional horse-drawn wagon coming onto the Plaza with *sacos de harina* and papas," Chávez said. "People from the area would come in and buy their flour, their potatoes, and drive them back where they came from, usually into the hills around Rio en Medio. There were a lot of Model-A's and Model-T Fords among the cars of the time. I remember one of the most striking cars was a convertible Packard. There was also a Duesenberg and a Cord—a real fancy car.

"My parents didn't have a car. Dad never drove a car or truck in his life. It could have been a case of finances, but my dad never had a desire to drive. The first car in the family that I can recall was a Ford Model-A acquired by my brother, Cuate. Dad used to walk a lot to get around for his work, and there might have been people who he did work for who gave him rides. Cuate probably also drove him around a bit. But because we lived just eight or ten blocks from downtown, we always walked back and forth. I spent a lot of time walking between home and the Capitol, and between home and the Palace of the Governors."

Ever industrious, Fabián usually tried to get something out of his walks before returning home. "I was eleven during Clyde Tingley's first administration as governor. It's when they installed the first elevator in the Capitol building. You had to place your hand on a crank to run it, and I remember the lady in charge of the elevator taught me how to handle it. I got so good at it that when she would take a break or go to lunch, I got to be in charge of the elevator.

"From time to time, they loaned out the house of representatives chambers for meetings of different political or religious groups. That was on the third floor of the old Capitol. Usually, when those meetings were held, they'd ask me to be the elevator boy and pay me anywhere from two to five dollars for my effort."

Young Fabián also turned a profit from his visits to the Palace of the Governors. "Artifacts in the Palace of the Governors were especially attractive to me. They had pictures of all the governors, the territorial governors and the early state governors. They had the old oxen-driven carretas. They had the fancy turn-of-the-century hearse that was pulled by horses. They had the chair that they claim was used by Lew Wallace while he wrote *Ben-Hur*. And they had little cards with captions under many of the exhibits, and I probably memorized almost all of them."

Chávez put his expanding knowledge to work. "I'd see all these people coming in from other places so I found ways to use my talents as a guide inside the palace as well as outside. I had this cigar box, and I'd buy some of these picture postcards at the Gans Indian arts and crafts store. It was a big curio store on the south side of the Plaza. They had several Indian jewelers who worked at a mini mass-production line. Some would cut the silver, others shaped it into bracelets, then came the placing of turquoise, and the polishing. They had quite a deal going in there. They also had big racks of color postcards that you could buy for very cheap. We're talking Depression days now; three for a dime or two for a nickel. I'd buy these sort of accordion postcards, hang them from my little cigar box, and sell them at a nickel a piece. I was making a profit.

"I was often the first thing that caught the tourists' eye. They'd see this little kid selling postcards, and before you knew it, I not only had sold them a postcard but was serving as their tour guide, too.

"In that same store where you could watch Indians making jewelry, they had this gentleman from Chimayó who wove Chimayó blankets right there in the big window. I remember being so fascinated that I hitchhiked to Chimayó one day, probably at the age of ten or eleven, to see more of the weaving. That gave me the idea of expanding my work as a tourist guide. I'd hop a ride with tourists and take them to San Ildefonso to see the pueblo and then up to Chimayó to see the weavers.

"I must have been a pretty cute kid because when I approached them to see if they wanted a guide, they'd smile and perhaps out of curiosity, they'd contract with me. I'd tell them they could pay me whatever they thought

I was worth when we were through. On the trip to Chimayó, I'd probably make a dollar and a half."

After a few ventures to Chimayó, Chávez was emboldened. "I started expanding the trips. Probably the longest one I ever took as a tourist guide was to the 'famous Taos Pueblo.' That's how I used to describe it to get people interested in the trip."

By the age of twelve, the entrepreneurial kid was turning increasingly curious and adventuresome. "I was very adventurous, and it must have made others in the family a little uneasy. Of the older sisters, Nora was the one who pushed more. She was nine years older than me, and she's the one who said, 'Learn, learn, learn.' I had only three brothers older than me, and Father Angélico was already in the seminary for twelve years so I really didn't get to know my brother, the priest, until he had already been ordained. My brother, Cuate, was the type who really didn't want to fool around with a young punk like me. 'Get out of the way,' he'd say whenever he felt like I was getting too bothersome. The third oldest brother, Francisco, was only two years older than me so we grew up together.

"Instructions to all of us had to come from mom and dad, but our older sisters were also involved," Fabián said. "Nora was the one who'd say, 'Get a good education.' But the one who was most strict in terms of good behavior was Adela. She's the one who'd always say, 'Don't bring mud into the house. Use your knives and forks properly.' My older sister, Marta, was more like a sweet, wonderful second mother. She'd buy us presents and take us to the movies.

"I had two younger brothers, Antonio and José, and I guess it never occurred to me that I might be setting a bad example for those brothers with my adventurous behavior."

Antonio said he never considered Fabián Jr., who was a little less than two years his senior, to be a bad example. "Not at all. He was never a negative influence on me," said Antonio Chávez, who is a retired attorney and judge living in Las Cruces. "Mostly, I admired the things he used to do. It's not like he was a thief or anything like that. Things like skipping class, well, he could have been the smartest member of the family, and he probably skipped class because he didn't think they were doing anything for him in the schools. He seemed to be above his class, above what they were teaching. He just had that kind of brain.

"When I'd see that he wasn't in class, I'd call dad to ask if he knew where [Fabián Jr.] was. Sometimes, when I'd see him leaving school, I'd trail him to try to find out where he was going. When he'd spot me, he'd say that I wasn't supposed to be walking around. He'd say he had business to do and that I should get back to school."

Antonio Chávez said Fabián Jr. always seemed to have business to do. "I used to look up to him because of the way he used to go the Plaza and walk into stores looking for ways to make money. He used to give little tours, sell postcards, or sell fruit from our trees in the backyard.

"He taught me during the Depression where to go for the good cardboard boxes that we could then take to the bakery in exchange for donuts and stuff. They were probably day-old donuts but as a kid, what would I know? The good boxes were the ones that were kept clean and even folded so that they would stay in good condition. Santa Fe Stationers had good boxes. So did J. C. Penney's and Kaune's grocery store downtown.

"Fabián just seemed to want to be in business all the time, and he seemed to do pretty well. He was always giving me dimes and nickels. That was a lot of money during the Depression."

Fabián Jr.'s thirst for knowledge and growth seemed to be constrained at school and, soon enough, in his own hometown. "It's like I was driven to learn what was beyond the next corner, the next turn in the road, the next town," he said. "I remember starting to feel like there was little new for me to do in Santa Fe anymore so I got curious about going somewhere other than Santa Fe. My first curiosity were the mines of Madrid south of town. I guess I was bored, and I just wanted to roam somewhere. I never actually went to the coal mines or the turquoise mines in the area. I was just curious about the town and the people."

Madrid was a growing community at the time. Its wood-plank homes lined the narrow road that wound toward the east side of the Sandía Mountains and were perched on hills blackened by coal. It all turned into a colorful wonderland at Christmastime, a spectacle that could not go unnoticed by a spirited boy.

"I also noted that Madrid is the name of the capital of Spain, and Spain was at least an occasional topic of discussion in our home where the family was very proud of its Spanish roots," Chávez said.

"When I found out how easy it was to hitchhike from Santa Fe to Madrid and back, I got venturesome one summer and decided to go all the way into Albuquerque. Albuquerque to me was a big city because it had a central avenue with several theaters and restaurants. There was more commotion. It was so different from Santa Fe."

And it did not take much for Chávez to recognize that he could get to Albuquerque pretty much anytime he pleased. "It was just a case of getting out on old Highway 85 and sticking out your finger," he said. "I'd walk out to around the Indian School and start hitchhiking because it was pretty much the edge of town. I figured anybody going beyond that was going to Albuquerque."

Commotion in the Duke City that was stirred by the railroad was of particular interest to Chávez. "There was no underpass at Central Avenue then. They'd simply block off the road when the train was coming. I'd sit for hours by the railroad station just to watch the trains go by. Albuquerque was an important stop. They had the Alvarado Hotel and the Alvarado Restaurant there, and passenger trains were very popular in those days. Not everyone could afford a Pullman or dining facilities of a long-distance train so they'd stop the train and give people forty minutes or so to get off and eat. I remember once some movie actresses on their way to California, I don't remember who they were, got off and stretched. Everybody was so excited."

As with many of young Fabián's youthful adventures, the railroads seemed to have to get bigger and better to retain the boy's attention. "The Chile Line was fun for a while," he said. "Many of us used to walk the line all the way into Española and then hitchhike back." That line served farmers and ranchers between Santa Fe and Alamosa, Colorado, until 1941, when it was abandoned by authority of the U.S. Interstate Commerce Commission.[11]

Also tugging for attention from Chávez was the regular gauge freight spur from Santa Fe to the community of Lamy toward the southeast. That spur was a sort of fluke, created after the Atchison, Topeka and Santa Fe Railroad in 1879 decided its new transcontinental tracks approaching from the northeast would bypass Santa Fe altogether.[12] "The hills below Santa Fe presented engineering difficulties which would cost more to solve than the line would pay," wrote Paul Horgan in *The Centuries of Santa Fe*. "The city's leading citizen—it was of course Archbishop Lamy—refused to lose the convenience and advantage of rail connections with the nation. If the main line would not come to Santa Fe, then Santa Fe must go to the main line."[13] Lamy petitioned the territorial government for a bond issue to raise $150,000, and the bond issue was carried by a three-to-one vote, Horgan wrote.[14]

The community that developed around the junction of the train's main line and its spur to Santa Fe was named in honor of the archbishop who pressed for the rail connection.

First serving the archbishop and his contemporaries, the seventeen-mile spur provided fun for Chávez but also helped him generate a little income. "I'd ride the freight car to Lamy, and then when the mail train came by, I'd help unload the mail then I'd hitchhike back to Santa Fe. Often I'd get a ride from people who were at the Lamy station to pick up relatives coming in on the train. Lamy had a hotel with a restaurant then. It was called El Ortiz. There was a general store, a post office, and an active church. A Super Chief would come by, and it had dining facilities with it. Still, some of the passengers would get off during the layover and go to the El Ortiz to eat. The building that served as a general store and post office later became a saloon."

Travelers and locals alike were treated to occasional displays that added spark to the small station. This account in the *Santa Fe New Mexican* told of one that occurred in connection with the Fiesta de Santa Fe:

> The mariachi de Jalisco, fourteen native musicians from Guadalajara, thrilled a crowd on the platform at Lamy and passengers on the southbound train last night with the crescendo finale of their stirring song of home entitled "Guadalajara," ending a short farewell concert at the saloon . . . As happened four years ago, this group of Jaliscienses from the most beautiful ancient city of Mexico found their visit to Santa Fe a high spot in their lives; and in Guadalajara it is the dream of every musico to go and play for the muy buena jente of Santa Fe, who are incredibly simpatico, en la Fiesta mas alegre del mundo.

Such commotion did not escape young Fabián's attention, but he knew the bigger action usually lay beyond. "The trains of the Santa Fe Railroad were the ones that passed through Lamy on their way to Albuquerque. But because Albuquerque was so much bigger and because there was so much more activity, everything about the trains just seemed to be more interesting there."

Train buffs like young Fabián had plenty to marvel at in the autumn of 1935. The *Santa Fe New Mexican* on September 9 of that year trumpeted the latest advancement on the rails in one long sentence:

> Announcement by the Santa Fe that it has just taken delivery from the Electro-Motive Corporation of the most powerful Diesel locomotive ever placed in service—and that the new giant, if exhaustive tests prove successful, will haul the road's crack flier, The Chief, between Chicago and California on a faster schedule than at present—marks another dramatic milestone in the spectacular drive by the management of major American lines to regain for the rails their old place in the sun with the traveling public.

Young Fabián might easily have concluded that the nation's railroads, or at least the one that served his corner of the world, were putting forth remarkable advances largely to satisfy adventuresome minds like his.

The boy's daring and independent ways left his parents stirring and increasingly agitated at home, however. "My folks didn't approve of my hitchhiking and I got castigated various times," Chávez said. "But I wasn't deterred. When dad saw I persisted, I think he took at least a little comfort in those times when he knew I was in Albuquerque because when I was there I often would visit with a granduncle on the Baca side of the family, Félix Baca. And we had other relatives and friends there. I could call and say, 'I'm here. Don't worry.'

"What bothered dad the most was when I would take off from school for a long period of time, say a week. Mother, I know, would worry about where I was. My dad's friends would always ask him, '¿Dónde está Fabiancito?' And dad would say, 'No sé, ese muchacho anda por los quintos infiernos.' Invariably the friends would then say something like, 'Sí es poco bribón, ¿no?'

"But there was something about dad after a while. I think he concluded, at least for a little bit, that the kid has chosen his way. Let's hope it works out."

It was a course that did not come easily for Fabián Chávez Sr., who had built his name on reliability, honesty, and hard work. The elder Chávez was born on a ranch in Ciruela in 1879, seven miles west of Wagon Mound, after his family had moved there from the Belén area in Rio Abajo. It was the same year that tracks for the railroad were completed along Wagon Mound, opening up opportunities for ranchers, tanners, carpenters, miners, and pretty much anyone who was not afraid of work. "Wagon Mound became a growing community," Fabián Jr. said. "Grandfather Roybal, on my mother's side, was drawn there from the Jacona area in the Pojoaque Valley by the business activity that was under way. That activity is what kept my father and mother close to that region for forty years except for a couple of excursions that seemed to promise better opportunities," Fabián Jr. said.

Fabián Sr. was proud to be of European stock that settled in what is now the United States years before Pilgrims landed at Plymouth Rock. He traced his ancestry to Pedro Durán y Chaves who in 1626 was the commanding general of royal Spanish troops in New Mexico.[15] A grandson of Pedro's, Fernando Chaves II, was a standard bearer for don Diego de Vargas, whom the Spanish crown in 1690 appointed governor of New Mexico. Two years later it was Vargas who helped resettle New Mexico following the 1680 revolt of Pueblo Indians that had sent Spanish colonizers fleeing south to El Paso.[16] The spelling of the family name in northern New Mexico was changed late in the 1800s from Chaves to Chávez as a result of an error a priest made on a birth certificate, according to Fabián Chávez Jr.

Fabián Chávez Sr. had only a sixth-grade education, but he learned from his father how to tend to a ranch and how to use his hands and mind as a skilled carpenter. It was as a carpenter that he made a living

≈ **FIGURE 1.** ≈

Fabián Chávez Sr. (right) with companions in Wagon Mound in the late 1800s.
Courtesy Palace of the Governors (MNM/DCA), negative no. 113653.

and shaped much of his surroundings. A lot of the rest came from his taste
for politics.

He married Nicolasa Roybal of Wagon Mound in 1909. Before that,
Nicolasa completed high school and secured two semesters of higher education at New Mexico Normal School in Las Vegas, which is now New
Mexico Highlands University, to become a certified public school teacher in
1904. "She was teaching in Wagon Mound when she met my dad," Fabián Jr.
said. "My dad's formal education was quite limited, but he loved to read,
he loved books. He especially liked reading out loud in Spanish. I'd ask
him why he seemed to read mostly the Spanish out loud. He'd say because
the words in Spanish 'tienen buen sabor.' He read and savored every word.
That's the best way to describe it. He also read and wrote in English because
he'd read the newspapers every day and complain like everybody else about
what was going on."

Nicolasa Chávez, at least as much as her husband, was proud of her
roots in Spain. "I recall having this long, even heated discussion with my
brother Cuate in the kitchen of our family home. Cuate, Father Angélico,

꧁ **FIGURE 2.** ꧂
Fabián Chávez Sr. around period of New Mexico statehood.
Courtesy Chávez family.

my mom, my dad, and I were having lunch," recalled Fabián Jr. "Cuate and I were talking about the mingling of Spanish blood with Indian blood after the Europeans arrived. Surely, I said, with so much mingling, there is Indian blood among the Chávezes.

"Cuate took exception. He said, 'No, we come from pure Spanish blood,' conquistadores and all that. To try to settle the argument, we turned to our brother, the priest and historian. I looked at Father Angélico and said we're bound to have some Indian blood, if not from the local Indians, then from the Indians that the Spaniards brought with them from Mexico— the *ayudantes*. Father Angélico said, 'Oh, yes, we're bound to have Indian blood.' To which mother said, 'If you do, then it's on your father's side.' My dad just smiled. He had smiling, twinkling eyes. I used to tell people that if there was ever such a thing as a Spanish leprechaun, dad was one."

In 1911, the allure of politics drew Fabián Sr. to the state Democratic Party convention, where William C. McDonald was nominated to run for governor. A state constitution had just been adopted in Santa Fe, even though New Mexico was still a mere territory of the United States. Statehood had been sought and denied since 1850. Former New Mexico state historian Robert J. Tórrez says one of the problems was that the area's predominantly Hispanic and Indian population was "too foreign and too Catholic for admission to the American Union."[17]

That issue and others were overcome by January 1912, when U.S. Pres. William Taft signed the proclamation that made New Mexico the forty-seventh state.[18] Nine days later McDonald was inaugurated as New Mexico's first governor under statehood.[19]

In timing that was interesting if not ironic for this family with ties so deeply embedded in the region's history, Fabián Sr. took his wife and their two firstborn children, Manuel Ezequil and Marta, to California just as New Mexico had won coveted statehood. Economic opportunity drove the move. Chávez went to work in San Diego as a carpenter at the Panama World Exposition. "Before long he ended up as a supervisor because he was literate and he could speak Spanish. Mexican immigrants made up a lot of the workforce," said grandson Thomas Chávez. "Fabián's dad became very valuable because he could read blueprints in two languages."

The excursion to the West Coast while New Mexico stepped uneasily into statehood was to be short-lived, though. "Dad was a solid northern New Mexican so I'm sure he always intended to come back," said Fabián Jr. "Neither he nor mom wanted to live in San Diego so one day they got on the train and came home."

Husband and wife with their two children settled in Wagon Mound, where the elder Chávez applied his just-secured worldly experience to local politics and with his wife, continued adding to the family. In 1916, Fabián Sr. was elected Mora County assessor as a Democrat in a region dominated by Republicans. He was elected county treasurer two years later. It was kinship more than politics, though, that drew Fabián Sr. and his family to the capital in 1924 following their brief sojourn to the Barelas area of Albuquerque.

"My mom's brother-in-law, Augustín Sosaya, was married to my Aunt Victoria. My uncle had built several adobe houses along what is now Acequia Madre in Santa Fe," Fabián Jr. said. "He had a substantial amount of property in the area, and he knew of this land that was adjacent to his and available for purchase. It was my aunt and uncle who told my parents of the ten acres on Acequia Madre. My parents bought it, and what they owned ran all the way from Acequia Madre up San Pascual clear to the hills."

The neighborhood in east Santa Fe was home mostly to some of the city's well-established families, but already outside influences were making their presence known.

"Much of the area back then was mostly milpas—fields and gardens. But there were also substantial properties. The Otero compound was owned by Judge Mike Otero and it included several beautiful, small townhouses. The family of Fred Herrera owned all the property that is walled in now by the Fenn Gallery. Fred was my contemporary, and he was a wonderful baseball player. At the left-hand side corner of Acequia Madre and East García was property that belonged to the Piatt family. It was this big family that had seven kids in World War II. They learned Spanish so they were bilingual and got along pretty well with people of the neighborhood. The property was later bought by Tito Griego, and he put a grocery store there. Now there's a bookstore on the site.

"Doña Filomena Ronquillo back in the thirties had a little grocery store along Acequia Madre. She was an aunt of Tito Griego, and Tito bought it after World War II, and he had that grocery store for a while before putting up his own place. On the 700 block of Acequia Madre is the Leonora Curtain property. It's all walled in now with beautifully tended buildings.

"Frank V. Ortiz Sr., the late ambassador's dad, owned one of the few other houses that existed on Acequia Madre at the time. The man who grew up to be Ambassador Frank Ortiz and I were neighbors. We knew each other since we were kids. From dad's house clear to where the Ortiz house was, we had apple trees, peach trees, apricot trees, and wild crab apple trees. My brother, Eugenio, and I used to come here to the acequia, and we carried a tub between us and a pail on our free side, and we would go water the trees as a regular routine."

It was just a place to call home back then, even though today it is one of Santa Fe's most exclusive neighborhoods, Chávez said. "It's gotten to be sort of like the Hamptons on the East Coast. It's the 'in place,' and it's recognized by people all around the country. We had no idea back then what was in store.

"After acquiring the land, dad built the family house in its territorial style. We built the wall in front of the house after World War II. Father Angélico helped; actually, he supervised us. We planted the trees that are in front of the house. Between here and the back of the house dad also planted vegetables, mostly carrots and radishes.

"Many of these newer houses came after the thirties. Some of the biggest milpas on the north side of Acequia Madre in the area where the elementary school is now belonged to the Francisco Rodríguez family. Wild spinach used to grow along the ditch there. There was a little corn, but the milpas were mostly alfalfa. The Rodríguezes used to have a home-dug well, and we used to go there to drink their water because it was so pure, so clean, so good.

"Dad got city water when we built the house. What we didn't have was natural gas or a sewer line. We had a septic tank behind the house. I remember when they closed the septic tank and connected to the sewer.

"Don Leopoldo Gonzales and his wife Elizabeth Gonzales were a very prominent family. He was county Democratic chairman. She was New Mexico secretary of state. Nearby, Francisco Delgado was a master tinsmith. The Valdés family owned a square block of land between Canyon Road and the Santa Fe River. All of this was on my way to school, church, or the Plaza."

These were all families whose names already were coming to mean so much to Santa Fe. "Sosaya Lane is named after my uncle Augustín Sosaya," Chávez said. "He owned so much property in what was becoming a landmark neighborhood in our historic community. All these other families—the Delgados, the Valdéses, the Ortizes, the Rodríguezes and Vigils—were landowners who would come to make a substantial mark on Santa Fe.

"In fact, I used to wonder why amid all these Hispanic names of the neighborhood, the names of families as well as names of the streets, why one of the streets ended up with the name East Manhattan. It just stood out as very unusual."

Back in 1945, members of the Santa Fe City Council and the mayor, Manuel Luján, expressed their own bewilderment that a street in the heart of old Santa Fe would be named Manhattan. It's inappropriate, Luján said at the time. People from back east are often fooled about what to expect after hearing the street name—"even the Latins from Manhattan," the *Santa Fe New Mexican* quoted Luján to have said.

In time, compromise followed, as it often does in politics at all levels. What was East Manhattan Street became an extension of Acequia Madre, but the name Manhattan Avenue survived just a few blocks to the west.

As time went on, the dissonance that poked at Chávez, Luján, and others became less of a concern among residents of the neighborhood.

"A large majority of the property in this neighborhood now is owned by people who moved into the city much more recently," Chávez said. "What can I say? It's changing times. To own a place on Acequia Madre, on Sosaya Lane, really has come to be equated with moving to the Hamptons back east."

Even while telling of the transformation of Acequia Madre, Chávez could not help but note that "so much remains the same." The observation is both conflicting and true. Chávez's own family home looks much as it did when Fabián Jr. and his siblings chased each other from room to room,

❧ FIGURE 3. ❧

The Chávez family included (seated) mother Nicolasa, father Fabián Sr.; (second row) Adela, Nicanora, Marta, Fray Angélico, Consuelo, and Clara; (back row) José, Francisco, Fabián Jr., Antonio, and Romualdo, "Cuate." Courtesy Chávez family.

much as it did when Fabián Jr. and brother Cuate reunited in the family kitchen for a tearful reunion upon returning from World War II to talk about where they had been and what they had seen while overseas. It is a far different home these days, though. Arguably by their own will, Chávez and his immediate family have been displaced from the neighborhood and the home Fabián Sr. struggled to reclaim following painful losses of the Great Depression. "We left the house to my sister Nora years ago. She was the last one to live in it. She'd say, 'Oh, I don't want to sell it.' I told her, 'Oh, go ahead. Sell it. Enjoy your life.'

"When she sold it, around 1990, she got three hundred thousand dollars for it. You couldn't touch it for that now. But with the money that Nora got from the sale, she was able to buy another house for her and her daughter and still had two hundred thousand left that she could use to travel and enjoy life."

If so much indeed is the same, as Chávez so generously observed, he must be referring largely to the blue sky overhead. In the first decades following New Mexico statehood, Santa Fe's Acequia Madre and adjacent Canyon Road neighborhoods were characterized by the occasional Anglo family living alongside the more prevalent native Hispanics. Families were aspiring even if for the most part not yet well-to-do. In recent decades, there has been great change in the neighborhoods' population and character. They are now mostly home to the wealthy. Many of the Hispanics have moved out, either by their own will or because of circumstances out of their control. Today, city zoning regulations and the still-rising price of property in the area are tantamount to "keep out" signs for so many who grew up knowing Santa Fe as their own.

For Fabián Jr., recollections of the family home are rooted in a natural bounty that molded the homestead's very walls. "There was so much around us: water from the acequia, fruit trees, vegetables, milpas. The soil itself was rich, and the adobes that were made for the family home came from that very patch of land."

Father Angélico wrote of the adobes and of the Chávezes' humble start in *Chavez, A Distinctive American Clan of New Mexico*:

> Our Chaves pioneer ancestors are most distinctive, if we must put it so, for having left no sumptuous mansions filled with all sorts of accumulated memorabilia like those found in other centers of Latin America and New England, no rare works of art which included painted portraits of each generation's haughty sire, no libraries crammed with learned tomes of the times besides stacks of documents detailing inheritances and other family fortunes. All

that the first pioneers left in this regard were bare adobe memories which time and the weather kept washing away. This is because their beloved land of New México, so much isolated for centuries as she was from the outside world, could offer them little else than that same perishable adobe which, in many ways, is part of her charm.[20]

His elder brother's words cannot help but resonate for Fabián Jr. He was brought up to have almost special respect for Angélico, the priest. "My mother would always tell me, 'Don't do anything that would embarrass your brother.' She meant Father Angélico, of course. I don't know that she said the same to my other brothers and sisters, but I guess I gave her plenty of opportunities to feel that she needed to admonish me that way.

"But even when I strayed, there was always that respect for everyone in our family, and it started with the respect we had for my father. The adobes for our home came from the earth beneath my father's feet, but he was responsible for all the woodwork—the frames, the windows, the doors. Dad designed the family home after seeing a general plan for a home in the Montgomery Ward catalogue. He sort of made minor changes, but he designed the house that he built, taking many ideas from that catalogue. He was very clever, and he used his contacts around town to his advantage.

"He was such a good cabinetmaker that he worked with a lot of home constructors in Santa Fe. He had connections with them so our home was a product of love and the contacts that my father had made in the city that would come to mean so much to us."

CHAPTER TWO

A Venturesome Boy
Rides His Thumb to California

Young Fabián Chávez Jr. took pride in being adventurous, often going well beyond what his parents and siblings considered wise, but he never thought of himself as reckless. At an age when many boys were still learning how to swing a baseball bat or field a ground ball, Fabián Jr. yearned to discover what life offered beyond the clearly defined boundaries of a ball park or those commonly accepted for lads so young that their voices had yet to change. The steps he took often alarmed his family and unsettled some who brushed up against his path. For Fabián, they were measured and calculated to enrich his life, not put it at risk.

At nine and ten, he ventured first from his home on Acequia Madre to Santa Fe's Plaza eight blocks away. From there, later, it was hitchhiking to San Ildefonso and Chimayó, then on to Taos, Madrid, and Albuquerque.

Life around young Fabián kept moving, too, even if somewhat more slowly amid the Great Depression. In Santa Fe's downtown area, Capital Pharmacy advertised speedy deliveries by motorcycle. Bell's advertised twenty-dollar suits for fifteen and pledged they were "styled to suit the best-dressed man."

My Life on the Frontier by Miguel Antonio Otero was on sale at the Villagra Book Shop in Sena Plaza. Spencer Tracy starred in *Murder Man* at the Lensic the same week that William Powell and Jean Harlow gave life to *Reckless* at the Paris Theater.

Chesterfield placed slick national ads locally that pitched the "cigarette halt."

"That's what men on the move call it when they stop for rest and a ciga-rette," the newspaper ad read.

For those more inclined to observe action than to create it, there was the brief visit of the Barnes Wild Animal Circus, promoted as having twelve acres of tents, two hundred acts, sixty clowns. It was all at the old ball park near La Tules's final resting place.

La Fonda at the end of the Santa Fe Trail regularly provided entertain-ment with its own dance and concert orchestra. Some occasions were spe-cial, though, like the one that unfolded on an autumn night in 1935 amid folk music and spectacular dancing on the hotel's roof. An account in the *Santa Fe New Mexican* described it this way:

> Gasps ran through the crowd as Jacques Cartier gave one of the best performances of his entire career in a dance that has made him internationally famous. The crowd was breathless at the beauty of the spectacle on the roof while he danced . . . Cartier did the voo-doo dance from the Congo but changed to the Montezuma cos-tume, that of a pillar of fire, all flaming red and gold. His entire body was painted red and silhouetted against the sky was the most gor-geous part of the program. He was accompanied only by percussion played by Ray Baldwin.

It was as if those in charge locally struggled to get people's minds off the Depression that was gripping the nation. Still, there were reminders every-where. Not only were men's suits marked down, Ballard's Grocery adver-tised peaches for $1.25 a bushel. Four tall cans of Pet or Carnation milk sold for the sum of 25¢. Mac Marr Stores had coffee at 25¢ a pound. The *Santa Fe New Mexican* sold for a nickel. The flow of visitors into Santa Fe slowed during those tough years and, Fabián remembers, so did automobile traffic. All the while, the young boy stirred.

"My brothers and sisters couldn't help but be aware of my hitchhik-ing. None of them ever came with me, but none ever tried to discour-age me, either," Chávez said. "My older sisters—Marta, Nora, Adela, and Consuelo—were good, solid members of the family. They were more con-ventional and very protective. They'd caution me, 'Take care of yourself. Don't get hurt.' They'd warn me that I might be running with strangers who might try to hurt me."

The more mature members of the family also knew of the random acts and senseless violence that could stop a life cold without warning. A September 1935 article in the *New Mexican* told of a man being held in the county jail after "running amok" and stabbing three others on a Sunday afternoon. The man "got hold of some bad liquor, got a knife and ran about the street, slashing at first one and then another," a policeman was quoted as saying.

At times it seemed as if terror might be all around, and it could not help but get noticed. Newspapers screamed of the assassination of Louisiana's U.S. Senator Huey Long in 1935. One news wire service report described "a year of disasters" in this manner:

> Drouth, black blizzards, flood, fire, hurricane, shipwreck, plane-wreck, tornado, lightning, battle, murder and sudden death have been striking at this country with unprecedented regularity and severity during the past year . . . One wonders why more clairvoy-ants have not come forward and claimed previous prediction of the appalling series of events.

As young Fabián rode his thumb to communities from Albuquerque to Taos, there was frequent news of death and injury inflicted on the roads. "Five persons were injured in two crashes on the Taos Highway out of Santa Fe over the weekend," a local news article reported. "All told there were six accidents on the road between here and Española on Saturday and Sunday."

Then, too, there was the dreaded toll of drunk drivers, as reflected in this passage from the *New Mexican*:

> Six months in the penitentiary for a drunken automobile driver who ran down a car and injured several people; and he will spend the six months there unless turned loose by 'a politically minded governor or a weak-kneed parole board,' quoth the vigorous and outspoken District Judge Mike Otero, who is occasionally available when not disqualified by his eminent district attorney or some of the ben-eficiaries of the rotten Hannett-Vogel law firm, to strike a blow for law and order. The carnage of the automobile is bad enough when drivers are sober; and the drunken driver is a menace which must be exterminated.

"These were the Depression years, so all my older brothers and sisters were pitching in to help the family," Chávez said. "They would help by buy-ing clothes or by providing spending money. Everybody was busy so my family didn't suffer from those hard times. And in all honesty, it wasn't hard times that got me to do what came next. To be truthful, I remained very inquisitive, and I had grown bored with Santa Fe."

It was 1936, and Fabián was twelve years old. His attention, ignited perhaps by the California actors he had seen get off trains briefly in Albuquerque, had turned to the movies, to the story-telling, the glamour, and refinement that seemed to be attached to the film industry even though most of the movies he watched had little to do with refinement and more to do with a young boy's imagination and venturesome interests.

"I was fascinated by movies, mostly the adventure movies, the short ones like Tom Mix and Flash Gordon. Of course, I also watched *Frankenstein* and Bela Lugosi and the vampire," he said. "Most of them were those serial movies they had every Saturday. They'd last a half hour and then continue the following week.

"I didn't have a girlfriend, and I felt pretty focused on this new attraction that was tugging at me, pulling me away not just from my home but

⊸ **FIGURE 4.** ⊱
Fabián Chávez Jr. at age twelve. Courtesy Fabián Chávez Jr.

from everything else I had done before. It was probably late August because I don't think school had started yet. I knew it was just around the corner, but I must have felt like I wasn't going to miss anything here.

"Dad was still working at his job as building superintendent at the state Capitol. Aside from that, he continued doing cabinetwork and other carpentry. One of the barter arrangements he had was with the José E. Roybal Store on Canyon Road. Dad would do carpentry work at the store and then charge it out in groceries.

"I knew that, so one morning I went to the store and got things like crackers, spreads, small cans of deviled ham. I got bread, a couple of apples, peaches, other fruit. I had decided I was going to California, to Hollywood specifically. Nobody knew what I was going to do. If they had, I'm sure they would have tried to talk me out of it."

Chávez said he recognized he would be facing a lot of unknowns, but he was certain of one thing. "I wasn't running away from home. I had beautiful brothers and sisters, a great mom and dad. As far as I was concerned, our family was well-off. We didn't lack for anything. Dad had this barter arrangement with different people so we never lacked for a balanced meal. We could count on old staples like pinto beans and chile, *carne molida* that could be done into anything. We always had vegetables, fruit in the house. I can't recall not being well fed, well clothed, and happy.

"Our entire neighborhood struck me then as a place that was escaping many of the hardships that we heard were being experienced elsewhere. We had the big alfalfa field but no animals so others would harvest the alfalfa and pay our family for what they took. You have to picture that part of the city as being the edge of country farmland just blocks from the state Capitol. Where Acequia Madre School is now there was a big wheat field, and there were orchards nearby. The Rodríguez family across the street from us on Acequia Madre Street had chickens and a cow that they milked. Out towards Canyon Road there was more farmland and horses. I remember our family's own trees of apricots and peaches.

"As you can see, I was very lucky to be growing up in a family that was able to take care of itself. There was extra help from my older brother, Cuate, and the older sisters, Nora, Marta, and Adela. There were good role models at home, good examples. As for my parents, well, I had great parents. We weren't rich, but I can't remember a day of suffering, a day of lacking anything."

None of that, though, satisfied Fabián's adventurous spirit.

"Somewhere in the house I had found a small suitcase made of strong cardboard. I left with probably three pairs of cotton pants, three shirts, underclothes, socks, and one pair of blue tennis shoes—good walking shoes. I had double bagged the little bit of food that I had gotten at Roybal's store. I was used to hitchhiking back and forth to Albuquerque and Taos. In fact, a lot of people hitchhiked back then. It was the Depression days so I really didn't feel overly concerned about what I was about to do.

"I must have had oatmeal or Cream of Wheat at home for breakfast that morning because that's usually what we had for breakfast. Without anyone knowing what I was doing, I got my clothes and my groceries, and I headed out to do what I had thought about for some time. I was going to see where they made the Hollywood movies. I was going to see the movie stars."

For Chávez, it was a mere natural progression in his attempt to learn about the world. "I wasn't being naughty or rebellious. I wanted to do good and to make my family proud, but I was taking my own path.

"Very simply, I was exploring what I considered to be a fascinating world. I guess I figured that if I could go from Santa Fe to Albuquerque, I could go to California. And I did. I walked out to the edge of town by the Indian School and stuck out my thumb."

Chávez recalls that the trip took him four or five days. "It was all along Route 66: Albuquerque, Grants, Gallup, Winslow, Flagstaff, Seligman, and on and on. Particularly as I got further away from Santa Fe, I tended to travel at night because it was so hot during the day. Imagine a kid of twelve making his way across several states in 110-degree heat! People would drop me off in different towns, and I'd find a place where they had a nice park, or I'd go to a public place like a city hall or a library where they had trees and a lawn. I'd mostly sleep during the days then clean up at bus stops, train stations, or filling stations where I'd look for my next ride. Every ride I got had at least a couple inside the car. I never recall getting a ride with just one person. I was never concerned about being kidnapped or molested or anything like that."

Nor was he terribly concerned in the beginning of his extraordinary trek to let his parents know what he was up to. "I don't know for sure when my parents became aware of what I was doing. I remember making a collect phone call from somewhere in Arizona to tell mom that I was OK. I don't think she could believe what she heard, and I probably figured it was best that I not talk with dad right then."

The same craftiness that served Fabián well as a young tour guide helped him make his way to the West Coast. "All the way along I told what you might call a little white lie," Chávez said. "Actually, I lied on the way to California, and I told the truth on the way back home. Both were very effective. On the way over, I told people I needed a ride to California because I was making my way home. Coming back to New Mexico, I said I was returning to my home in Albuquerque. I used Albuquerque because it was along Route 66 and Santa Fe wasn't as well known at the time.

"People who gave me rides didn't lecture me because I was doing the right thing in their minds: I was a kid who was returning home. They'd buy me a candy bar at the filling station before we headed out or when they'd stop to get something to eat, they'd invariably get me a hamburger or a hot dog, too."

Except maybe for one stretch on the trip over, Fabián did not look back. "There was one place where I felt a little touch of depression," he said. "It's when I got a ride from Flagstaff to Seligman. It was a very small town that didn't have the conveniences that I looked for in bigger towns so I hung around the railroad yard. I knew I couldn't allow myself to be deterred; I had to keep on going. I spent the night there and then got a ride to Needles just beyond the Arizona-California border. I was finally in California, and, boy, it was hot, pretty barren, too. But I remember crossing that big Colorado River. When you do, you never forget it. The river sure looked big to me. It was much bigger than the Rio Grande.

"Getting into Needles gave me my first image of California but I wasn't disappointed even though it didn't even come close to what I was expecting. I remember seeing that big road sign that said 'Welcome to California,' and I couldn't help but be excited about what was yet to come. I spent a day in Needles. It was big enough that there were facilities I could utilize and get ready for the next leg of my trip. The same was true in Barstow, San Bernardino, and into Pomona. The Mojave Desert wasn't very inviting, but I kept thinking of what was ahead."

Pomona just outside Los Angeles came far closer to tracking with Chávez's imagination. Surprisingly, though, the community with a population that was approaching thirty thousand also had a feel to it that reminded him of home. "The town of Pomona intrigued me because on that main street there was the big farmers' market and down the street not too far was the Catholic church," he said. "The Los Angeles County Fair was being held in Pomona. It was not too unlike the state fair in New Mexico. It was big with a lot of things going on.

"I found a nice place with a big lawn in one of the parks, and that's where I stayed for a few nights. Then there was a used-car lot where I could get in the back of a car to sleep because they didn't lock the cars then. Very quickly I made friends with an elderly lady who was the housekeeper for the local parish priest. She had gray hair, and I think she was Irish. When I got acquainted with her, she made sure I called home to tell my folks that I was OK. I remember the first call I made from there. Mother said, 'Hito, come home.' I said, 'I'm all right momma. Don't worry.' I think she felt at least some relief when I called from there and told her I was at a priest's house."

Pomona was one of the first chartered cities in Los Angeles County, and Latinos were a growing part of its population by the mid-1930s.[1] The city's population was growing rapidly around its agricultural base, which interestingly enough began when a citrus grower suggested that the town be named after the ancient Roman goddess of fruit.[2] The name was taken for the community reportedly even before a single orange tree had been planted within its boundaries.[3]

Pomona organized the first Los Angeles County Fair on a forty-three–acre site the city purchased.[4] Other activity was budding as well. The Fox Theater, which was built for three hundred thousand dollars, opened in 1931 and was on its way to becoming a landmark art deco movie house.[5] It was the fair and the activity around it, though, that unexpectedly transformed Chávez's journey to California.

"I got a sort of job at a farm just outside of town where I was allowed to live while I picked tomatoes, cucumbers, and other stuff," Chávez said. "Suddenly, I had this place to stay, and I got real cozy. I was able to make a little money on the side, and I was able to go to the local priest's house where I had made the acquaintance of that elderly lady who let me use the phone. And since I was an altar boy in Santa Fe, I was even able to serve Mass on several occasions while in Pomona. I remember I ate real well on the farm. There were plenty of oranges, of course, but I never lacked for good food. It was homey. On weekends, along with walking to the church, I was able to walk to the fair."

One of those walks onto the fairgrounds brought young Fabián into contact with someone who, much as the priest at the church, drew upon the boy's experiences of home. "I came upon this Indian who was either from Cochiti or Santo Domingo Pueblo, but he was dressed up like a Navajo," Chávez said. "He wore this colorful maroon Navajo-style shirt, and he had a little booth from where he sold pottery and jewelry and little trinkets.

"I approached him. I was a very up-front kind of a rascal. I asked him, 'Where are you from?' I had gotten to know Indians. I'd seen them working in Santa Fe, and I had seen them walk all the way from Tesuque to Santa Fe or come in wagons or on horseback.

"He looked down at me and said, 'Where are YOU from?' I said I was from Santa Fe. 'What are you doing HERE?' he wanted to know.

"'Oh, just visiting relatives,' I said. I lied to him because I figured he might call authorities or shoo me away if I told him the truth. I asked if I could do some work for him. He said, 'Sure,' and then he dressed me up like a little Indian in an outfit that included even a little ribbon around my head.

"People would stop and take pictures of this cute little 'Indian boy.'

"In all, I don't know how much money I made working for that man or for the man who owned the farm outside of town. But I remember I always had a lot of change in my pocket. I always had enough change to do whatever I needed to do."

Chávez recalls thinking that others around him must also be doing pretty well.

"If there was poverty in Pomona, I guess I didn't see it. What I remember are the lawns and flowers and all those buildings with red tile roofs between Pomona and the Los Angeles County Fair. There was so much in Pomona that made me think a lot of Albuquerque."

There was comfort in that because Albuquerque always made Chávez feel safe. It was big but safe. So was Pomona.

Los Angeles turned out to be far more than Chávez had bargained for. "I knew I was real close to the big city of Los Angeles and that I could go there simply by putting coins into the trolley car, but it took me several days before I went. I'm not sure why. I just didn't have that great urge anymore. It's as if my curiosity had been taken over by things I had come upon in Pomona," he said. "In the end, I made several trips into Los Angeles, but I never stayed there overnight. I'd leave to LA in the morning, but I'd be back in Pomona by four or five in the afternoon.

"Los Angeles scared me. It was too big. It was intriguing but too big. I'd take the trolley for fifteen or twenty-five cents and go to downtown Los Angeles. By downtown, I mean the big, beautiful railroad station. Then once you're in Los Angeles, there were all sorts of ways to get around. But it was the railroad station where I spent a lot of time. I was fascinated watching so many people come in there and unload their things."

As he watched, Chávez, of course, saw opportunity. "I was able to make a buck or two every time I was there by offering to carry luggage for people," he said. "There was always somebody who needed help."

What Chávez did not see during his trip to the West Coast was the glitz and excitement of Hollywood. Carol Lombard was big in Hollywood at the time. The Marx Brothers were stirring up laughter in *Yours for the Asking*. And 1936 was the year that Snow White and the Seven Dwarfs came to life.

"I went to Hollywood only once, and I didn't find it that fascinating, after all. Oh, I had heard of Hollywood and Vine so I had to go there but all I could say was, 'Huh! So this is it!' I guess I said to myself, 'Big deal,' because I didn't find it that attractive. I went to Grumman's Chinese Theater because I had read about that. That was a must. And I was very impressed by it. It was like what I had seen in the movies. I remember seeing it in the news as well as in the movies, all the lights flashing and stuff like that. But I wasn't as impressed as I was with the railroad station.

"I saw the outside of Paramount Studios, but I never made an effort to get inside any of the studios. I was outside Paramount, I think, more by accident than anything else, and I guess seeing it from a distance was good enough for me."

One of the big hotels on Pershing Square gave Chávez a closeup look at the lifestyle he figured went along with glamour. "I walked into the lobby, and it had murals all over the place. I was fascinated by the corridors and by a large ballroom where I imagined many of the famous Hollywood stars who I had seen in the movies back home had actually danced and partied with their friends.

"Still, Hollywood didn't grab me like I thought it would. I don't know that I could use the word 'disappointed.' It just didn't impress me all that much. I had all the adventure I needed in Pomona. It was a good, friendly town, and I had taken to the environment."

Then in a haste that surprised even him, Chávez concluded he had taken in enough of California for his first visit. "One day, I just decided it was time to come back home. I started my journey in the evening about six or seven o'clock. I walked to a service station and came upon this couple that was in their thirties. They were on their way to Las Vegas, Nevada. I told them I was from Albuquerque and that I was hitchhiking back home. They said they'd take me as far as Barstow because that's where our paths would part. But before we left, they stopped at a restaurant there in Pomona, and they bought me a hamburger and a Coke. They treated me real nice.

"They must have sensed my adventurous spirit and that I wasn't in any hurry to get home because when we got to Barstow, they asked if I wanted to go with them to Las Vegas. I had never been there, but already it had a reputation so I decided it would be an interesting detour. The Vegas strip didn't exist yet, and, frankly, the place didn't fascinate me that much. We were there a couple of days. I ate well and looked around but nothing really captured my attention.

"I left Las Vegas with a couple who drove me as far as Boulder City. There I met another couple that was going to Kingman, Arizona. We drove over Boulder Dam, which was later renamed Hoover Dam, and ended up stopping there. The couple I was with paid for me to go down with them to see the big generators. I suppose people looked at us and figured we were a family.

"Because of my side trip to Las Vegas, it took me a couple of days longer to get home than it did to get to California, but I got an extra experience or two that I wasn't expecting."

Nor had Chávez expected to come away from the trip with a fortified sense of confidence in himself and his world. "As I think back on those days, I guess if I had to describe my lessons from the trip in a single word, it would be 'survive.' In retrospect, I'm lucky to have survived. It was a damn foolish thing for me to do. But it didn't occur to me at the time or I wouldn't have done it. I was twelve years old. I made it all the way to Los Angeles and back. I found ways to get there, places to sleep, places to clean up. I found work and made a few bucks. I guess I had a natural instinct for survival.

"I have to say, though, I was never bothered in any way during the trip. That's where I was really lucky—and blessed. It all must have imbued my soul with a positive feeling for humanity because I got treated so well all the way over and all the way back.

"The big difference between going and coming was that at this end, I bought a ticket on the Greyhound Bus from Albuquerque to Santa Fe. Actually, I had enough money in California that I could have bought a bus ticket there for the entire trip. That's not what I wanted, though. Still, the money in my pocket was more evidence of how I did all right for myself on that trip—a twelve-year-old kid. Of course, it wasn't until later that I started feeling remorse for the anxiety that I must have created for my parents, especially my mother. But even with the remorse that came years later, I couldn't help but feel that it was a heck of a trip."

CHAPTER THREE

Springer

An Exasperated Father Looks for Reform

Young Fabián's parents, though unaware that their wayward son had taken a detour into Nevada's fledgling gambling and entertainment strip, had received a phone call telling them he was on his way back home from his furtive venture to California. "I had called from the priest's house in Pomona and told mom I was coming," Chávez said. "She let me know she was eager to see me but didn't let on about what I might find when I got in.

"'¡Bueno, hito! ¡Apúrale!' she told me. They knew I'd be there sometime. They just didn't know when, and it's not like they sat around the house looking out those French windows that dad liked so much to see when I might walk up."

In fact, nobody was home when twelve-year-old Fabián stepped off Acequia Madre Street and crossed the ditch that separated the narrow road from the Chávez home in that late summer of 1936. "They were on a picnic over by a creek up the canyon when I got home," he said. "I found things quiet at the house so I walked over to my sister Marta's place. My brother-in-law took me to where the family was picnicking. I walked onto the scene and must have said something like, 'Hola, here I am.'

"Big deal! That was kind of the response I got: Big deal! I didn't get a hug from mom. But I didn't get a swat from dad, either. Not there. There were too many people around. The swats came later."

So did something else, something that young Fabián could not have imagined or prepared for. "School had already been going on for at least a couple of weeks, and I don't even know if I enrolled when I got back. Things started moving pretty quickly."

The red-brick Roman Catholic school just a few blocks from the Chávez home was unable to harness young Fabián's extraordinary spirit despite all the discipline imposed within its walls. Chávez's father had come to recognize that. Fabián Jr. also found that his father no longer was inclined to simply allow his son to grow out of this streak of independence that had him straying so far from what was accepted at home. "What I remember more than anything was dad's determination to do something that might get me onto a different path."

Father and son one day walked from their east side home past the milpas and beyond the little river that dissected Santa Fe. They crossed the Plaza and approached the county courthouse on Grant Street just south of the First Presbyterian Church. As they walked, young Fabián could not help but look upon the Plaza and all its surroundings, thinking of the entrepreneurial opportunities and other experiences he had drawn from the site, and still uncertain about where his father was leading him at such a determined pace.

"We walked into the courthouse, and we went directly to see the district attorney, David Chávez Jr., who was a friend of my father's and the brother of Dennis Chávez, who had just begun serving as U.S. senator," Fabián said. "My dad had good connections. He knew both the district attorney and the judge, Miguel Otero. Dad was known as don Fabián, and he was a highly respected gentleman.

"Dad must have talked to the DA ahead of time because my father got right into the discussion as soon as we arrived. He told the district attorney that he just didn't want me getting into deep trouble or getting hurt in any way. I guess, in his eyes, I was sort of incorrigible. I know he was worried that I was going to stray into something serious.

"The DA asked my father in Spanish, 'Are you sure that you want to put the boy in Springer?' Judge Otero later asked pretty much the same question. My dad's response both times was, 'Yes, he has to learn.' He said he had lectured me and whipped me before, and it hadn't done any good.

"Once the decision was made, things went smoothly. They walked me down to the sheriff's office and arrangements were made to drive me to Springer."

Even in the mid-1930s, the name of Springer had its connotations, particularly among wayward boys and their families. It was a reform school more than a detention facility in the thirties. Still, merely mentioning the name struck fear in boys across New Mexico. Imaginative minds regarded

Springer as a sort of farm club for places like Alcatraz, Leavenworth, and Sing Sing.

That was not the way it started out, of course. The small community about 125 miles northeast of Santa Fe got its name from two brothers, both of whom were accomplished men of the community: Frank Springer, a lawyer for the railroad, and Charles, a rancher who worked land that included portions of what was once the two-million-acre Maxwell land grant.[1]

Part of the rolling prairie on the western edge of the Great Plains, Springer grew into a busy trading point for livestock after tracks were laid for the Atchison, Topeka and Santa Fe Railroad in 1879.[2] Locally crafted leather goods, like boots and saddles, were a staple of the community. Springer served briefly as the county seat for Colfax County, and the courthouse around which government business was run later served multiple purposes after voters moved the seat northward to Ratón.[3]

There was an edge to the community in its early years, to be sure. "People thought with the coming of the railroad that law and order would be better enforced and that the day of the desperados was past but each man was more or less his own law," wrote school teacher Lorrena E. Keenan in *A Brief History of Springer, New Mexico*.[4]

Still, over time members of the community looked to cultivate the best from their surroundings. The Colfax County Fair in August and the Cowboy Ball held in the old Springer Opera House on Colbert Street were main events each year.[5] The "boys dressed in white silk shirts, red silk ties and sashes," wrote Keenan. "It was the only affair at which it was permissible for gentlemen to dance without their coats."[6]

Skating parties on the Cimarron River entertained townspeople in the winter when cold winds were not blowing across the open plains.

The courthouse became a public library after the county seat was moved in 1898.[7] The library was displaced in 1909, three years before New Mexico statehood, when territorial Gov. George Curry issued a proclamation creating the New Mexico Industrial School for Boys.[8] It was meant to serve as a detention home for troubled youths, who were confined to the one-time courthouse until 1917, when a new facility was built about ten miles outside of town.

"For a long time, all you had on New Mexico's northeastern plains were a few cattle ranches on the Maxwell Land Grant," wrote Anselmo Arellano, a historian and descendant of one of Springer's original families.[9] "But by 1874, five different railway lines were under construction leading to the area. The Atchison, Topeka and Santa Fe Railway won the race when it crossed the Ratón Pass on December 7, 1878, and entered into New Mexico. Within weeks it arrived at Willow Springs, a stage coach stop that became the town site for the community of Ratón. From Ratón, the railroad continued to the site that was also being planned for the new community of Springer.[10]

"Springer quickly became a shipping and transportation center for northeastern New Mexico and parts of west Texas that reached the Dalhart-Amarillo area," Arellano wrote.[11] "Elizabeth Town in the mountains to the north had been founded as a gold mining community in 1868, and a lot of the machinery, equipment and supplies destined for the community were unloaded from the trains at Springer and hauled to E-Town by wagon.[12]

"Springer also became a shipping outlet for sheep, cattle, wool and hides," according to Arellano. "Porter and Clothier established itself as the first major mercantile outlet to serve this sector of New Mexico and the Texas Panhandle. Other merchants, such as the Floersheims, followed to establish Springer as a major trade center."[13]

Springer Irrigation Company served many of the local farms and ranches, but dry farming was also quite common, Arellano wrote. Sugar beets were a staple.[14]

"East of Springer at Bueyeros on the Old Tascosa Trail to Texas, oil drillers hit carbon dioxide which was almost 100 percent pure," he wrote. "It led to development of dry ice plants in that area close to Mosquero. Many local jobs were provided in the plants that were considered to be the purest CO_2 fields in the United States."[15]

It was a vibrant and varied life around Springer, but much of it was lost on the state's residents who lived beyond the eastern plains. Springer often translated into the boys' school, plain and simple, and the school grew to take on a substantial presence amid New Mexico's political circles, largely because of its role as a source for jobs.

In September 1935, the longtime Springer mayor, Irwin C. Floersheim, was ousted as superintendent of the school and replaced by John Peck, former sheriff of Chaves County to the south, according to news reports. A member of Springer's early mercantile families, Floersheim was aligned with Democratic U.S. Rep. John Dempsey. He told newspapers that he suspected that a political opponent had been "working on" Gov. Clyde Tingley to oust him from the school.

"But I felt differently when Tingley named four district judges to the [school] board and believed politics would not sway them," Floersheim told a reporter. "I find now that the nonpolitical board is playing politics harder than the former board did."

The newspaper account told how Floersheim's firing was more evidence of the growing split between Democratic power brokers Dempsey and Tingley.

As evidence of his dedication to the school, Floersheim told of work on a new refrigeration plant, a sewage disposal system, and the reroofing of all buildings on the campus—all accomplished for three thousand dollars less than estimates. "That was done by using the boys as workers instead of letting the work out on contract," he said.

It all was part of the atmosphere that awaited young Fabián Chávez Jr. at the Springer boys' school. Though he was destined for the school on an order his father initiated and endorsed by both a district attorney and a highly regarded state judge, the boy and the sheriff's officer who transported him out of New Mexico's capital city took a sort of casual route on their way out. "The officer and my father were very good friends so I didn't feel scared or intimidated in any way as we left Santa Fe," Chávez said. "We passed over the Pecos River near San José, drove past Las Vegas, and then as if to take a well-deserved break from our journey, we stopped to visit some of my relatives in Wagon Mound. It was one of my dad's younger brothers, my Tío Tomás, and his wife. I don't know if the officer knew them before that day or if he was simply acting on instructions from my dad, but we pulled into Wagon Mound in that small Ford and visited for probably a couple of hours. There was no sense at all that I was this young prisoner on his way to face some kind of dreaded punishment."

Chávez recalls his arrival at the boys' school in the latter part of September 1936 as anything but intimidating. "It was real nice, in fact," he said, and, again, he found himself in the company of a family friend. "We drove up to this two-story building, and I was greeted by the superintendent and his wife along with a lady by the name of Aurora Lucero White. She was a schoolteacher there. She happened to be a good friend of the family and was an especially close friend of my older sister, Nora. So, right away, I guess, I became a teacher's pet.

"There were no walls or anything like that around the place. They had the dormitories. They had the main buildings with the kitchen and other facilities. The schoolrooms were on the second floor. Out in the yard they had a barn. They had cows. They had chickens."

Though he would never sit in its classrooms, a new public grade school was being built at a cost of forty-three thousand dollars on the grounds of the old Springer courthouse as young Fabián arrived in the community. Not counting the boys at the detention school, the community of Springer had close to four hundred school-age children at the time, historian Arellano said. It was about a fifty-fifty mix of Anglos and Hispanics.[16]

The school that would take Fabián in was out of town, isolated mostly from Springer's daily activity. Still, young Fabián never felt inferior in his extraordinary surroundings.

He stayed in a dormitory with boys who ranged in age from ten to six-teen. Older boys were housed in a different building. "I especially remem-ber an older boy from nearby Las Vegas," Chávez said. "He was one of the guys you knew you didn't fool with, but mostly it wasn't hard to stay out of fights and other trouble. In fact, I got into only one fistfight while I was there. This one kid would go around grabbing other boys by the hair. He did it to me once, and the only way I could get him to let go was to hit him in the stomach. I remember him gasping because I knocked his wind out."

During more recent years, the boys' school at Springer took in some rough juveniles, including rapists and murderers, as documented repeat-edly by news reports. Chávez was never in that kind of company. "I don't think there were any real bad guys at Springer when I was there. If there were, I sure didn't know about them," Chávez said. "To tell you the truth, kids back then were sent to Springer mostly for discipline. I had the sense that I was there for discipline; I wasn't being punished. Punishment to me was getting whipped. Discipline nowadays, you might call it getting grounded. Well, back then, when discipline didn't take at home, they'd send you to Springer.

"It's what gets a lot of boys sent to New Mexico Military Institute in Roswell, even today. Springer was very much like a military school without the uniforms. A family friend told me many years after I had left Springer that if my dad had had the money, he would have sent me to the Military Institute. He said I was lucky because the Military Institute was much tougher than the boys' school at Springer."

As Chávez recalls, kids could end up at Springer because of circum-stances at home not entirely of their making. "I met these two boys from Santa Fe, the Walsh brothers, and once they found out I was from Santa Fe, too, we became very close friends. We played together and kind of looked out for one another. The two boys had gotten into some sort of trouble in Santa Fe, but mostly I think they wound up in Springer because these were the Depression days and they came from a family that was left to be run by a widow. Times were hard on a family like that, and Springer probably was used to help lighten the widow's load. They were good boys, and I was lucky to have such good friends there."

When Chávez was not flanked by newfound friends, he was under the watchful eye of someone who paid special attention to his progress, much as the nuns had at St. Francis Parochial School in Santa Fe. "Aurora White was my only teacher while I was there. She had taught school in Santa Fe before going to work at Springer. She was nice to everybody at the boys' school, but I was lucky because she happened to know my family.

I remember she gave me the lead in the Christmas play. My stay at Springer was not an unpleasant experience for me at all."

Still, the daily routine was a far cry from the independence that young Fabián had sought over and again to his family's distress. "I had to adjust to the discipline, no doubt about it," Chávez said. "By that I mean the uniformity of the processes that were established, like what time to go to bed, what time lights went out, what time they wake you up in the morning. You get up, clean up, brush your teeth, fix your bed, and go to breakfast. After breakfast, you come back and brush your teeth again and prepare to go to school.

"In the afternoon, they'd let you out of school. You had time to play. Then it was off to supper. Then came study time, then lights out. It was like a rigid boarding school in many ways. I was there because I hadn't adjusted to some of the disciplines of life, like going to school. It's not that I didn't want to learn. I've had, even to this day, what you might call a rewarding fault in that I've had the capacity to learn well those things that I found attractive and to ignore, or just barely learn out of necessity, the ones that I don't find attractive. Simply, I was a bad student but a good learner.

"I'd gravitate toward the liberal arts. I could study history and have fun. After Springer, I'd study philosophy, The Great Books—Socrates, Aristotle, Shakespeare. I'd read the *Federalist Papers*. Yet, whenever I could, I'd ignore subjects I didn't like, subjects like science and math, even when they were required.

"At Springer, I couldn't ignore anything. We had study periods. The teacher would say here are the classes, here's the homework. You did it, or they'd cut you off from going to the movies at Springer. It's one of the few incentives they had for you to stay in line. If you did your schoolwork, if you gathered the manure and cleaned up the stables and the chicken poop, if you stayed out of fights, every other week or so they'd take you to movies in downtown Springer."

Local employees of the Pastime Theater greeted boys of the detention school when they arrived. Standard dress for the boys at the time, as the *Springer Tribune* reported, included blue overalls and blue shirts. The theater, as Chávez came to know it, was on its last legs. It was temporarily closed soon after Chávez left the community late in the summer of 1937. It underwent major renovation and was merged with the Gibralter Theatre network to become one of the premier theater houses in New Mexico under the new name, Zia Theatre.[17]

"On Sundays, the boys' school had two kinds of services," Chávez said. "One was a regular Mass, and the other was a Protestant service. I had been trained as an altar boy by the nuns in Santa Fe so I was able to help sometimes with the masses at Springer. I also attended some of the Protestant services and remember that they did a lot of singing. That's what I liked the most about their services."

With little effort throughout his stay at Springer, Chávez was able to integrate himself into activities he liked most and learned to adjust to those that had a distinctive edge of discipline. If he missed home, it was only for fleeting moments that he was able to push aside. "I didn't get many visits from the family while I was at Springer," he said. "At Christmas, families would buy their sons round-trip tickets on the bus, the school placed you on trust, and you were allowed to visit home. I was supposed to go home for Christmas, but I turned it down. I didn't go because the teacher gave me the lead in the Christmas play and I took the assignment seriously." Chávez's parents and younger brother, Antonio, drove to Springer that Christmas to view the play.

"By the time the new year began, I think I had adjusted to pretty much everything at Springer so that it was just like being at any other boarding school. When the time came for me to leave at the end of the spring semester, it was my brother-in-law, Vincent Matt, who picked me up. Vincent was married to my sister, Marta, and he had this nice car, a Pontiac, I believe, so he's the one who made the long drive out.

"I remember I was waiting in the front office of the main building. Mrs. White might have been there to say good-bye, I'm not really sure. But it was a very pleasant departure, even though it was a routine kind of thing. I remember I had my little sack or suitcase with my clothes. Vincent walked up and said something like, 'Hey, junior, how are things going? How was school?' We had easy conversations on the drive back. I never felt any negativity from him. And I didn't have any apprehension about facing my parents. I felt completely relieved, and I was glad to be going home. It was May and summer vacation time."

Chávez's thoughts, again, turned to making a buck. "I didn't have any specific plans for the summer. I thought I'd try to find ways to make some money, of course. I thought maybe I'd deliver newspapers, run errands. After all, I was still a little enterpriser. Springer didn't change that. I don't think anything could."

Chávez's parents were both at home, along with several other family members, when young Fabián and his brother-in-law arrived. "My parents greeted me with hugs and kisses. It was a sharp difference from the day that I had returned from California. After Springer, everybody was happy to see me. Later that day, I can remember somebody remarking how neat I was while eating. It was little things, like placing my knife and fork on top of the plate, things that I must have picked up at school. Frankly, I guess my manners improved while I was at Springer and members of the family noticed it."

Once back, neither of Chávez's parents lectured him about his stay in Springer or the conduct that sent him there. "We just went about life, picking up where we had left off in terms of chores around the house. I'd help water the trees, the plants, keep the little garden outside in good shape."

When the fall semester approached, a year after Chávez had ventured off to California on his own, he enrolled in the seventh grade at St. Francis Parochial School. "I had no trouble integrating with the rest of the kids. My experience at Springer didn't seem to be a factor. Not only was I accepted, I had become a better student, probably because of the discipline that I got at Springer," Chávez said. "The nuns had a certain way of teaching that I guess I had always found attractive. They worked with me to improve my reading, writing, arithmetic. And I became good in all the subjects.

"I don't know if it was because I was the kid brother to a priest, but again the Loretto nuns spent special time with me. They just seemed determined to get the best out of me, and I think it worked."

Following his year at Springer, Chávez completed the next two years at the Roman Catholic elementary school. He enrolled at the city's public Harrington Junior High School for the ninth grade and to his surprise came upon a fond acquaintance.

"Aurora Lucero White had left Springer and came back to Santa Fe to teach at Harrington," Chávez said. "My older sister, Nora, was administrative assistant to Raymond Patrick Sweeney, who was city school superintendent at the time. When I signed up to go to the ninth grade, Nora called up Mrs. White and said, 'Make sure that Fabián takes these courses: algebra, English literature . . . ' None of the easy ones, in other words. I still had some oversight from my family.

"Nora had always been almost like a second mother to me. She sort of guided me after I got out of St. Francis Parochial School. She worked a lot on discipline with the other kids in the family, too, the way we dressed and sat at the table, things like that."

For several years after Springer, Fabián's life cooled from his bright hot days as a very young boy. "I studied and got good grades, especially in the subjects that interested me. I played a little softball while I was at Harrington as a catcher, but I wasn't big enough to be a sports hero," he said. "But I was a damn good dancer. When I moved on to high school, I wound up winning a lot of dance contests."

High school for Chávez was not at St. Michael's, despite his parents' fondness for the city's Roman Catholic schools. Guided again by his sister, Nora, Chávez enrolled at Santa Fe High.

"It didn't reflect any defiance against my parents, nothing like that," Chávez said. "I had great respect for my parents, my entire family. It's just that my sister Nora had assumed considerable responsibility for me. She was in a position with the public schools where she thought she could help provide guidance, and it all must have made sense to my parents.

"I had settled down from my earlier years, but I remained intensely curious. Even though I wasn't hitchhiking across several states anymore, I was still very interested in what was happening in the world around me. These were the Depression years, remember. And there was great unrest abroad. War was raging in Europe, and I developed an intense interest in that war. The big headlines about the war coming in from overseas were inescapable."

Chávez sensed the world shifting under his feet. "For me, so much seemed to happen so quickly. Pomona and southern California were a distant memory. Springer came later, but I didn't even think of Springer anymore. My youth seemed to come to an abrupt end, and I couldn't really say when it happened. I had begun to wonder not only about what lay beyond the city limits or across state lines. I was thinking about events across the oceans. I was still adventurous and daring. I was still a boy, but increasingly I sensed that I was entering a huge new, important stage of my life."

CHAPTER FOUR

Five Battle Stars

Jumping into World War II at Sixteen

War was raging in Europe, and for Fabián Chávez Jr. it created a new opportunity to expand his knowledge of the world. News of Hitler and Mussolini was splashed daily on papers with datelines that included Rome, Tirana, London, and increasingly, Washington, DC.

"Germany and Italy were involved in aggressive expansion activities," Chávez recalls. "In this county it was becoming obvious that it was just a matter of time before we would be involved against the Germans, especially. More and more young men from New Mexico were volunteering for service. I couldn't help but notice that, because many of my own friends who were a little older than me were among those who were lining up for duty, either as volunteers or after having been drafted."

The headlines of 1939 were ominous as young American men left their homes to prepare for the uncertain:

> "Nazis Attack Poles by Land and Air"
> "British Plane Carrier Sunk by Sub"
> "Nazi Threat Issued to Allies"
> "2 Powers Split Poland's Spoils"[1]

The United States was not yet a part of the fighting, but this country was already taking sides. "Activity was really getting hot in Europe. Around my home, for sure, the Germans—los alemanes—were the bad guys," Chávez said. "I remember my parents saying in Spanish, '¡Esos alemanes son bárbaros!' More and more volunteers were going into the armed services, including some of my neighbors and friends.

"I remember specifically going to a sort of family party for neighbors whose son had come home on furlough around the fall of 1940. He was two years older than me, and he was dressed up in this nice army uniform, very impressive. Almost immediately I wanted to be a part of what was going on. That's when I asked around and found out that when you reach your eighteenth birthday, you can be drafted and they would send you to whatever branch of the military they want but if you volunteer, you could choose your service. I liked that, the opportunity to choose where you would go."

The eighteenth birthday: it seemed like an eternity away for the restless sixteen-year-old Chávez. Meanwhile, he found the excitement surrounding the fighting in Europe inescapable. "Along with listening to members of my family, I learned to hate the German Nazis by reading the newspapers and listening to the radio. We'd also see them on the newsreels at the movies, of course. I'd go to the movies once a week, sometimes twice a week. The newsreels that ran before the movies would show pictures of German battalions, tanks; we'd see the artillery, the screaming bombers, and the damage they left behind. I'd say to myself, 'That's one mean bunch of guys!'

"Was it military propaganda? You can say that it was, if you want. But it wasn't propaganda in my mind when you also read about the invasion of France, the invasion of Poland, the bombing of England. No, that's not propaganda. That's reality."

Again, headlines reflected the atmosphere that had Americans stirring:

"Danes Submit Without Fight"
"Nazis Warned on Air Threat"
"U.S. Arms Program in Full Swing"
"Germans Renew Bombing of Britain"[2]

"We saw that Italy had taken over Ethiopia, that it was going in with artillery, tanks, and guns, and fighting people who had only bows and arrows and spears," Chávez said. "At that age, I can't truthfully tell you that I envisioned the Germans crossing the Atlantic. But there was information about them sinking ships with U2 submarines.

"There was war news everyplace. I was still selling the *Albuquerque Journal* in the mornings and the *Santa Fe New Mexican* in the afternoons. I read a lot in those papers, and I learned from what was being reported that it wouldn't be long before the United States would go in on the side of England and France. They were the good guys. We fought on their side in World War I.

"I was stirring. There's no doubt about it," Fabián Jr. said. "I specifically remember there was this family by the name of Tafoya that lived on Delgado Street near our home and their father was a veteran of World War I. He had this album with all these pictures of that war. The pictures that impressed me the most were the ones that showed the big artillery, especially the picture that showed what came to be called Big Bertha."

Big Bertha was the name given to 420-mm howitzers that developed a wicked reputation and towered over men. Their muzzles were more than twenty-two feet long. The wheels on which they rolled were taller than some of the men who had to break them down and then reassemble them each time they moved. Germans used the big guns while advancing through Belgium in 1914.[3]

For Fabián Jr., the activity that was stirring around him—beginning in his own family kitchen and extending to foreign lands across the Atlantic—was too much to ignore. "I remember it was the Christmas season of 1940 when about six or seven of us from the neighborhood decided we would volunteer for the military," he said. "Some of the guys were seventeen going on eighteen, just months away from eligibility. I was sixteen going on seventeen, but we were all contemporaries. We were neighbors who used to walk to school together from our homes on Acequia Madre, Canyon Road, Delgado Street, East García Street.

"We decided to go to the federal building and post office that was right across the street from St. Francis Cathedral, where the Indian art institute museum is now. We got applications, and we filled them out right away. There was a portion at the bottom of the form that called for parental authorization. Our parents didn't know what we were doing so we signed each other's papers; we forged each other's parental signatures. It was something that was being done a lot in those days, actually, all over the country."

Chávez and his friends submitted their paperwork and awaited word as the holidays unfolded. "The next thing we know, we were called up within about two weeks," Chávez said. "I don't remember if it was a phone call or a letter, but I think they sent us a letter. We got together and went to where the army museum is now on Old Pecos Trail. It was actually an army installation at the time. We got in, and soon there were about fifteen or twenty of us lined up for physical examinations. I recall saying to myself, 'This thing is going to work.' The signatures on our forms were a ruse, but we felt patriotic doing what we had done. We were going to beat the hell out of those Germans!"

Suddenly Chávez and his boyhood companions found themselves on the fast track to war instead of preparing for another semester of high school. "Nobody in the military questioned our age, our documents, or the forged signatures," he said. "There were a lot of people volunteering, and if you were in good health, they took you. People all around New Mexico, all around the United States, could attest to that. Heck, a lot of guys going in with me didn't have fuzz on their face.

"I got through my physical, and I remember a bunch of us were trucked to Albuquerque on January 2, 1941. We were then placed on a train that took us to El Paso. At El Paso, there was another truck waiting for us at the railroad station that took us to Fort Bliss. There we filled out another set of documents, and since I had volunteered, I got to choose where I wanted to go. I signed up for artillery; it's what I wanted all along. I was assigned to the Sixty-first Field Artillery Battalion, First Cavalry Division. We were given uniforms, and, officially, my records show that I enlisted on January 3, 1941."

German bombers raided Ireland that very day, as if to fortify Chávez's hatred of the Nazis.[4]

~ **FIGURE 5.** ~
Fabián Chávez Jr. at Fort Bliss, 1943. Courtesy Fabián Chávez Jr.

Chávez's entry into the military and his transport to Fort Bliss all came as a surprise to his parents. "Mom and dad didn't learn that I had signed up for the military until I called them from Fort Bliss. I remember talking to mom on the phone. She said, 'Cuídate mi hito.' I think news of my going into the military might have prompted a sigh of relief on their part, figuring that it surely would continue adding structure in my life.

"My enlistment was nine months before Pearl Harbor. Also before Pearl Harbor, the Two Hundredth Coast Guard Artillery was activated and moved into the Fort Bliss area. They maneuvered there and then were shipped to the Philippines. That shows how much activity was going on related to World War II prior to Pearl Harbor. You couldn't escape the feeling of war, and then the Axis formed of Germany, Japan, and Italy. I got through basic training and was at Fort Bliss for at least eighteen months while fighting raged on overseas."

Chávez was in training for just a few months when Germany announced the surrender of the Yugoslav army in April 1941.[5] A few days later, the Germans attacked Athens and then Crete.[6] In May, Pres. Franklin Roosevelt proclaimed an unlimited state of national emergency in the United States.[7] By summer, Germany, Italy, Romania, and Finland declared war against Russia.[8] The Japanese moved into French Indochina, and in mid-August Roosevelt and Winston Churchill, the British prime minister, announced the eight-point Atlantic Charter following what had been a secret conference at sea.[9]

Chávez could do little more than adjust to his training. "The first year, especially, was a very intense period, but I have to say that the discipline and things like that weren't much of a change for me. The reason was that the nine months or so that I spent at the boys' school at Springer were very similar. At Fort Bliss we got up in the morning to answer to revelry at 6 a.m.; we'd dress up; they'd call your name; you're dismissed; you go back in and shower and shave; you fix up your bed then go to breakfast. That's discipline. I got all that at Springer. Having to do it at Fort Bliss was no big deal. Since everybody has to do the same thing, it's no big deal. It's not like you're being punished. It was kind of fun in a way. I blended in very easy.

"Our battalion still relied on horses to pull cannons and the caissons so I spent a lot of my time around horses those first few months in the military. In truth, a lot of our time was spent shoveling horse manure. One of the very first things they assigned to you at the fort was two horses. Each man had to take care of his horses. I had to learn not only how to ride a horse but how to lead a horse. I learned the lead, the swing, and the break—two horses in each of three rows. We had to learn how to maneuver them all. Between learning how to maneuver the horses, how to march, taking orders, and all that other stuff that goes with the military, there was no escaping the horse manure. Man, we spent a lot of time cleaning up behind the horses. Our monthly pay was thirty dollars."

If events at Fort Bliss were less than stirring, people back at Chávez's hometown were reminded daily of intensifying hostilities across the ocean. On July 24, 1941, a banner headline and accompanying story in the *New Mexican* reflected the patriotism that was being fanned even in the smallest of U.S. cities. The main headline read: "Thousands Celebrating Defense Day Hear Governor Miles Warn of National Peril." The drop headline followed with: "America Facing Real Threat to Life and Freedom, Throng Told."

The story's lead read: "'Hitler hopes that we will continue to be suckers,' stated Governor Miles, warning thousands of people in the Defense Day rally in the Plaza this forenoon against Isolationist Propaganda. 'There is a real threat to our lives and our freedom,' said the governor. 'Do not be lulled to sleep by talk of a defensive ocean between us and the enemy.'"

Judge David Chávez Jr., the same man who had helped get Fabián Jr. admitted into the Springer boys' school a few years earlier, introduced Miles at the rally as well as Adjt. Gen. Russell C. Charlton and former U.S. attorney W. J. Barker, the *New Mexican* reported.

Fabián Jr.'s division went on maneuvers in Louisiana in July and August 1941 before Chávez got his first furlough home nine months after he had left. "I was dressed up in uniform as a private first class. My folks thought that I was a very handsome young man. I sensed by looking at them that they had concluded I did the right thing by going into the military. I remember thinking that the week I had there went by quickly. I arrived on a Sunday and left on a Sunday."

By then, the summer's public rallying in Santa Fe had turned to practice blackouts. The Capital Pharmacy ran an ad in the local paper on September 12, 1941, that encouraged residents to participate in the practice blackout so that it might be "a success."

"If possible, remain at home until after the blackout period is over. If you happen to be in a car, park immediately and turn out the lights when you hear the warning whistle," the ad read. It said further, "There will, of course, be no deliveries during the blackout tonight. We ask that you anticipate your needs prior to the blackout (warning whistle)."

Local theaters ran ads reminding people that blackouts would not affect indoor movies, encouraging them to sit out any drills while watching the latest films. Dorothy Lamour and Jon Hall starred in *Aloma of the South Seas* at the Lensic as September drew to a close. On September 28, people not distracted by the movies were stirred by the day's headline and accompanying story in the local paper. "Unparallel Victory Claimed by Nazis" read the main head. The drop head announced: "Berlin says Soviets All But Knocked Out; Turning Point in War." Then the story began with this information: "The first anniversary of the Germany-Japanese-Italian tripartite pact was marked yesterday by the German announcement that five Soviet armies had been annihilated."

None of the boys from Santa Fe who enlisted with Chávez were part of his battalion. He sensed great transition in his young life. "The first year in the military was a good year. I was happy, and I saw my life changing very much. The major change I began to see was just how different things were from home even though home was little more than three hundred miles away. When you go into the armed serves, in my case the First Cavalry Division, and you're intermixed there with guys from all over the country, you find out that many of your countrymen speak funny, boys from Mississippi, Louisiana, from Pennsylvania, California, everywhere.

"I was glad to experience all of that but I was also fortunate to come upon someone who offered something more familiar. A guy named Jesús Pacheco from Santa Fe had enlisted about a year before me and was in the Sixty-first Field Artillery Battalion. I knew the Pacheco family. They were very well known in Santa Fe. Jesús was about three or four years older than me. He sort of took me under his care and helped guide me through the early stages. Later, he was in charge of the horses used by our battery commander. He wasn't as restricted as those of us in the barracks so on weekends, if I wanted to, I could go over and stay with Jesús, catch a trolley car, and go down to El Paso or Juárez. Believe me, it was nice to know someone from Santa Fe who already knew the routine."

If the routine of life surrounding basic training had become easy and even enjoyable for Chávez, however, some of the routines of war were changing. "After our furlough in 1941, we had to get rid of the horses because we got mechanized. It wasn't easy. In fact, I had tears in my eyes as I watched the horses leaving. I don't know what they did with the horses. They were transferred somewhere because the military had to make room for the machinery that was brought in to replace them. Up until that time, we didn't even have enough artillery, enough rifles. Suddenly, we were looking at modern equipment."

Then came the real change for Chávez and every other American in and out of the military. "I was down in El Paso," Chávez said. "It was a Sunday so some of us had taken a trolley into town to relax or have some fun. Suddenly the broadcast came over on all radio stations: 'All soldiers get back to Fort Bliss.'

"It was December 7, 1941, and Pearl Harbor had just been attacked. That changed everything."

It was a horrendous period for many, including the Europeans who were fighting thousands of miles away from the Japanese assault. The day before the attack, news reports said, soldiers were fighting in Moscow in minus-thirty-degree weather.

"We at Fort Bliss were told to send home all our civilian clothes because from that point forward we would only be using our army uniforms," Chávez said.

Headlines in New Mexico screamed of the surprise hit by the Japanese. "Congress Declares War on Japan; 3,000 Casualties in Raid on Hawaii," read one headline the day after the surprise attack in the Pacific. Four days later, New Mexico headlines reported massive new escalation. "Germany, Italy Declare War on U.S.," read one. "Hitler and Mussolini Praise Japan in Announcing Joint Action Against America and Britain," read another.

Santa Fe, like communities across the United States, was stunned. On the very day of the attack, the lead headlines in the *New Mexican* read: "FDR sends personal note to Jap Emperor; Message Viewed as Last Resort to Avert Break with Japs."

As if to signal that life apart from war still went on, another story on the paper's front page reported that Charles J. Ekert, a cashier at First National Bank, and insurance man Manuel Luján had just been nominated to serve as vice presidents of the Santa Fe Chamber of Commerce. On the sports page that day, the leading headline read: "Horsemen Basketball Prospects are Bright."

Back at Fort Bliss, Chávez quickly came to recognize that the war machine of which he had been a part would suddenly shift gears. "Suddenly much of my basic training had become obsolete. I hadn't been trained with modern equipment, but that's what came into the fort after Pearl Harbor. Nineteen forty-two was very interesting because they started bringing in more trucks, newer artillery pieces, like the 105 howitzer. I had trained on the old famous French 75. I had been trained in the old-type army, but suddenly the war effort had magnified, and I quickly went into a modernized army that our country was converting to."

That modernized military required transformations throughout U.S. society. There was massive retooling of Detroit's auto plants so they could produce tanks, planes, and other weapons instead of the cars and trucks upon which Americans were becoming increasingly reliant. An April 9, 1942, story in the *Detroit News* told of the effort:

The battle of production, the battle to forge the weapons of war for the men at the fighting front is being won.

It is being won by the sweat and toil of tens of thousands of men and women in the grime and smoke and the glare of the mass production factories which the genius of the automotive industry developed to set men free from the narrow boundaries of their own immediate neighborhoods—the same genius that now seeks to set men free from the threat of tyranny.

The tanks are rolling off the assembly line. The assembly line technique has been applied to the manufacture of immensely intricate anti-aircraft guns.

"I felt like now we really had a war on our hands," Chávez said. "I guess I became more militaristic. What impressed me the most at the time was the whole tenor of our training. It turned more aggressive. The first time I went home on furlough before Pearl Harbor I brought home my uniform so my parents could see how cute I was. After Pearl Harbor, there was no more cuteness. There was a strong sense of military purpose that was imbued into us by Pearl Harbor."

A special sense of purpose was also being instilled in citizens back in Santa Fe following the attack on Pearl Harbor. Their local paper reported that construction of combat ships and work on all munitions industries at various points around the country would go on seven days a week on President Roosevelt's orders. The *New Mexican* also told of local officials out to discourage anything that might detract from challenges seen to have been sparked by the Japanese attack. The story read:

To refrain from repeating baseless war gossip, to keep calm and to aid in civilian defense were the pleas addressed last night to a crowd that practically filled the armory by several speakers, including Governor Miles and Archbishop Rudolph A. Gerken, and which, at the close, repeated the oath of allegiance led by Justice Howard L. Bickley of the state supreme court.

"Once aroused, we're the greatest fighting nation under the sun," said Governor Miles, "and just as sure as I am standing here, every single living citizen of Japan will have cause to regret what they started at Pearl Harbor."

Former judge Miguel Otero Jr. called upon New Mexicans to respond to challenges before them. Said he: "We have enjoyed the privileges of citizenship. Now let us not forget its obligations."

Chávez was months into training with the new weapons of war and waiting for the inevitable orders that would send him into the heat of battle overseas. Something else came first, though: word of events in the Philippines that served to further boil the blood of Americans at home as well those serving abroad. After surrendering to the Japanese army, seventy-six thousand American and Philippine troops, including more than eighteen hundred members of the New Mexico National Guard endured brutal treatment on a ten-day march to internment, news reports told. Thousands of the prisoners died, and many others fell gravely ill or were seriously injured.

"It was the image of brutal Germans that drove me to lie about my age and enlist in the U.S. military, but Pearl Harbor and then the Bataan Death March just a few months later made it abundantly clear that when it came to fierce enemies, we had more than we could count," Chávez said, "Pearl Harbor and the Bataan Death March also erased any doubts that I might have had about war being a very brutal undertaking."

Training assumed greater intensity, and the U.S. military took steps to ensure it would have the leaders needed to take troops into battle. Chávez got summoned as part of that effort. "I remember it was shortly after my real eighteenth birthday in 1942," Chávez said. "On the military record, I was twenty years old at that time, but, of course, I was just eighteen. I was told to report to the main headquarters of the First Cavalry Division of Fort Bliss for an interview of some kind. It turned out that I was one of numerous soldiers who had been called in for the interview because we had scored fairly high in the IQ test when we first went into the service."

Chávez thought it was at least a bit ironic when he was told of his high test score. His background prior to the military, after all, had strayed far from what was considered acceptable. "Remember, I was in and out of grade school with the nuns. I skipped a lot of days when I should have been in class. I'd get Cs, and the nuns would work harder with me to do better. I always look back at the nuns when I think of my education. They pushed me to think.

"Then, no doubt, I learned a lot by being around mom and dad and my older brothers and sisters. But here I was in the military, still wet behind the ears. I had been sent off to Springer, returned to the nuns, and then had gone only through the tenth grade in high school before I did something that was against the principles taught to me by those same nuns who did everything they could for me as a young boy: I lied to get into the military. The nuns would have told me that it was a big sin. They always taught me not to lie, to tell the truth.

"Now I had been summoned to appear before a lieutenant colonel for an interview that I had earned because of a high score on an aptitude test that I took when I was sixteen early in the first month that I went into the service. Dozens of soldiers from the fort were called for similar interviews, but I suspect I was the youngest. The lieutenant colonel asked me a lot of questions specifically related to artillery. I had had training on the 75-millimeter. I had learned some techniques in basic surveying. I had learned some of the very basics in doing forward observations. I answered the questions as best as I could. After it was all done, I asked the officer what it was all about. He said they were interviewing several of us for officers' training school.

"It was training for three months. They referred to soldiers who went through the training as ninety-day wonders. The army developed a lot of officers through the ninety-day-wonder program. If you did your course successfully, you would be commissioned a second lieutenant. I knew about those guys because I got to know some of the men who had become ninety-day wonders. They weren't always held in the highest esteem, especially by those who had gotten their commissions at West Point, at Texas A&M—people who had gone through a college degree program before they got their commission."

Chávez did well in his interview and seemed enveloped by the momentum of it all. In December 1942, he was ordered to report to Fort Sill, Oklahoma, for officers' training school. "I asked if I could go to Oklahoma by way of Santa Fe to vacation with my family a little," Chávez said. "I told my folks when I arrived home that I had been selected for officers' training school. My sister, Nora, was especially proud. She said that if I completed the course, she would buy me my first second lieutenant's suit and bars."

Chávez was in training at Fort Sill when Gen. Douglas MacArthur's troops occupied Buna village, New Guinea, and U.S. forces occupied Amchitka Island in the Aleutians. Also during that period, President Roosevelt and Winston Churchill met at Casablanca for what was called the "Unconditional Surrender" conference, and bombers made the first All-American assault on Germany.[10]

That and other wartime activity swirled as Chávez progressed through the ninety-day-wonder program. It was not long, though, before he began doubting his course. "Remember, I was just eighteen years old," he said. "About two-thirds of the way into the training, I personally began to feel that I wasn't capable or mature enough to be an officer giving orders to more mature soldiers, men with a lot more experience and knowledge than I had obtained during my first eighteen months in training. I was still fuzzy-faced, and I feared the responsibility of being an officer with three or four soldiers at my command entirely depending on me to give orders. I had a tremendous amount of respect for the sergeants and these tough corporals who had already been hardened by the military, and I would have felt out of place as their superior. So I went to the commanding officer and asked permission to return to Fort Bliss.

"The officer I went to tried to talk me out of withdrawing, but I had made up my mind and even though I was a young kid who might easily have been intimidated in those surroundings, I stood my ground."

Chávez said the weeks he spent at Fort Sill proved useful after he returned to his division. "While I was in Oklahoma, they taught me more about how to be a forward observer, how to use logarithm books and things like that.

"There were no hard feelings when I left. In fact they gave me authority to stop for another brief vacation at home on my way back to Fort Bliss." When Chávez got home, he found that not everyone felt the same about his decision to abort officers' training. "My parents didn't tell me anything about my decision, but some of my older sisters were disappointed that I had decided not to be an officer. They were getting money together to buy me a new uniform."

For many, thoughts of the road not taken often fuel thoughts about what might have been. For Chávez, the mere fact that he fought in World War II and lived to talk about it is evidence enough that he made the right decision to withdraw from officers' training. "In retrospect, I ask was I scared or was it good instincts? I really don't know. I just knew I didn't want to be an officer. When the war was over, I had been in major battles for which I received five battle stars and came back home alive. But what would have happened if I had made different choices? I might not be around to tell my story."

Besides, Chávez surmises, the lie that paved his entry into the military might have caught up with him had he remained in officers' training. "The major who was interviewing me thought I was twenty years old. He and everybody else thought I was two years older than I was. If the major had known that I was eighteen and not twenty, he might have gotten me by the hair and told me, 'Get out of here squirt.' He might have done it for two reasons: One, because I was a squirt and, two, because I lied."

When Chávez returned to Fort Bliss, work was under way there to form a new battalion, the 153rd Artillery Battalion. It was the battalion in which Chávez would serve for the remainder of his military life. "They brought soldiers in from different places, including these two men who came in from the cavalry side and would become my dearest, dearest friends.

"They had very different backgrounds from mine. One was from South Philadelphia, Tobias 'Toby' George. You didn't say Philadelphia. You'd say

South Philadelphia when you talked of Toby. He came from the Italian-Lebanese section and was half-Italian and half-Lebanese. The other dear friend was, Cecil J. 'C. J.' Reed, from Memphis, Tennessee. For a three-year period, we were inseparable. The three of us, you couldn't get three people who had come from such different places, three different backgrounds, and yet meld a friendship that is so absolute. It sure broadens your horizons, your overall view of humanity."

Much of humanity was entangled in the day-to-day fury of war thousands of miles away as Chávez and his compatriots at Fort Bliss continued preparing to join hostilities. "We couldn't lose sight of why we were there, of course. It was military training, and we knew that the time would come when we would have to put it to use under very dangerous circumstances. But we were also young men, and we needed relief from the pressures we faced every day."

Indeed, it was one of those outlets for pressure that brought Chávez and his two newfound friends—Toby George and C. J. Reed—closer together. "Amazingly enough, I think it was dancing that drew us together. I considered myself a damn good dancer and even won contests to prove it," Chávez said. "Toby and C. J. were also damn good. Girls would come onto the base from El Paso to dance with the guys, and I think the three of us ended up connecting with one another by dancing with the same girls. As a matter of fact, it wasn't long before we even worked up a dance routine for the three of us like what you might see on a Broadway stage and stuff like that. Some of it came from dances that Toby learned about in Philadelphia."

Thousands of Chávez's countrymen, meanwhile, kept fighting deeper into the war that troops back in the states mostly yearned to join. Others in Chávez's family joined the military as events of the war went on. "I followed my brother, Cuate, into the service. He was a member of the 111th Cavalry of the National Guard. Then in 1942, Father Angélico went in as an army chaplain with the Seventy-seventh Infantry Division. Cuate was in the European theater; Father Angélico was in the Pacific and at the invasion of the island of Leyte. Then in 1943, my brother, Francisco, who was studying to be a priest like our oldest brother, left the St. Francis Seminary in Cincinnati to join the U.S. Army Air Corps in Texas. Then Antonio joined the U.S. Marines and was part of the invasion of Okinawa. My sister, María Consuelo, became a navy nurse in Hawaii. My sister, Adela, worked as staff at Fort Bliss after I left."

Antonio was just sixteen when he enlisted and recalls being influenced by Fabián Jr.'s ability to get into the military before reaching the legal age. "When Fabián went in, I knew I was going to go in as soon as I could," he said. "Besides, that Bataan Death March got everybody fired up."

The patriarch of the family also got drawn into the war activity.

"Dad went to work in Los Alamos in 1942 as the national laboratory up there began taking root," Fabián Jr. said. "He was a carpenter and built special cabinets for the laboratory. He worked in Los Alamos all week long before coming home on the weekends. There were times that he had to work Saturdays and Sundays so he couldn't come home. He stayed in the barracks and used to keep with him a picture of one of his children while he was up there. He'd swap the picture for the picture of another child each time he came home."

There was another Santa Fean who went to work in support of the war effort and before long would step into Fabián Jr.'s life. Coral Jeanne Rustenbach graduated from Santa Fe High School in 1942 and promptly went to work as a military aide in a commander's office at the Kirtland Army Air Base in Albuquerque.

The United States and its allies made key gains as 1943 unfolded. The Sicilian capital of Palermo fell to the Allies in July 1943. "Sicily is Invaded in Sea-Air Smash," read one headline.[11] Mussolini, the Italian prime minister, resigned days later.[12] By mid-August, the conquest of Sicily was completed, and General MacArthur had occupied Vella LaVella.[13]

September was a week old when an oversized headline in the *New Mexican* screamed, "Italy Gives Up." The United Press story under it reported: "The announcement came as dispirited Italian troops by the hundreds surrendered to British and Canadian troops advancing up the Calabrian peninsula, where the Allies landed last Friday on the heels of a 39-day . . . victory which sent the Germans fleeing to the mainland."

Roosevelt, Churchill, and Russia's Joseph Stalin met in Iran in December 1943 and signed a pact to coordinate their attacks on the Germans.[14]

After leaving Fort Bliss in 1942, the 153rd Battalion had gone to Camp Phillips and Fort Riley in Kansas for more training. There were maneuvers in Tennessee before it was sent to Fort Bragg in North Carolina. It was there that the battalion in January 1944 was equipped with powerful eight-inch guns drawn by M6 tractors. "We were probably the first in the army to make that conversion," Chávez said. "The eight-inch guns shot shells as far as thirty-eight thousand yards. Remember, I had been impressed by Big Bertha. But our guns weren't like those old German guns. Bertha was a howitzer that shot bigger shells, but they were lobbed shorter distances."

A 1944 article in *Life Magazine* told of the new eight-inch weapon:

This gun is the most accurate and most destructive weapon of siege warfare ever devised. Major-General Barnes, one of the world's greatest experts on gun design, has said, "It'll drop a projectile right on the courthouse steps.

The article said the "great battle-axes of invasion" weighed many tons but could be put into action in two and a half hours and could be moved again in forty-five minutes. They were said to be capable of firing 240-pound shells every sixty seconds.

"Our training on the new guns began immediately, and by March we were inspected in position by the U.S. secretary of war and two high British generals," Chávez said. "We were getting closer to being shipped overseas, and we could all but smell the European air."

In April, the battalion moved by train from Fort Bragg to Fort Slocum, New York, and ten days later it was on the high seas headed to Europe. "We were on ship for thirteen days before arriving at Bristol, England," Chávez said. "We were greeted by what would be the last German air raid over England." The battalion was promptly moved by rail to Bournemouth on the coast of the English Channel. Final preparations for combat were completed on June 15, and it is believed that the 153rd became the first eight-inch gun battalion to enter combat in the European theater. "We were told a lot was expected of us as the Allied invasion of Western Europe began," Chávez said.

News reports told how in the first days of June 1944, Allied troops landed on the Normandy coast of France, claiming beachheads and moving inland in a massive show of strength, according to the Associated Press. The AP reported the assault this way: "The seaborne troops, led by Gen. Bernard L. Montgomery, surged across the channel from England in 4,000 regular ships and additional thousands of smaller craft. They were preceded by massed flights of parachute and glider forces who landed inland during the darkness. Eleven thousand planes supported the attack."

By the middle of June, reports swirled for what the news media called "the most sustained task force assault of the Pacific war" on the Marianas Islands, including Guam. On the same day back in Europe, Allies were reported to be engaged in their fiercest fighting since their landing in France. Germans had sent four armored divisions in what was termed a "furious counterattack," and the Nazis claimed that the fighting was approaching a climax.

That was the state of the war that greeted Chávez before his first battle. "We stayed in the area of the English Channel for a couple of months until we were shipped to France. The Allied landing on Omaha Beach was June 6. Our battalion didn't get onto it until June 28 because the troops ahead of us had to get enough land for us to bring in our heavy artillery. Carentan was the name of the town in France where we parked for a while after we landed and waited before we set up our big guns. Carentan reminded me a little bit of Santa Fe because it had a plaza, and like all French towns, there's a church and everything else is situated around it.

"The time came for us to move in and set up our guns. This was the Battle of Normandy, and our battalion started firing our artillery the first week of July. It's amazing. I guess it has something to do with being so young, but I really wasn't scared at first," Chávez said. "When we landed on Omaha Beach and we went in a couple of miles, there's this air raid by Americans heading into France, and there's a lot of German antiaircraft fire going on.

"I remember the order to hit the ground, and at first I did. I crawled into this little hole maybe two feet deep that I had dug with a little shovel and said, 'Hail, Mary, full of grace . . . ' But then later I stood outside the hole watching the display of antiaircraft fire. It was kind of like a Fourth of July display, and it was fascinating. The sergeant from our unit came by and shoved me back into the ground. 'Get into that damn foxhole, you fool!' he shouted. We were instructed that antiaircraft fire actually shot up into the air and exploded into fragments that were supposed to hit the planes. Well, those fragments come back to earth so we were told to protect ourselves. To me it was all just very exciting that first time, but I'll guarantee you, I quickly became more cautious.

"Our battalion during that period faced heavy shelling from the famous German artillery. It was our first experience of shells coming at you. Your body bounced as the artillery shells exploded."

Working with the forward observer, Chávez's role at times was to help calculate angles and direct the fire of his battalion's guns. At other times, he helped load those same guns. "It was a massive display of power on all sides," Chávez said.

Leaving Normandy thrust new challenges on U.S. troops. On July 11, 1944, Americans began their drive for St. Lo at the entrance to the peninsula, according to news reports. "On July 26, practically every Allied artillery in the area aimed their guns at St. Lo, and all the planes were dropping bombs," Chávez said. "The First and Third armies broke through the St. Lo gap, and that's what opened up the movement in northern France. It was momentous to see all those shells and bombs exploding at the same time. What was left of the German soldiers, they came out surrendering. The bombing and artillery fire on our part was so heavy that when we moved out, I remember seeing Germans who were dizzy, wobbly, and giving up with blood coming out of their ears because of the horrific blasts. We're talking about men who were forty, fifty years old. But there were also boys thirteen or fourteen years old. Really anybody who could handle a rifle was sent in to fight.

"There was death everywhere as we moved out of Normandy. Dead Germans, dead Americans. It's the first time I recall that we used to stop and pick up blankets from dead American soldiers and save them because we could trade them later for fresh food and other things from French civilians. We weren't supposed to but we did it anyway. Everybody did."

The dead bodies meant far more than mere blankets that could be used as barter, of course. "As we started coming upon these bodies, I developed a sharper instinct for survival. No more silly things like standing up to watch the display. I was much more cautious. I never really thought of dying, but in the eventuality that I was seriously wounded, I kept my rosary and prayer book in my satchel. I'd read the book, not every day, but from time to time. We had a Catholic priest assigned to the battalion, and whenever we could, we'd have a Mass on Sunday. Periodically, I'd help serve the Mass."

From St. Lo, Chávez recalled that the American army moved quickly through northern France because of the path heavy shelling and bombing cleared. "We had to wait for a while until they settled down somewhere so it gave us time to rest," Chávez said. "I remember two stops the most. One was a small town called La Pallu. We were there four or five days, and I came upon a little priest. He was a Frenchman, but he had spent twenty years in Spain and spoke perfect Spanish. When I introduced myself with the little French that I knew, 'Je m'apelle Fabián Chávez,' he asked in French if I was Spanish. I said, 'Oui.' He then replied in Spanish, '¿Pues cómo estás, hijo?'

"I told him my brother was a priest, and we quickly became good friends. Actually, that became a pretty good entree wherever I went and came upon priests. I'd tell them that my own brother was a priest, and it opened things up. In La Pallu, I gave the priest some army blankets that we had picked up from dead soldiers, and he gave them to parishioners so they could make sweaters and other clothing. He also wanted some gasoline for his tractor to work his farm. We gave him several gallons from some of our five-gallon cans, and he gave us some eggs, nice French bread, and sweet cakes that he had baked.

"We left La Pallu for Versailles, which was just about seventeen miles outside of Paris. In the middle of war, we were surrounded by these beautiful gardens and other magnificence. We were there for about two weeks, and it was vacation time for us, even though some of the truckers from our battalion were used to run food, gasoline, ammunition, and other supplies to the front lines in what was called the Red Ball Express. General Patton was advancing so fast that he needed a steady flow of these things going in his direction. I remember my friend, Toby, and I were glad for the rest. We even were able to make our way into Paris to take in the sights and visit some of the cathedrals.

"In mid-September, our entire battalion started moving toward Germany. It was September 22 when we crossed over from Belgium and took our first position within Germany near a town called Aachen. We stayed there till the middle of December. Aachen was the historic capital during the Charlemagne era of the Middle Ages. Charlemagne became a symbol of justice and good government, and there we were fighting an enemy that symbolized a threat to justice as we had come to know it centuries later. We fired at enemy defenses throughout the period of several months, which also saw heavy bombing of German positions."

It was during this period that Chávez had not only his first near-brush with death but perhaps his first sense that he had made the right decision to abort his stay at officers' training school. "Part of the officer's job is to work as a forward observer for the artillery. I had been trained as a forward observer while at officers' school so I was assigned to accompany our lieutenant, Lieutenant Frye, as his backup in case anything happened to him. We would work in front of the guns, always looking through binoculars to see what we could spot. We'd give information to our fire directions center, which could then direct fire for several sites.

"One day Lieutenant Frye and I were observing from a second-story building near Aachen when the lieutenant noticed a certain pattern of artillery coming in from the Germans. Lieutenant Frye ordered everyone with us down to the basement, and there was this mad scramble as shells came in. As I was going into the basement, I saw Lieutenant Frye get struck and killed by part of a shell. It was at about that time that the entire house that was above ground collapsed. We recovered the lieutenant's body from under the rubble after the shelling stopped.

"Lieutenant Frye was doing what an officer does: He was to have been the last one into the basement. Had I been the officer in his place, I would have had the same responsibility, and I would have acted the same way that he did. The superior responsibility of an officer is to take care of his men. As an eighteen-year-old, I wasn't mature enough to assume those responsibilities. Lieutenant Frye died while ensuring our safety, and to this day I can't remember his first name. It's the way war is. People drop at your side in the middle of battle, sometimes while saving your own skin, and all the time you've known one another it's by your last names."

Before December was over, Chávez's battalion was back in Belgium and firing its artillery to help eliminate the bulge in Belgium near the German border. "The Germans in great numbers tried driving a wedge into the Allied forces in that area, and when we stopped them with our own massive numbers, it created a bulge," Chávez said. "We were in firing position for five weeks, and a lot of the time we were in snow up to our hind ends. Temperatures below zero were common. The Germans were all over the place, and they were merciless. They didn't take prisoners. That was the toughest battle for a lot of us because fighting the cold took up 80 percent of our time and fighting the enemy took up 20 percent. We used to joke: If you can't stay alive in the cold, you can't fight.

"For me, it was the bitterest experience of the war because of the nature of the forest land that we were in, the heavy snows, the bitter cold, and merciless enemy. We were relentless in our own fighting, too. We fired so many big artillery shells that we ran out. We had to send a convoy to Antwerp, Belgium, for eight-inch artillery shells that the navy guns used. It was maybe eighty miles one way. We could use navy shells because our own guns were a copy of what the navy used. It added an interesting twist to our situation because the navy shells had tracers on them. When you'd shoot them, you could see them as they went out to their targets."

The 153rd Battalion moved back into Germany after having helped win the Battle of the Bulge. "It's when I first got the feeling that the war might be coming to an end," Chávez said. "We had moved through France so fast. We were so good, so powerful. I felt it was just a matter of time before the Germans would collapse and it would all be over.

"Back in Germany, our battalion took position at Mannheim in late February 1945, and we became engaged in the Battle of the Rhine. During coming days we fired from both sides of the river. Some of the firing during the battle was so intense that it had to be stopped periodically so that the guns could cool off to prevent premature bursting of the shells.

"Once we crossed the Rhine, then I knew for sure that it would be just a matter of time before it was all over."

As the war neared its end, the 153rd Battalion helped in the elimination of the Ruhr pocket, firing at enemy traffic sometimes thirty-eight thousand yards away, utilizing the full range of its guns. Its success added to its many commendations, this one from the XVII Airborne Corps:

The 179th and its attached Battalions 153rd F.A. Bn. Performed in a superior manner their missions in the battle of the reduction and elimination of the Rhur Pocket. Their mastery of technique of their arm was clearly demonstrated. Particularly outstanding was their aggressiveness, which always kept them well forward. The entire group functions smoothly and well throughout the period.[15]

The battalion spent V-E Day, May 8, 1945, in Roddenau, Germany.

Along with battle stars earned at the Battle of Normandy, the Battle of the Bulge at Ardennes, and the Battle of the Rhineland, Chávez was awarded a battle star for fighting in northern France and another for fighting in central Europe.

Fighting raged on in the Pacific theater, but Chávez was among troops designated to return home. "Soldiers who had accumulated a certain number of battle points could be shipped back home, and I had more than enough points. But I was able to stay in Europe for a while so I took advantage of being free. I did a lot of gallivanting around Germany. I remember visiting airplane factories and different communities and, of course, churches."

Chávez was still in Europe when the atomic bombs were dropped on Japan. "The bomb exploded in August, and I was on my way back home in the latter part of September," he said. "I hadn't heard anything about the race to develop the atomic bomb. I had no concept of the bomb. It was almost impossible to imagine. To this day they argue: Could we have found some desolate island to demonstrate its power without sacrificing so many lives? I don't know the answer. I only know that we're told we would have lost tens of thousands of American lives with many more injured if we had had to invade Japan. Putting an end to fighting in the Pacific theater required one of the great horrors of war, without question."

When it was over, Santa Fe rejoiced as did communities throughout the country. On the fiftieth anniversary of V-J Day, Helen López-Perry of Santa Fe told the *New Mexican*: "All the church bells were ringing—the Cathedral, St. Anne's, Guadalupe. We just followed the sound of the bells."

New Mexican reporter Bob Quick, who has written extensively about World War II, repeatedly has expressed admiration for the troops who fought in it. "I would say the New Mexicans who served in World War II were driven by their patriotism and their desire to fight tyranny to join the service," Quick said for this biography. "The ones that I have interviewed were eager to serve and often couldn't wait to graduate from high school before they joined up. Their attitudes have remained consistent over the years: They saw what they had to do and they did it; no second guesses or regrets at all, even by those who were captured and spent years in captivity.

"The people back home were behind those in the military 100 percent. They did everything they could for the men and women in the service, not the least of which was prayer," Quick said.

Reporter Greg Toppo, who wrote for the *New Mexican* before moving on to *USA Today*, interviewed Chávez for the fiftieth anniversary of the war's end. He wrote: "For Fabian Chavez and his brother 'Cuate,' their sweet tearful reunion came in their mother's kitchen, where they sat down and talked about what they had seen and where they had been during the previous three years. Fabián remembered: 'We figured at one time we were only 22 miles apart. We got stars from the same battles, but we didn't know till we got to mother's kitchen.'"

Chávez's younger brother, Antonio, told Toppo that when he left for the service at sixteen he remembered his father had a full head of thick black hair. "When I came back two years later, he was completely white," he said.

Boston was Fabián Jr.'s first stop back in the states following the war. There, he and other soldiers boarded a train headed west. "I got to Fort Bliss and within about a week they had all my papers processed. It's amazing how they got everything ready so fast.

"As I left Fort Bliss, I saw another trainload coming in. When my brother, Cuate, and I met up later in mother's kitchen, we figured that Cuate was on that train."

Fabián Jr. spent a night in El Paso and Juárez, Mexico, before heading home. "I had a couple of tequilas and a nice dinner, and the next day I caught a Santa Fe Trails bus to Albuquerque. From there I had to shift to another bus to Santa Fe."

Chávez spent a few weeks in Santa Fe readjusting to civilian life before the restless feet that got him into trouble as a youth returned. "Toby George had asked me to spend some time with him in South Philadelphia. I spent a few months there and was able to get by in part with money that we had been sending to Toby's mom during the war. While overseas, we got our monthly pay of forty bucks or so. We didn't need it for food or any of the other basics because we were able to swap the army blankets that we collected on the battlefields with Frenchmen and Germans as we came upon them in their communities. I also remember going into Belgium for a little R and R, and I took as many blankets as I could along with army socks and shirts, stuff that people had taken out of knapsacks of dead soldiers, and I converted them into Belgium franks. On top of all that, Toby was an accomplished gambler. He never knew a poker game or dice game that he didn't win.

"We really had no use for money while we were overseas so it was Toby's idea that we send what we had to his mother. But Toby's mom really didn't need the money, either. She and her husband had a nice home and a shoe shop where Toby's dad made and repaired shoes. He had a major business going with the big department stores. I remember going into his shop for the first time and seeing thousands of wooden shoe forms.

"Toby's mom had saved all the money we sent her, and she gave it back to us when we were in South Philly. I don't remember how much it was. All I know is we had enough to spend while I was there and I came back with a few hundred bucks in my pocket, even after having bought my bus ticket home."

Chávez's buddy had made every effort to keep Chávez from buying that ticket. "Toby was a Catholic too and said that if I wanted to go to college, there was a good Catholic school right near Philadelphia: Villanova. But I told Toby the big city was not for me. There was too much traffic, and I missed the mountains.

"I got home and after I spent all the money I had, I knew it was time that I go to work and go to college. Remember, I left the tenth grade to go to war so I hadn't graduated from high school. It was 1947 when I went to Highlands University in Las Vegas and got my GED, then signed up at St. Michael's College in Santa Fe. By signing up, I got my seventy-five dollars a month from the military plus they paid my tuition and paid for my books. I was able to sell shoes on weekends for extra money. I worked at Khan's shoe store, The Guarantee, and Feldhake Shoe Store. They were all on or near the Plaza. I was still living at home so I had no rent to worry about."

Compared to what Chávez had just been through, life suddenly was pretty smooth sailing. "I was still a very young man and along with thousands of others like me, I had been through a remarkable experience, but I really didn't have any trouble putting the war behind me," Chávez said. "In a sense we were propagandized ahead of time before going into war so once we were in, we were ready to take on those Germans. You're in a fighting mood. Then you get into an actual war. Violence and death are all around you. I'd see German soldiers and American soldiers die in front me. Every time I'd see a dead body I'd repeat the names: Jesús, María, y José."

"I remember seeing a German soldier lying dead with half of his body still leaning forward out of the top of his disabled German tank. Toby and I climbed the tank to see who it was. We pulled out his wallet, we opened it, and there was a picture of a woman and two kids, obviously his wife and children. Our enemies became more human after situations like that. They happened to be soldiers fighting on the other side. They tried to kill us, and we tried to kill them. And then there were times that we'd walk through French or German villages between battles, and we'd see elderly people with little kids—often their grandkids, I suppose—begging for help or food. It struck me in a sad way because I'd say, there but for the grace of God go my own grandparents. We're very lucky that such fighting has not occurred on our homeland."

Chávez's brother, Antonio, observed major changes around Santa Fe upon his return from the war, but Fabián Jr. saw more of what had stayed the same. "With the exception that the city now had Bruns Hospital, Santa Fe had not changed that much in my eyes," he said. Bruns Hospital, situated on what would become the campus of the College of Santa Fe, was mostly frame buildings that at its peak was capable of housing fifteen hundred patients, according to news reports.

"I'd see a lot of soldiers in town because of the hospital, but for me, Acequia Madre was still the same. The fields around the old homestead were still the same. My Santa Fe that I had left hadn't changed that much even though there had been tremendous change within me."

Change was gaining momentum in Chávez's surroundings. It was change that already had dug in well before the war, largely along the upper Rio Grande Valley. Its presence would grow more profound after the war, change that Chávez, himself, would embrace and help promote later in life. Journalist Harvey Ferguson wrote of it this way for the book *The Spell of New Mexico*: "The latest invasion of this much invaded land has been an influx of painters and writers and of all those various types of men and women who are the camp followers of every cultural movement. This westward migration of the men with paint and ink on their fingers has given New Mexico a new type of society and a new spurt of life, just as the coming of the beaver trappers and the wagon traders did . . . They have been followed by a troop of tourists with money in their pockets. They have boosted rents and bettered business."[16]

Historian Paul Horgan wrote in *The Centuries Of Santa Fe* that "the migration to Santa Fe of people of leisure began before World War II, and increased in numbers and pace after it . . . Many of those who came to live built Spanish Colonial houses of much beauty, or took ancient Mexican houses and with fine effect converted them into dwellings in which every luxury and rarity of furnishing took its place comfortably against old plain walls of plastered adobe . . . The city has always been, not only a political capital, but a center of opinion and an example of style. Now, with its increasing drift of a luxury class into town, the airs of national, and even international, chic began to tell in the local scene."[17]

If change in Santa Fe were to be accommodated after the war, for many there was first the business of giving thanks for the hellish war's end.

"Mother just kept on going to Mass after we were all back, thanking St. Anthony and St. Francis. Throughout the war, mom had kept a statuette of St. Anthony in the living room and a perpetual candle. She prayed to St. Anthony that her kids would come home alive. Both mom and dad, of course, were very thankful that all of us came back alive and unwounded, but mom showed more emotion than dad.

"There's no escaping the fact that the war was devastating. It was hell for the people fighting it as well as for the civilians who were caught in the middle. I've come to recognize that wars are not created by people against people but by governments against governments. Governments fan emotions of their people as they're led into war, and then there are the great events like Pearl Harbor and the Bataan Death March that lead people to think that there are no alternatives to war.

"World War II was fought against evils that had to be stopped, and I don't think they could have been stopped without the kind of fighting that we saw. If there is such a thing, World War II was a 'good war.' It produced great-thinking Americans that went on to do good things for our country. New Mexico got its share of such people. I personally have worked with people of very different political perspectives who in the end came together to support issues for the common good.

"I can point specifically to Mack Easely and Donald Hallam. Both were state representatives from Lea County, and both became speakers of the House of Representatives. Mack later became lieutenant governor, state senator, and chief justice of the state supreme court. One of the big issues during my first year in the legislature was integration of our schools. Schools were still segregated in the southeastern counties. Mack and Donald were from the east side so I didn't expect their support. Yet, they both worked to end segregation, and I personally thanked them for their help. Mack answered: 'It was easy. We're veterans of World War II.'

"So many people from that war developed not only a special bond but on so many important issues, a common view of what is right and wrong.

"And it's what many of us took with us into the remainder of our lives."

CHAPTER FIVE

Turning Friends and Foes into Political Allies

The military had kept him away from Santa Fe's day-to-day occurrences for nearly five years, but at the age of twenty-two, Fabián Chávez Jr. had gotten himself elected president of the Young Democrats of Santa Fe County as well as chairman of one of the city's major political precincts. In both cases, prominent party members who told him they recognized his budding talents asked him to seek the positions.

Despite his youthful promise, much of his work went into maintaining well-oiled, grassroots practices that had kept Democrats as well as Republicans busy for years. "We'd buy liquor and pint bottles of wine, cases of it, and stick them into trunks of the cars that would be driven around on election day looking to sweep up votes wherever we could. The booze was for the alcoholics in town who likely wouldn't have gone to the polls if they hadn't been given a ride," Chávez said.

"We knew who they were, and, incidentally, they knew whether they were Democrats or Republicans and were honest enough to get their rides from the appropriate party. They'd cast their votes and then take that pint of wine before stepping back into the community from where they had been picked up.

"It was totally appropriate in terms of how politics was approached in those days, certainly not out of the ordinary. And, again, Democrats and Republicans battled each other to do it better."

Indeed, longtime Santa Fe County Republican leader Willie V. Ortiz looked back on the practice decades later as an important element of election day practices. Ortiz, Chávez's contemporary in Santa Fe politics, served Republican and Democratic governors in appointed positions during four decades beginning in the 1950s. He was roundly recognized for serving with distinction. Serving with distinction was something to which Chávez aspired even while briefly prolonging old-time political practices that soon would be frowned upon.

Before his elevation to local political leadership positions, Chávez worked as a volunteer in two 1946 campaigns he considered important to the state party's future.

"One was the primary battle to get U.S. Senator Dennis Chávez reelected against Gov. John J. Dempsey," he said. "The other was the campaign of the senator's brother, David Chávez Jr., who had just come back from military service and was running for district judge in the first judicial district. In those days, the district was composed of Santa Fe, Rio Arriba, San Juan, and McKinley counties. The county of Los Alamos had not been created yet. It was still part of Santa Fe, Rio Arriba, and Sandoval counties.

"Dennis Chávez was one of my top heroes. He was, after all, a United States senator. He was a native-born New Mexican with my same surname, and he was a distant relative. He dropped out of high school to help his family during hard financial times; I left high school to join the military. We had little things like that in common. But mostly I admired him because he was in the Senate during the Franklin D. Roosevelt era, and FDR was my superhero.

"Dennis Chávez's brother, David, I knew from the fact that he was district attorney when my father approached him for help to get me sent to the Springer boys' school. He was running in the Democratic primary against Harry L. Bigbee, who was a young lawyer in Santa Fe and had been appointed district judge by Governor Dempsey. David Chávez had been district attorney and then was district judge before he enlisted in the military to serve in World War II. When he came back, he challenged Bigbee for the judgeship that used to be his. I got behind David mostly because he was the U.S. senator's brother, but also because I knew him when he was district attorney. It doesn't matter that he played a role in sending me to Springer. He simply did what my father asked him to do. I looked at David as a model public servant and worked hard to get him elected."

Dennis Chávez, after winning the U.S. Senate primary, faced Patrick Hurley in that year's general election. "Patrick Hurley was a high-profile candidate because he was a U.S. general and a former secretary of war. It required the best of us as we worked to get Dennis Chávez reelected. As it turned out, I had more contact with General Hurley soon afterward in my own political career."

Fabián Chávez Jr. would also develop a much-fuller relationship later with the man he worked to defeat in that year's race for judge. "I came to meet Harry Bigbee as a result of working on David Chávez's campaign. In an interesting twist of fate, Bigbee would become one of my strongest supporters and almost like a big brother to me for the remainder of my political activities. I was able to rely on him for support and advice ever since the end of that race in 1946. It was a relationship that I truly valued."

✒ **FIGURE 6.** ✒
U.S. Senator Dennis Chávez. Photo by John LeRouge Martínez.
Courtesy Palace of the Governors (MNM/DCA), negative no. 057271.

The extended family of Dennis Chávez seemed to have a finger in many political pots, engaging in activity that over time would buttress the man's standing not only at home but in Washington, DC. In his twenties, Dennis Chávez actively promoted statehood for New Mexico in 1912. His father already had developed a reputation as an enthusiastic Republican in a state that was all but full of Republicans. From 1869 through 1912, eight of the nine men who served as U.S. president were Republican, and it was their administrations that had filled most of the political positions in New Mexico during that time. "All the territorial governors, the territorial supreme court justices, all the territorial managers were Republican appointees with the exception of those appointed by Grover Cleveland," Fabián Chávez Jr. said. "The general populace of New Mexico knew practically nothing but Republicans.

"Interestingly, the constitutional convention that wrote our state constitution was 75 percent Republican, yet the first governor and lieutenant governor elected in our state were Democrats." It is widely believed that voters were upset with Republicans for how the new constitution was written and expressed their disfavor by electing Democrats William C. McDonald governor and Esequiel C. de Baca lieutenant governor in the state's first election. In the ensuing years through 1930, however, Republicans filled the governor's chair during ten of the fourteen years.

Fabián Chávez Jr.'s own father was one of the few Democrats of the era who was able to help keep hopes of the Democratic Party alive. "My dad got elected county assessor in Mora County in 1916," Chávez said. "He was the only Democrat on the county ticket to get elected, and he ran against a guy who was supposed to be the Republican powerhouse in the area, don Demetrio Medina. Two years later, don Demetrio decided to run for county treasurer and defied my dad to run against him. Dad did, and he won. He had what you might call grassroots support because he was a cantor for the Penitentes. He wasn't a member of the Penitentes, but he was a cantor who knew all the group's prayers. When he ran for office, he had their support, which made for a substantial block of voters."

Interestingly, the Penitentes were known to have provided strong, reliable support to Republicans in New Mexico at least through the late 1800s. They traced their origin to the confraternities established in Spain to provide for needy members, assisting at funerals, and caring for widows and orphans, wrote Warren A. Beck in *New Mexico: A History of Four Centuries*.[1] "Although it cannot be proved, it is more than likely that the virtually solid Republican support by the Spanish-Americans was delivered through the backing of the penitentes," Beck wrote. "It is alleged that at one time no one could be elected to public office in New Mexico without the blessing of the society."[2]

More than a decade unfolded following the fluke successes of Fabián Chávez Sr. in Mora County, though, before Democrats were able to wrest control away from factionalized Republicans in New Mexico, and Dennis Chávez played a central role in the transformation. Without a high school diploma, the man destined to become a U.S. senator passed a test required for acceptance at Georgetown University.[3] He obtained a bachelor of law degree from Georgetown in 1920 and served several terms in the New Mexico Legislature as a Democrat from Albuquerque, winning friends in the party along the way.[4]

As part of a national Democratic landslide, Dennis Chávez was elected to the U.S. House of Representatives in 1930.[5] Democrat Gov. Clyde Tingley in 1935 appointed Chávez to succeed Democrat-turned-Republican Bronson Cutting in the U.S. Senate.[6] Chávez was a man of slight build with his black hair combed flat and to the side. He spoke in a soft, pleasant voice that easily transformed into a loud, clear tone when the man addressed crowds. "Dennis Chávez had campaigned for one thing or another all of his adult life, and he often did it in front of crowds in communities around New Mexico where there were no microphones," said Fabián Chávez Jr. "So he knew how to speak loudly, and he knew when to do it."

During much of his first decade in public office, Dennis Chávez spoke mostly to an anemic state Democratic Party. For years beginning in 1926, "the role of the Democratic Party in New Mexico was one of political servitude to Bronson Cutting,"[7] wrote Arthur T. Hannett, who served as a Democratic governor from 1925 to 1926. He wrote in his book *Sagebrush Lawyer* that "there were 55,000 Democrats in the state qualified to vote, but it was nevertheless true that we had neither a Democratic Party nor a Democratic organization."[8]

New Mexico Democrats, wrote Hannett, were divided between two factions: one controlled by Tingley and Dennis Chávez and the other by Cutting and Arthur Seligman, who was state Democratic Party chairman before serving as governor from 1931 until his death in 1933.[9] Seligman and his supporters sought to strip the Tingley-Chávez faction of influence first at the Bernalillo County convention in 1930 and again later that year at the state convention in Clovis, according to Hannett.[10]

"At the Albuquerque convention both sides came prepared to do physical battle; Clyde Tingley, for instance, hired a group of former football players for his defense. Before the normal convention procedures had been concluded, a fist fight erupted. When I saw a large set of knuckles come close to my upper dentures, I decided that I had no desire to fight. I unceremoniously climbed to the top of the grand piano and threatened anyone who came close . . . I stayed on the piano until the ruckus calmed down."[11]

Cutting, by then a Republican, first took office as a U.S. senator in 1928.[12] Dennis Chávez narrowly missed defeating Cutting in the 1934 general election and had accused Cutting of election fraud.[13] Cutting died in a plane crash between Washington and New Mexico on a trip made to respond to those allegations.[14] Chávez's entry to the Senate at a time when there were no Hispanic members was not without theater, resentment, nor, seemingly, at least a bit of ethnic prejudice. Reportedly, half a dozen senators turned their backs on Chávez and then left the chamber in protest as he was to be sworn in by Vice President John Vance Garner.[15] Author and historian María E. Montoya wrote for the book, *New Mexican Lives*:

> Chavez's induction has been seen as emblematic of how poorly New
> Mexicans, particularly Mexican American and Native American citizens, had been treated by the federal government and eastern lawmakers . . . The U.S. Senate probably did not view Dennis Chavez,
> a young Mexican-American from a poor family, as an appropriate
> replacement for the older, dashing, and patrician Bronson Cutting.
> Chavez represented a kind of populism and ethnic politics that the
> Senate liked to believe it was above.[16]

Closely aligned with Pres. Franklin D. Roosevelt, Chávez served as chairman of the Senate Public Works Committee and was successful in landing many New Deal initiatives for New Mexico, further solidifying his party's control of the state and his own standing among New Mexico voters. The state Supreme Court Building and the Santa Fe County Courthouse, where the decision was made to send young Fabián Chávez Jr. to the Springer boys' school, were built as part of the New Deal's Work Projects Administration. Fabián's brother, Cuate, was among many New Mexicans gainfully employed as a youth by the New Deal's Civilian Conservation Corps, earning thirty dollars a month for his efforts.

"Supporting Dennis Chávez against Governor Dempsey in 1946 was, for the most part, a very positive effort with solid intentions," Fabián Chávez Jr. said. "Chávez was a good man, and I wanted him reelected. But I had an added incentive to work especially hard against Dempsey. My father had had a personal negative experience with Governor Dempsey.

"In 1942, Dempsey had been elected governor, and he called in some of the main Democratic politicians who were part of his administration, two of which were my father and our good friend, Frank V. Ortiz Sr. The governor told them that when he got through with his gubernatorial terms, he intended to run against Dennis Chávez for the U.S. Senate seat. 'I want you to know ahead of time,' he told them. 'Those that are with me can stay in this administration. Those that would be with Dennis can leave.' Several people left, including my dad and Frank Ortiz. By the way, my dad, because of his talents as a cabinetmaker, went to work in Los Alamos and made much more money there than he did as superintendent at the state Capitol."

Dennis Chávez survived the challenge from Dempsey in 1946 and had developed a solid political machine to back his ambitions by the time he was elected to a third full Senate term that year. His relationship with Tingley had soured years earlier.

The machine included members of his extended family and others well entrenched in Santa Fe politics. It was those people who gave young Fabián his start in party leadership posts. "I was very intimately involved with that Chávez clan," Fabián Chávez Jr. said. "I had been doing a lot of political work and was getting deeply involved in politics even though I was doing it without any titles yet.

"Barbara Chávez Sena, the senator's sister, ran the Senate campaigns for Dennis Chávez and the David Chávez campaigns for judge in Santa Fe County. She had been a schoolteacher in El Rito and knew northern New Mexico very well. She was a fantastic lady, and she ran campaigns effectively because she knew the intimacy of operations from the precinct level up. Her two sons, Robert and David, were responsible for electing me president of the Young Democrats of Santa Fe County in 1947. Both were a few years older than me. Robert had been president while I had been active working in my precinct and doing other party stuff wherever I was needed. One day, Bob told me he was resigning as president of the Young Democrats and that he wanted me to be the next president. They nominated me, and I won. I had no competition. Bob and David had it so well organized that I was elected by acclamation.

"Earlier that same year, 1947, my next-door neighbor, Frank V. Ortiz Sr., approached me at a meeting of what was known then as Precinct 3. He said, 'Son, we're going to make you the next precinct chairman.' I told him, 'Mr. Ortiz, I'm young, and I'm new at this.' He said, 'We'll help you, but we need to have young people more involved in the Democratic Party.'

"Frank V. Ortiz had long been one of our Democratic leaders in Santa Fe County. He had been state tax commissioner. His wife, Margaret, had been county clerk. His son was already going to Georgetown School of Foreign Service in Washington, DC. With or without title, though, Frank V. Ortiz was a person you looked up to. He was someone you looked up to close to home. Dennis Chávez was someone you looked up to far from home."

Fabián Chávez Jr. got the sense he was being drawn into important matters of the community, and he liked it. "Getting these two positions— precinct chairman and president of Santa Fe's Young Democrats—was my first real sense of accepting positions of responsibility and trust outside the military," he said. "It made me feel like, by God, I better do a good job because they trust me to take over."

With newfound responsibilities, Chávez sensed he had the wind at his back. "These were strong days for Democrats in New Mexico. Herbert Hoover was president during the Depression, and Democrats ran against Hoover well into the 1940s. The Democrats always used to play to the fact that in Hoover's days one could buy ham and eggs for twenty-five cents but who had the twenty-five cents? For a long time under the Republicans, there were no jobs. Then came FDR and the programs that created jobs. That's the era that I grew up in politically.

"I didn't give any thought to being anything other than a Democrat. My mother was raised as a Republican, but she registered as a Democrat when she married my dad. I not only thought as a Democrat, but I evolved into a liberal very early on because of Roosevelt and what he did to pull us out of the Depression. I already had the perception that the Democrats were the party for the general public, the party with a soul, and that Republicans at the time were more concerned about the rich.

"Besides, while I was growing up and dad was working in the state Capitol, he introduced me to a long string of governors beginning in 1931 with Arthur Seligman. Then there was A. W. Hockenhull, Clyde Tingley, John E. Miles, and John J. Dempsey. When I came back from the war the governor was Thomas Mabry. All were Democrats. I had a mind-set that, God, the Democratic Party is undefeatable. I had grown up with nothing but Democratic governors, Democratic congressmen. FDR had four terms. When I voted for the first time, as a soldier overseas, I cast my first vote for Clinton P. Anderson for the U.S. House, position one, and Antonio Fernández for the U.S. House, position two.

"I can't say I had a dislike for Republicans. There were Republicans who I admired, like Manuel Luján Sr. and Frank S. Ortiz, both of whom were very fine mayors of Santa Fe and successful businessmen. My aunts and uncles on my mother's side were all Republicans. No, I didn't scorn Republicans. I just had a strong love for Democrats. And many people were converting around me. One was Frank Sosaya, who was my uncle Augustín Sosaya's brother. Another was Armando Larragoite Sr., who served on local school boards and ended up having an elementary school named in his honor. Biterbo Quintana, the county sheriff who served while I was in Springer, was a Republican who converted to a Democrat and became a leader in our party."

The ascension in local Democratic politics came fast and furious for a young man who had not even graduated from high school. "Being that I was a dropout—actually, I don't like the term 'dropout' because I withdrew from school at age sixteen to do something else with a purpose—I had to get my GED before I could enroll in college," Chávez said. "Among other places, the GED test was offered at Highlands University so that's where I went to take it, because my aunt Floripa, my dad's youngest sister, lived on Bridge Street just a couple of blocks from campus. I stayed with her for about a week to prepare for the test, which had to be taken over a two-day period. I passed with flying colors, especially the part that called for us to read articles and then tell what the message was.

"I enrolled at St. Michael's College and promptly went to work campaigning the Christian Brothers and other students. I made sure they were registered and made sure they knew about the Democratic Party and what it was doing for the people. My math teacher was Brother Cyprian Luke, who later became president of the college and served for twenty-five years. I studied history and philosophy under Brother Raymond, who I could tell was a Democrat, but I made sure he was registered to vote."

Along with social sciences, Brother Raymond taught Chávez something that would guide him throughout his life. "He said early on that he would teach me how to think, not what to think. Actually, I believe, it was an approach that I had been following even in the early grades of education. I had no problem thinking. I had no problem learning. It's just that I had little or no interest in some subjects, so I chose to apply myself in other areas. It creates problems, of course, when teachers at the early levels are required to teach you the so-called three Rs, not just one or two of them.

"Anyway, I was further inspired by Brother Raymond and used that inspiration to talk with other Christian Brothers on the faculty and with students who were living in the dorms and preparing to become Christian Brothers. I talked them up and got some of them to register as Democrats."

Chávez continued his studies at St. Michael's College even as he got deeper and deeper into politics of the state Democratic Party. It was not merely books that occupied his time on the campus on what was then Santa Fe's south side. Work he did outside of traditional classrooms proved to be as helpful as most information he picked up off a page. "There was a professional actors' summer studio at the college known as the Ann Lee Theater. They would bring in professional actors from New York and California to come and act under professional directorship in various plays. Since they were using the theater at the college, they frequently would get some of us students to help, and in some cases, if we fit into certain parts of an act, we would be used either as stand-ins or in actual speaking parts.

"I volunteered for speaking parts in three different plays and was given the parts. The first play was *My Sister Irene*. It was a famous Broadway show that was made into a movie. In that one, I actually played two parts. In the first act, I was an Italian flower vendor. In the third act, I was a Brazilian ambassador. The next play was *The Man that Came to Dinner*, another famous Broadway show that was later made into a movie. In that one, they whitened my hair and put on a false beard, and I played the part of a German professor. The third one was a lesser-known play, *Candlelight*. In that one, I played the part of a room service assistant in a hotel whose job was to serve a couple of lovers who were staying in the hotel.

"I did it all under professional directorship, and it gave me the experience of stage presentation that came in handy during my political career. I gained confidence and worked to create a presence while addressing masses of people or debating with opponents. The experience that I gained in that theater was very valuable throughout the rest of my life."

The college studies, the acting, the politics—all were challenging but in sharp contrast to the years Chávez had just spent as a soldier. "They couldn't help but be very different," he said. "But if there was any commonality, it probably was my drive to compete in whatever I did."

As a Democratic precinct chairman, Chávez came up against seasoned and well-known opposition. "My aunt Victoria Roybal de Sosaya, who along with her husband convinced my parents to move to Santa Fe in the twenties, was the Republican chairman of Precinct 3. Her brother-in-law, my uncle Frank, converted from Republican to Democrat, but my Aunt Victoria and my uncle Augustín remained very staunch Republicans.

"Precinct 3 ran all the way from what was then College Street east clear to Three-Mile Reservoir, and my Aunt Victoria worked it like it was her front yard. She was in her early sixties and was my mom's youngest sister in a family of three daughters and one son. I learned a lot from her, and I couldn't help but have high respect for her. She was a tough opponent, without question.

"We were at what you would call political loggerheads but with all the due respect that is exchanged between an aunt and nephew. On election day, we'd meet very early at the polling place, and I'd give her a kiss and say, '¿Cómo estás, tía?' And she would say, 'How are you, junior?' She wasn't being disrespectful or trying in any way to put me in my place. That's what people in the family called me: Junior."

Victoria Sosaya learned the old style of Santa Fe politics, neighborhood politics that had worked well not only along the Sangre de Cristos but in big cities like Chicago, Boston, and New York, where politicians honed the art of maintaining contact year-round with the people whose votes they would need on election day.

"My Aunt Victoria worked the precinct from January through December year in and year out. She wasn't around just on election day," Chávez said.

"She worked the Christmas season and other holidays, helping those families that might need a little boost. She knew when there was sickness in a household and would visit to see if there was any way she could help. That's why when she'd show up at these homes on election day, offering a ride or a friendly reminder to get out to the polls, she wasn't appearing out of the clear blue. She developed a rapport with her voters, and she was able to turn to them for help when the time came to beat the Democrats.

"The old-time members of the Democratic Party, of course, were just as good at that routine. These precinct leaders were usually elderly folks. If somebody in the neighborhood needed medicine, these people would make sure it was obtained. They'd get turkeys for people around Thanksgiving; they'd help out with a little money come Christmastime. I didn't have their kind of connections, but I was lucky enough to have people working under me who did, and I made it a point of staying out of their way."

Precinct 3 was divided into three divisions—A, B, and C—while Chávez waged political battle with his esteemed aunt. Democrats had a distinct numerical edge countywide, but Republicans maintained a considerable presence in neighborhoods of the east side. "I was successful in beating my aunt in divisions A and B in the first couple of elections, but I had difficulty in division C. After two or three elections, we won all three divisions, and I thought it was quite an accomplishment. No matter how good it felt, though, I had too much respect for my aunt to be boastful. And she was always very sweet to me."

In his precinct battles, Chávez also got encouragement along the way from one of his heroes in politics. "Dennis Chávez would come to the political rallies at Seth Hall and make the rounds as U.S. senator. I met him in 1932 during his race against Bronson Cutting. I remember my dad introduced me to him by saying, 'Senador, éste es mi hito.' He remembered me, I suppose, because he remembered my dad. He'd come up to me at those rallies, put his arm firmly around me, and ask, '¿Cómo está tu papá? ¿Cómo está tu mamá?'"

It seems encouragement was around every corner for Fabián Jr. as he climbed Santa Fe's political ladder in his midtwenties. "Victor Salazar was the state director of taxation and revenue, and he was commonly known as the second-floor governor during the Tom Mabry administration," Chávez said. "The governor's office was on the first floor of that old Capitol that was built in 1900. Victor's office was on the second floor. If you wanted anything done within the framework of state government, you went to Victor Salazar.

"And he had great influence over me. He was a very well attired gentleman, and he wasn't like other politicos that I had known who were a little more casual. He always had a coat and tie. He was very well educated and had run a real estate and insurance business in Albuquerque.

"Here he was with all this influence, and I was just president of Santa Fe's Young Democrats. But he called me into his government office and asked, 'What can I do to help you work more closely and more effectively with the parent organization?' He wanted us to organize and be more active."

The fact that what was purely a political meeting occurred in a state government office was of little if any note. "It's the way people in authority tended to do things in those days," Chávez said. "Back then, don't forget, there wasn't the press coverage that we have today. Reporters didn't spend a lot of time nosing around Victor's office or even the governor's office, as I recall.

"I came out of that meeting with Victor mindful of at least two things. One was the importance of involving all segments of your organization, all segments of society, in what you are trying to accomplish. He furnished us with money so that we could travel around the state to recruit more Democrats, and he was instrumental in integrating the young members into the parent organization. We ended up with a strong Democratic organization that was active at all ages, something that we've rarely had since.

"The other thing that struck me during that meeting was something that I already knew, but it was reinforced in me. Here was a man with great power but he used it with a gentle hand. He didn't say, 'Fabián, I want you to do this or do that.' He said, 'What can I do to help you so that together we can be more effective?' He didn't have the title of Democratic Party chairman, but we knew he was the leader. Can you imagine me going into his office hearing him ask, 'Fabián, what can I do to help?' It conveyed a brand of leadership that I admired."

As Chávez recalls, he admired the old style of neighborhood politics for its ability to deliver on election day, and he respected the people who were able to make the system work, sometimes even hum with effectiveness. He, though, was casting an eye for models who seemed intent on moving politics in a new direction. Salazar, he thought, personified both approaches.

And there was another man, a politician originally from Mora County, whom Chávez followed and admired from an early age. "Don Casados never got close to being governor, but he looked to me like what a governor should look like. He was stately looking. He commanded respect just the way he comported himself. He impressed me as a kid and later on in my years, too."

Indeed, Casados had a sterling reputation, columnist Will Harrison, who wrote Inside the Capitol, noted upon his retirement. Harrison wrote that Casados had served in public jobs for more than thirty years "without a smear that anybody around here can remember." At sixty-five, Casados retired after seven years on the state Public Service Commission, sixteen years on the Corporation Commission, and jobs in the State Tax Commission, the state bank examiner's office, the legislature, and the Mora courthouse, Harrison wrote.

Harrison recalled in the same column that "second-floor governor" Victor Salazar purged Casados from the Corporation Commission in 1948 with the intent of replacing him with J. O. García of Rio Arriba. Signals were crossed, and the party's much-traveled Seven-Foot Pickett was nominated, instead, according to Harrison.

"Don Casados had this presence about him even though he worked his way through night school as a bellhop at the old Alvarado Hotel in Albuquerque," Chávez said. "He met Teddy Roosevelt there and wound up being the hotel's assistant manager before enlisting for World War I. But what really stands out for me is that report that says he didn't have a smear on his record. Not a smear. That's my kind of hero."

There was something else that Chávez thought would serve him well along with his desire to elevate practices that often had characterized old-time politics in northern New Mexico. "I think I've always felt that you can get further not by punishing your so-called enemies, but by converting them. And it's a principle that served me well as a precinct leader, even in the little things," he said. "As elections approached, party officials would bring me money to buy gasoline for the people who drove voters into the polls and for other related expenses. When it came time to eat, I'd go out and get hamburgers for my workers, but I'd also bring some for Republicans who were working the same site. Their own people, maybe, would bring them cold sandwiches. I made friends that way, and it helped me later on."

It did not lessen political competition at the time, though. "The Republicans at the precinct knew what they had to do, and I knew what I had to do. I had this idea of pushing for reform in policies and laws, but the first thing at hand was the matter of winning your precinct. Like I said, that included rounding up alcoholics in town, bringing them to the polls, and leaving them with a pint of wine when we dropped them back off. The bad part about it, of course, is we were feeding the alcoholics' vice and that was wrong.

"I personally never saw anybody buy a vote with money, but there were practices then that, with good reason, are scorned today. As I was getting started, I took part in the old-style politics. But I also played a big role in pressing for reform as I went along."

Changes that Chávez sought fit in with his glorious image of the Democratic Party. "Whenever dad made speeches as I was growing up, he'd always say that the Republicans were the party of the rich; Democrats were the party of the poor. This was a man who married a Republican, remember. My mom never really got involved in politics, not like my dad, my brother, Cuate, and myself. We had this image that the Democratic Party could make a difference in the lives of people you came upon in the streets.

"I had my heroes in the Democratic Party: FDR, Dennis Chávez, David Chávez, Frank V. Ortiz Senior, don Casados . . . my own father. I wanted to contribute to their work. And the goal I set for myself was to do it with pride and dignity."

CHAPTER SIX

Escorting Love through a
Reluctant Family and Church

Santa Fe pharmacist Morris Yashvin comes quickly to mind when Fabián Chávez Jr. considers people who played influential roles in his early years.

"Morry had four wives while I knew him, and I knew him since I was a very young boy," Chávez said. "His first three wives died of cancer. He took his fourth before time claimed him in October 1991 at age ninety-three.

"He was married to his third wife, Ann, for nineteen years. A week or so after she died, I invited Morry to join me on a trip that I had to make to the southern part of the state. I wanted him to get out and into different surroundings for a few days. Somewhere between Truth or Consequences and Las Cruces, he suddenly looked at me and said, 'You know, son, I'm one of the luckiest guys in the world.' I said, 'How do you figure that?' He said, 'I've had three such beautiful wives in one lifetime.'

"That's the way he was all his life: very kind, understanding, and very generous. He had a remarkable influence on me."

Yashvin, who came to Santa Fe from Denver in 1927, was a one-time city councilor in Santa Fe and longtime state chairman of the March of Dimes. "He was chairman of the March of Dimes from its inception under FDR until the polio vaccine was developed in 1955," Chávez said. "He also served on the board of Carrie Tingley Children's Hospital and contributed time and effort to children's health issues for half a century."

Yashvin worked the drug counter at Capital Pharmacy just a few blocks from Chávez's home. The pharmacy was between the boy's house and St. Francis Parochial School on a path that Chávez walked several times a week.

"Capital Pharmacy was more like a Mexican curio shop than a pharmacy," Chávez said. "Martin Gardesky was the owner, and he was a great lover of Mexico. He made trips down there constantly. In fact, he was the first person to bring a Mexican mariachi to Santa Fe for the fall fiesta.

"The pharmacy had Mexican candy, Mexican straw dolls, Mexican jumping beans, Mexican limes. Being a kid, I couldn't resist the temptation to grab a handful of jumping beans and run away. I did it often. On one occasion, Morry spotted me and grabbed one of the limes. He threw it at me and hit me in the back of the head. I found out later that Morry up to his late twenties had played semiprofessional baseball as a third baseman in southern Colorado."

Chávez grew up knowing not only Yashvin but his wives, too. "His first wife was Iola. She was chief clerk at the state supreme court. His second was Lyna Jewel, a redheaded Irish woman who came to Santa Fe from Kansas. His third wife, Ann, arrived in Santa Fe from New York and owned a classic women's wear store in the city. His fourth wife was a lovely widow, Frannie Berntsen, who was an original owner of the Pantry Restaurant."

Of the four, the second wife, Lyna Jewel, was the one Chávez came to know best. Yashvin and Lyna Jewel lived in a comfortable apartment on Castillo Street, which later became part of Paseo de Peralta where it intersects with Canyon Road. It was near both the pharmacy and the Chávez home. Chávez, just as he had been as a boy, was attracted to Capital Pharmacy because of its unique ambience even in the years after returning from the military.

"By then, Morry called me Cuate," Chávez said. "That was my older brother's nickname, of course, because it means twin. But it also means buddy, and that's what Morry came to call me. I was in the pharmacy one day, and Morry says, 'Hey, Cuate. I have some information for you. We're all going to dinner at the San Juan Club this Saturday.' I said, 'We are?' He said with all the confidence in the world, 'Yes, we are.'"

The San Juan Country Club was an upscale restaurant north of the city located where the Santa Fe Opera is situated today. The dinner to which Chávez was unexpectedly invited was to be on September 5, 1949. It was the twenty-fifth birthday of Yashvin's stepdaughter and Lyna Jewel's daughter from a previous marriage, Coral Jeanne Rustenbach.

Coral Jeanne recalled the setting up of the date fondly decades later. "My parents and I were discussing what to do for my birthday. Papa said he wanted to take us to the San Juan Country Club for dinner and dancing. I asked papa, 'Do you know Fabián Chávez?' He said, 'Oh, sure!' I said, 'I'd like to have him for my date,' and papa said, 'Oh, well, we'll fix that up right away.' I guess he felt fondly of Fabián."

Coral Jeanne said she never really thought of asking Chávez herself for the date. "Oh, gosh! I guess in those days, girls weren't as forward as they are today. There was a little more restraint, I guess. Having papa ask was sort of the proper thing to do."

Chávez and his young date recalled the night as a wonderful evening of dancing. It was not their first time together on a dance floor. Their first time had been months earlier in 1949 at a night spot that Chávez and a close friend had sort of staked out as their own. If it was theirs, it also belonged to a substantial portion of Santa Fe's evening crowd.

"My old friend and golfing buddy Charlie González and I would go batching at El Nido in Tesuque. Charlie and I both liked to dance. El Nido and the New Mexican Room at La Fonda in town were our favorite places.

"The New Mexican Room at La Fonda actually had a small dance combo composed of a violinist, a guy with an accordion, and Freddy Valdés on the piano. Billy Palu played the violin. He was originally from Colombia, and he had a very impressive stage presence. He wrote a lot of music, including the Santa Fe Fiesta song, which is sung to this very day. Jimmie Palermo was the accordionist. Jimmie, of course, went on to be a partner in Tiny's Restaurant and Lounge after he married Tiny's daughter. He loved playing the accordion until he died.

"Dancing music at El Nido, on the other hand, was strictly from a nickelodeon, a jukebox. They had a variety of records: sambas, rambas, foxtrot. You name it, they had it. They also had some of the most excellent steaks you ever tasted. The place was owned by a French couple, Charlie and Mimi Besre, who got it just at the beginning of World War II.

"Many of the dancers at El Nido were married couples. Charlie and I would usually go without dates. We knew a lot of people so we were constantly on the dance floor. Our friends would ask us to dance, or we would ask them. Charlie was about ten years older than me. He had worked at the State Land Office before going out on his own, dealing in oil and gas leases. He's the one who taught me how to golf out at the public course, which also doubled as the Santa Fe Country Club."

When it came to pastimes, González taught Chávez more than golf. "We were at El Nido one night, and I had had a bit to drink, mostly things like whiskey sours or Seven and Sevens. I ended up getting sick so I stepped outside to hug a tree," Chávez said. "Charlie came out and said, 'You know why you're sick? Because you're drinking garbage.' He said I needed to get accustomed to Scotch. I told him I had tried it before and that it tasted like iodine and burned cork. But beginning that night, I began developing a taste for good Scotch."

Chávez was sipping Johnnie Walker Red Scotch one evening in the spring of 1949 at the bar in El Nido while he and González scouted surroundings for possible dance partners. "Joe Guthman was there with his wife, Shirley," Chávez said. "Joe was a lawyer in town and shared office space with former district attorney and former judge David Chávez as well as with Harry Bigbee, who had run against Chávez for district judge in 1946."

Shirley Guthman after a while approached Chávez at the bar with more than one mission in mind. "Shirley, who was a successful real estate broker, was a very happy, outgoing kind of person. She walked up and tapped me on the shoulder and said she wanted to dance with me. We were on the floor for only half a dance before she told me, 'I want to introduce you to someone who wants to dance with you.' Then she led me over to the booth where Coral Jeanne was sitting. Shirley introduced me to this stunning, beautiful brunette. I wanted to play gentleman, but I'm not sure that I did. I kept looking at her beautiful face. I was very impressed. You couldn't help but be impressed.

"It was a very simple introduction. Shirley had known Coral Jeanne since they were at Santa Fe High together. Shirley said, 'I want you to meet a friend of mine.' I asked Coral Jeanne to dance, and off we went. Our first dance was a fox-trot, I think. Then Coral Jeanne said she'd like to try a rumba so we went and put some money in the machine.

"I had won dance contests while in the military so I was confident I would do alright on the floor that night even though I was awestruck. When we danced the fox-trot, Coral Jeanne followed me perfectly. She followed me real good in the rumba. Then I decided, let's try a samba. A good dancer can almost lead a female partner without any instructions for simple dance steps. When you get into more intricate steps, it's a different story. Then you have to teach, train as you go. I didn't have to do any teaching with Coral Jeanne that night. She was wonderful."

That first night of dancing was unforgettable for both partners. "It was mutual admiration, I guess," Coral Jeanne said. "I sensed it right away. I was sitting there with Shirley and her husband, and she said, 'Oh, look. There's Fabián, and he's such a wonderful dancer.' She said, 'I'm going to ask him to dance,' and I said, 'If you do, please ask him to ask me to dance.' I love to dance so it was really nice to meet somebody that was such an excellent dancer.

"He was very polite and gentlemanly and just really sweet. Not pushy or anything, just a real nice guy."

Chávez said he tried his best to impress. "She was wearing a dress that came in at her waist, and she had a beautiful figure, but even as we danced

꒜ **FIGURE 7.** ꒜

Fabián Chávez Jr. and Coral Jeanne Rustenbach as dance partners in the late 1940s.
Courtesy Fabián Chávez Jr.

there was very little body contact," he said. "We didn't have much conversation while we danced. There was no need for talk. I think she was enjoying it very much and so was I.

"In those days, she combed her hair straight back with a chignon in the back. She had this beautiful profile, and I remember being stunned by her good looks. In heels that night, she was about five feet six. I was about five feet ten, five feet eleven.

"Before it was all over, we talked a little bit about ourselves, but the most I got out of that first night was her phone number. I asked for it. I said something like, 'It would be nice to go out dancing with you again.' She said she'd like to, so I asked for her phone number."

Chávez phoned about a week later. "I called and said I'd like to come visit prior to our first date. I went to see where she lived. It was a ground-level apartment in the same complex where her mother and stepfather lived.

"We were neighbors, really. I had seen her before but only casually.

"When I walked into her apartment, that's when I remember meeting this beautiful little creature named Christine. She was two years old. Beautiful, just like her mother. If there was ever a love at first sight, it was between me and that little child. That little kid took a liking to me; maybe it was because of my big nose, or maybe because I have a way with children. She had sparkling eyes and a sense of energy. I picked her up to hold her. She smiled at me, grabbed my nose, and twisted it."

Coral Jeanne, a divorcée, had been on her own, making a new life with the child Chávez was moved to embrace upon their introduction. Chávez

❧ FIGURE 8. ❧
Fabián Chávez Jr. and stepdaughter, Christine. Courtesy Fabián Chávez Jr.

Escorting Love through a Reluctant Family and Church   ❧   87

said he and Coral Jeanne spoke little about Christine that day, but before long the child likely cemented Coral Jeanne's attraction to Chávez.

"We went back to El Nido on our first date, and as we started dating more often, we'd go to La Fonda. And then there was a rumba club on West Agua Fría Street that played beautiful Latin music," Chávez said.

Chávez and Coral Jeanne both dated other people during their first few months of courtship. Hours before one of her dates, Coral Jeanne found herself unable to secure someone to watch Christine. Chávez volunteered so that Coral Jeanne could keep her date.

"I should say, it scored some points with me," Coral Jeanne recalled. "It told me what a wonderful guy he was."

The relationship quickly grew more serious. "I was impressed by his intelligence, his feelings about the things that mattered," Coral Jeanne said. "He felt very strongly about civil rights and things like that, things that so many young men weren't really thinking much about in those days. He just had a different outlook on life than so many other people that I knew. And through it all, he remained very sweet, very thoughtful, very kind to everybody."

Chávez said his attraction to Coral Jeanne seemed to be rooted in the deep respect each had for their families. "She's as proud of her heritage as I am of mine," Chávez said. "Her father, Ralph Rustenbach, was a first-generation German-American. Her grandfather on her father's side came from the Bavarian region of Germany. Her father was born in Tennessee and somehow found his way to Kansas, and there he met a beautiful red-head Irish woman by the name of Lyna Jewel Humphrey.

"Coral Jeanne's grandfather on the Humphrey side owned hotels in small towns like Greensburg, Kansas; Kingman, Kansas; Macon, Missouri. It was in one of those hotels in Greensburg, Kansas, population 157, where she was born. An only child, she and her parents later moved to Kingman, Kansas, where her father opened up a dry-cleaning shop. Her parents divorced years later."

Mother and daughter settled briefly in Santa Fe in the early thirties after being charmed by the community during a visit. Coral Jeanne was twelve and enrolled as a sixth grader at Catron Elementary School, just northwest of the Plaza. She studied in Santa Fe, but most of her school years were in Kingman, Kansas. She graduated nonetheless from Santa Fe High School in the spring of 1942 and promptly went to work at Kirtland Air Base in Albuquerque as a military aide. It was at about the time that Chávez was being interviewed at Fort Bliss as a possible candidate for officers' training school: Neither Chávez nor Coral Jeanne was yet aware of the other's existence.

Coral Jeanne's mother, Lyna Jewel, developed a relationship with the widowed Yashvin, and the two were married in 1948.

Although their paths would cross once or twice in Santa Fe in the years immediately after the war, Chávez and Coral Jeanne did not actually meet until that first night of dancing at El Nido.

"It took a few months before we really got serious about one another," Chávez said. "But it was clear to me from the beginning that we were moving in that direction. By the time Morry stopped me in Capital Pharmacy in September 1949 and said, 'Hey, Cuate, we're all going to dinner at the San Juan Club,' I think Coral Jeanne and I both had begun thinking about spending the rest of our lives together.

"The dinner was to celebrate Coral Jeanne's twenty-fifth birthday. I had turned twenty-five just five days earlier, so we ended up celebrating both our birthdays that night with Morry and his wife."

Chávez and Coral Jeanne each celebrated one more birthday before Chávez, on the last day of December 1950, and once again in the company of Coral Jeanne's parents, proposed marriage.

"We knew we were very much in love, and I think marriage was something that we knew was going to happen," Coral Jeanne recalled. "We ended up getting engaged on New Year's Eve. We were going out to La Fonda with my mother and papa. They lived in this nice apartment, and they had this huge dressing room-bathroom combination with a chase lounge and everything.

"When Fabián and I got there, my mother was still in the dressing room putting on her makeup. We all ended up talking in that dressing room, and that's where Fabián gave me my engagement ring. He was going to wait and give it to me at midnight, but he thought it would be a perfect time there in the dressing room because it was just the four of us and we had already gotten very close.

"Everybody always got a big kick out of the way things happened that evening."

Indeed, at times the courtship seemed to be enveloped in a storybook setting, but serious concerns were never far away. They shot to the surface almost immediately and lasted throughout the approach to marriage.

"It was kind of difficult, no question," Coral Jeanne said.

Chávez knew as the courtship unfolded that there would be issues to address both within his own very traditional home as well as in the Roman Catholic Church that meant so much to his family. "Dad and mom had opposed me dating a divorced woman," Chávez said. "Along with that, Coral Jeanne's propensities were toward the Catholic Church, but she had been baptized a Presbyterian.

"She and I didn't immediately start talking about these issues as obstacles even when we were getting very serious about one another," Chávez said. "I really didn't think they were going to be big obstacles. But I knew the first question at home after we were engaged was going to be: 'So you're going to marry a divorced woman?'"

The question indeed was raised on the heels of the announced engagement. It came up both in Chávez's home and in his church. Eventually, he was able to win support on one front but not the other.

"I went to people who were high in the archdiocese and argued against the church's assertion that Coral Jeanne's divorce constituted a sin," Chávez said. "I argued that Presbyterians don't play by the same rules that we play by so how could she be found to have broken them? And I hadn't broken any rules, I argued, because I had never been married."

Attempts to win converts to his mission became one of Chávez's most demanding challenges. "During a period of more than four years, I addressed our situation in great length with officers of the church. I even got one of the church's ranking officials to agree that I made good arguments. But the church was really rigid then, and in the end, I guess I knew that the rules of the church were going to stand. So Coral Jeanne and I got married outside the church."

The wedding came after an unexpectedly long engagement and with Chávez's family still cool toward the relationship. In the end, Chávez and Coral Jeanne were married on April 18, 1954, at the Santa Fe home of David Carmody, a state supreme court justice. No one from Chávez's family was present. Yashvin was the only witness. Coral Jeanne's mother was gravely ill at home with cancer and died three months later.

"The wedding was simple, private, for more reasons than one," Chávez said.

Father Angélico, Roman Catholic priest and Chávez's brother, wound up providing the opening needed between the family and the new couple. "About three or four months after the wedding, Father Angélico came to visit us at our home on San Antonio Street, which was just half a block away from dad's and mom's," Chávez said. "He had been visiting with our parents, and after he knocked on our door, he said something very casual, something like, 'I just came over to say hi and to see how you guys are doing?'

"He was an easygoing charmer of his own, and it turned out that we had won him over. Actually, it must have been Coral Jeanne who won him over because he already knew me and the situation I was in. He came to realize what kind of woman Coral Jeanne is."

Chávez had given Coral Jeanne a gold charm bracelet, whose small adornments included one with Christine's image and inscribed birth date.

The bracelet had not escaped Father Angélico's notice. "My brother had a Newman Club key that I believe he had been given when he was chosen as one of the top Catholic poets in the nation," Chávez said. "It meant a lot to him, but he gave that key to Coral Jeanne to put on her bracelet. That was a very moving thing for him to do for my wife. Once we got his blessing, his support in marriage, everything opened up with the rest of the family."

Father Angélico's respect for the couple in decades to come remained a cornerstone for the relations that developed with other family members. The priest signed a copy of his book, *Chavez, A Distinctive American Clan of New Mexico*, "To my kid brother Fabián Chávez Jr. and his darling wife Coral Jeanne with the affection of aged Fray Angélico Chávez."

Coral Jeanne recalls Father Angélico's involvement warmly. "Father Angélico, bless his heart. He certainly was wonderful to me. He was such a terrific man."

If initially tested under fire, the marriage was forged into a strong relationship where neither love nor respect faded.

"We're still as much in love as we were when we first met," said Coral Jeanne. "We're so close and care so much about each other. I don't know what I'd do without him."

She said there have been few quarrels during the marriage. "Maybe when I tried to get him to quit smoking, things like that," she said.

Chávez used to smoke both cigarettes and cigars. Asked how long it took her to get Chávez to quit in 1994, Coral Jeanne replied amid laughter, "Just one day."

The decision to quit smoking, indeed, came suddenly, Chávez recalled. Coral Jeanne, who smoked cigarettes briefly early in the marriage, had been urging Chávez to stop for some time, he said. "I never smoked more than half a pack a day and rarely smoked an entire cigarette. I would take three or four puffs and then throw the cigarette out. The late state senator, Eddie López, used to say, 'You can always trace where Fabián's been by the long cigarette butts he leaves behind.' I enjoyed smoking cigars but eventually realized it was repugnant because it would leave my clothes saturated with the smell of cigar smoke.

"Coral Jeanne, actually, was constantly after me to stop. For example, I couldn't smoke in the house. I'd have to go outside, even in the middle of winter. Coral Jeanne would show me articles about people who died of lung cancer because of smoking. She was consistent but loving in her attempts to get me to quit. One day while at work, I was coughing real bad and went into the restroom of the PERA Building. After I coughed up a lot of brown stuff, I reached in my pocket, pulled out my pack of cigarettes, and threw it in the garbage. That was it. It was a happy day for Coral Jeanne."

Daughter Christine Jewel Barrett has taken it all in since Chávez stepped into her life while she was still a toddler and said she has felt nothing but love for Chávez since the first day they met. "He's just the best guy in the world. He's always been there for me and our family," she said.

If you listen to Chávez, the relationship that developed when he was a young man has been musical without interruption. "I started dancing with Coral Jeanne in 1949, and we've been dancing ever since," he said.

CHAPTER SEVEN

Into the Legislature
Producing Victory from Defeat

Encouraged by support he had gotten at an early age from some of Santa Fe's established Democratic Party leaders, Fabián Chávez Jr. looked to the state legislature as the first stepping stone for what he already was hoping would be a long political career.

It was nearly a year before he would be introduced to Coral Jeanne Rustenbach at El Nido. Though early into his studies at St. Michael's College, he was less than entirely dedicated to the course work. He was president of Santa Fe County's Young Democrats and chairman of one of the city's major political precincts. Politics dominated much of his conduct and more than a bit of his thinking.

"Santa Fe County had three seats in the state House of Representatives in 1948. Actually one of them, the Twenty-eighth District, was spread out to include parts of Santa Fe, Guadalupe, and Torrance counties," Chávez said. "Almost invariably, that district would elect someone from Santa Fe. Santa Fe's other two house districts had incumbent Democrats seeking re-election. District Twenty-eight had no incumbent; it was an open seat, so I chose that position to be the target of my own first election campaign."

It was an appealing target to two other men who joined Chávez in filing for the Democratic primary, including fellow Santa Fean, Henry Trujillo. "I knew Henry Trujillo would be the man to beat. Henry was about ten years older than me and also had served in the military during World War II. Like me, he was a student at St. Michael's College. He had a lot of connections and even had close relations with some members of my own family. He'd say repeatedly during the campaign that I came from a good family and that I was a good young man. 'Fabián es muy buen joven,' he would say as a way of presenting himself as a more mature person to deal with responsibilities associated with a seat in the state house of representatives. It was his subtle way of pointing to the main difference between us. That's about as negative as the campaign got. And, as you can see, it really wasn't negative. He knew mom and dad and Father Angélico. He wasn't going to do anything dirty."

Chávez's father helped some with the campaign, but he left the heavy lifting to his son. "Dad gave me a list of his contemporaries in various parts of Santa Fe County, and they came in handy. He helped like that with personal contacts, but he didn't campaign for me actively."

Fabián Jr. figured he could run strongly in the Santa Fe County precincts, largely because of his well-regarded family and because of support he hoped would come from members of U.S. Senator Dennis Chávez's organization. He also turned for support from a man whom he had helped the senator's organization defeat just two years earlier. "Harry Bigbee had come to Santa Fe from Torrance County, and he had taken a liking to me ever since his unsuccessful race for a state judgeship in 1946. I asked him for names of people I could contact in Torrance County. He gave me names from there, and he also gave me names of people he knew in Guadalupe County."

Despite Bigbee's help, Chávez was pounded in Torrance County, where he finished a distant third in the three-man race. Pedro Zamora collected 353 votes in Torrance County; Trujillo received 95, and Chávez got 48. Chávez failed to get any votes in four of the fifteen precincts.[1] He did better, though, in Guadalupe County, collecting 404 votes while Trujillo got 318 and Zamora, 252.[2]

Chávez's expectations were dashed in Santa Fe County, where he actually had expected to win. Instead, totals showed Trujillo with 1,707 votes; Chávez, 1,382; and Zamora, 553.[3] At home, Chávez lost to Trujillo, 40–28, in Precinct 3-A. But he won, 74–27, in Precinct 3-B, and 50–22 in Precinct 3-C.[4]

At the end of the night, Chávez finished 286 votes behind Trujillo.[5]

"Here's what's important about that 1948 race," Chávez said. "I knew I could run strong in Santa Fe County, but I had to divert campaign time to Torrance and Guadalupe counties. I won Guadalupe, but there weren't a lot of votes there. Henry lost in both of the smaller counties, but he won enough votes in Santa Fe to carry the day. Two years later I smartened up. Politically, mathematically, I saw the solution: focus all my attention in Santa Fe County."

As Chávez pondered the future, his father wanted to make sure school figured into his boy's plans. "Acaba tu escuela, hito," the elder Chávez told his son after the 1948 primary defeat.

Fabián Chávez Jr. did continue his college studies, but he kept at least one foot in the state Capitol. "Even while I was taking classes at St. Michael's, I worked as a student aide to state Senator Tibo Chávez of Valencia County," Chávez said. "I was twenty-five years old, and I saw in Senator Chávez a man who was deeply committed to equal rights and equal opportunity. In 1949, he introduced the first fair employment practices act in the history of our state. It called for eliminating discrimination in the workplace, and as we've come to learn, that's a constant, ongoing battle. But Tibo Chávez's bill sounded the call: We need to begin moving aggressively in that direction. Democrats dominated both the senate and the house, but there were conservative Democrats who weren't fond of the legislation.

"It passed comfortably in the senate, but we knew it would face stiffer opposition in the house. The legislation stalled in the house, largely because of opposition from legislators of the conservative southeast. Rep. Sixto Leyva from Sandoval County was carrying the bill in the house so he started a filibuster, and on the final day of the legislative session, it threatened to deny votes on other key measures, including the state budget. Sixto wanted an assurance that the fair employment bill would be heard on the floor of the house and that it would be given a vote up or down before the end of the session. Lacking such an assurance, he said that he and his allies in the house would keep the filibuster going.

"That's when Victor Salazar, the so-called second-floor governor, called me in Senator Chávez's office and asked me to see if Tibo was willing to meet with speaker of the house John Simms and others to resolve the impasse. We all met in the speaker's office, and John Simms pledged to us that if we'd let the general appropriations act move along for a vote on the floor, then he would make sure that the fair employment practices act would be heard by the full house and voted upon.

"When the floor session resumed, Representative Leyva explained his position and his understanding of how things were going to unfold. Speaker Simms explained his commitment, and business of the house went on as time for mandatory adjournment approached. Time came for a vote on the budget. It got the vote and passed. Then quickly, a motion was made by one of the conservative members to adjourn sine die, which means no more business would have been taken up, even though Simms had explained he had promised that the fair employment bill would get a vote once the appropriations act had been passed. There was a quick second to the motion for sine die. The speaker ruled it out of order and made the fair employment bill the next item on the agenda. There was a long debate and in the end, the act passed.

"You talk about an education. Here I was a student in college, a World War II veteran, and in a matter of hours, I got a practical education on a tough legislative process that led to adoption of a significant piece—actually, a historic piece—of legislation. They don't teach this stuff in the schools. You have to experience it. Arguably, that was the first civil rights bill in the history of New Mexico, and I was intimately involved because of political contacts that I had made on my own. It gave me courage to continue fighting for civil rights for the rest of my life."

That lengthy fight for Chávez would unfold over years in the state legislature, where the young Santa Fe Democrat still yearned to serve as a member.

In 1950, Chávez felt he had a good chance of winning one of the two house seats that were carved entirely within Santa Fe County. The downside was that Santa Fe is a big county, stretching from the Stanley area in the south all the way up to Chimayó in the north, eighty miles or so, depending on which roads are traveled. "If you think of some of the communities—Stanley, Edgewood, Golden, Chimayó, Cundiyó—it's two different worlds. There is great diversity in the people," Chávez said.

Amid the diversity, a familiar face came to the fore again early in the campaign. "I approached Harry Bigbee for help and told him why I thought I had a better chance of winning this time," Chávez said. "He gave me a hundred dollars, I believe, and said, 'Good luck, son.' I took it down to the Schifani print shop to buy some little eight-by-ten-inch posters and some cards. Louis Schifani gave me time to pay for my full order because he knew my family, especially Father Angélico."

Chávez waged an effective campaign despite lacking the endorsement of Santa Fe County's influential Democratic Party chairman Santos Quintana. "Santos was a big, formidable figure. He looked like an athlete, and he sought to have control over who ran for what and what would be done every step along the way. I was working hard to be a legislator because I had wanted to be one since I was a kid. I was nine or ten years old, and by myself I was already playing the different roles of legislators going through procedures to get make-believe bills adopted. It was almost in my blood. I wanted to be in the legislature badly to do things as I had envisioned them in my own mind over the years while growing up, so I was not going to be dictated to by anyone, not by Santos, not by anyone."

Chávez felt political momentum building at his back as the 1950 primary went on. "I was running exclusively in my home territory, as diverse as it was, and it didn't take long for me to build a sense of confidence," he said. "I'd go to El Rancho, for example, and I'd come upon Tobías Gómez, who'd greet me with a handshake and say, '¡Oh, tú eres hijo de Fabián!' And I'd get similar greetings in other communities like Cuarteles and Chimayó, too.

"I knew I was benefiting from the reputations that others in my family had already established. I not only was Fabián Chávez Jr., I was the kid brother of Father Angélico, who was famous as a priest but also as a historian and poet. I was a member of a large family that included members like Cuate and Nora, who in their own rights had already gone on to be highly respected and loved."

Chávez and Ruth Taichert won nominations in the 1950 Democratic primary to compete in the general election for the two all-Santa Fe County posts in the house of representatives.[6] Like Chávez, Taichert benefited from an established family name. Taichert's husband, Dan, owned and operated Taichert's five-and-dime store on West San Francisco Street. Votes Chávez and Taichert collected more than doubled those of Democratic Party competitors.[7] On his way to victory, Chávez settled for four votes in Stanley, two in Edgewood, and finished without any of the thirteen votes cast in Cow Springs.[8]

As expected, Chávez ran strongest within the City of Santa Fe and in the county's northern precincts, including El Rancho, Cuarteles, and Chimayó.[9]

By Chávez's own account, Santa Fe County Democrats rarely had to worry about difficult races in general elections. "Once you won the primary, you were home free. You'd win the general election hands down," he said. Still, he and Taichert both had spirited Republican opposition in 1950. Chávez beat Claude Sena, 6,909–6,154.[10] Taichert beat Elizabeth Cable, 7,244–6,572.[11]

Republicans showed strength in other races that year, too, largely because of bitter fights that had developed within the state Democratic Party organization. Party divisions grew out of a messy and emotional governor's race in the 1950 Democratic primary. "Mr. Democrat" John Miles won the primary over David Chávez Jr., U.S. Senator Dennis Chávez's younger brother,[12] but lost in the general election to young Republican legislator Edwin Mechem of Las Cruces.[13] It marked the first time that Republicans elected a New Mexico governor in twenty years and the beginning of what Fabián Chávez Jr. described as the hara-kiri period of New Mexico Democrats, the subject of this book's next chapter.

Chávez's first term in the state legislature was marked more by what he learned than by what he accomplished. One of his major lessons came from an unlikely mentor who told him, essentially, that he talked too much and was hurting himself in the process.

The lesson came amid other attempts from more senior members of the house who tried to pull the reins in on Chávez. "I had a tendency to talk a lot on the floor, and I really didn't have a sense of what the effects were.

I guess I felt that if I talked long enough, people would eventually see things my way."

The Associated Press in February 1951 reported on one such winded debate in which Chávez had at least a little company. "Somehow or other, the members of the New Mexico house of representatives got off the main issue of a bill being debated. They began arguing about the use of the term politician.

"Rep. Fabian Chavez (Dem.) of Santa Fe began quoting Webster.

"Rep. Albert Amador (Dem.) Española suggested the House adopt a rule that 'we call ourselves statesmen instead of politicians.'"

Amador's suggestion fizzled, but a house memorial offered by the chief clerk and his staff later referred to Chávez as "he of the silver tongue, already well on the road following the oratorical tradition of the late George Washington Armijo." It said Amador, an educator, did "a good job of teaching—plus a little preaching—while in the Legislature." House speaker Calvin Horn of Albuquerque was referred to as "one of the outstanding figures in the history of the House, handling a most difficult job with dexterity, knowledge and personal ability."[14]

⊰ **FIGURE 9.** ⊱

Fabián Chávez Jr. and Coral Jeanne Rustenbach in chambers of the New Mexico house of representatives, 1951. Courtesy Fabián Chávez Jr.

Chávez's gift of a "silver tongue" was evident almost daily as reflected in these remarks the *Santa Fe New Mexican* reported: "I have at times been accused of being selfish for Santa Fe, but after all it was the constituents of Santa Fe who sent me to the Legislature to advance as well as protect their interests. If all of the legislators approach the Legislature with the same feelings then it must follow that the collective thinking, knowledge and conclusions of the majority will more than often result in a net gain for the state as a whole."

Gifted orator or not, Chávez as a rookie lawmaker needed occasional checks with reality, including times marked by long-winded remarks.

"Ike Smalley sat to the left of me in the last row of the house of representatives during my first year. He'd reach over and grab me by the jacket and say, 'Sit down before you lose your bill.'

"I was learning from things like that, but the real positive step that was taken to make me a better legislator came from Rex Kipp, who I barely knew at the time. Kipp was a rancher and Democratic state representative from Lordsburg. He spoke Spanish fluently because he dealt a lot with Mexican Americans along the border. For some reason, he took a liking to me, and he took me out to dinner during my first legislative session in 1951."

Kipp made the invitation in Spanish as if to assure Chávez that it would be a friendly meeting. The two dined at El Nido, where Chávez recalls sipping Scotch and eating a thick steak during a two-hour meeting. "I was a twenty-six-year-old kid, and I remember Representative Kipp looking at me across the table. He started out by saying, 'I want to give you a piece of good advice.' He said, 'I've watched you during the past few weeks. You're very bright. You have a complete grasp of the issues. You're blessed by being articulate. But have you noticed that you haven't passed or killed a single bill during the first thirty days of the legislative session?'

"He told me I had to put my talents to greater use. 'Don't stand up and speak on every issue, and if you must speak, try not to be negative. This legislature is composed of the entire society of the state of New Mexico, and you must respect where legislators come from as individuals.' He said, 'If you have objections to a piece of legislation, approach the sponsor first and tell him that you have some serious questions about his proposals which you may be able to resolve ahead of time. If you can't resolve them, you at least will gain his respect for having contacted him first before you stand up on the floor to proclaim your opposition.'

"He also told me, 'If there are legislators who have legislation that you support who are less articulate than you, stand up and give them support whether they are Republicans or Democrats.'

"I changed, and I saw the difference in my relations with other members of the house during the last thirty days of the session.

"That was Rex Kipp's lesson to me, and I've lived by it all my life. And, boy, has it paid off!"

It was helpful to Chávez as he worked later in that year's legislative session with Rep. Lilburn Homan of Estancia and others to push through a measure that created the Legislative Council Service. "I must have been making some kind of impression, because here I am a young kid and Homan, a Republican from Torrance County, comes up to me and says, 'Fabián, we've got to do something other than depend on lobbyists and volunteer lawyers who help us research and draft legislation. We need a service for the legislators where we can go to get assistance in establishing the proper procedures for our legislation.'

"It wasn't a new idea. It was new to me, but it wasn't a new idea. I liked it because I used to rely a lot on two people, two people that I trusted implicitly. One was my good friend Harry Bigbee and the other was Brian Johnson, a former state Democratic Party chairman who also had served as state judge. Brian had big clients, like Santa Fe Railroad. Harry had big clients, like Mountain States Telephone. They very seldom lobbied me but always said I should come to them for help when I needed it. I also turned to lawyers Lorenzo Chávez and Edwin Felter on labor and workers' compensation issues.

"And there were others who helped me research and write legislation, lawyers like Bill Federici, Kay Montgomery, and Oliver Seth, who volunteered their services through the attorney general's office. These same people would later help the governor analyze bills after they had been passed by the legislature and were sent to the executive for his signature. That in itself created conflicts that had to be addressed."

The bill creating the Legislative Council Service passed easily, and the new agency initially consisted of three staff members: Dir. Jack Holmes, Dep. Dir. Inez Bushner, and a secretary.

"There was this wave of reform at the time among legislatures around the country," said Paula Tackett, who began working at the Council Service as a staff attorney in 1982 and became director in 1988. "Legislatures in the early 1950s began providing staff that could work with them on legal research and analysis as well as on bill drafting."

Richard Folmar, who began working for the Council Service in 1959 as deputy director, said the idea for providing professional staff to legislators probably originated in Kansas. "The idea was to have a nonpolitical staff that would set up a uniform, equal-treatment type of bill drafting service," Folmar said. "Before that, if legislators couldn't get someone in the AG's office to draft a bill for them, they'd turn to lobbyists. Once the Council Service was created, legislators knew staff wouldn't go out of their way to express bias while drafting bills other than what the requester himself wanted."

The council in New Mexico by 2006 had grown to fifty full-time employees who alternate shifts around the clock during legislative sessions.

"The legislature simply couldn't work without the Council Service," Chávez said. "And to this day I can point to it as something that I helped create while following the wise counsel of Rex Kipp."

That positive lesson from the Lordsburg lawmaker was in sharp contrast to what Chávez learned about the seamier side of politics during his first term in the legislature. "Rex Kipp, this Anglo rancher whom I had barely known, gave me some very important advice that influenced me the rest of my life," Chávez said. "On the flip side, a man with deep Spanish roots, someone whom I had known for a long time, was at the dealing end of a major disappointment for me as I began my service in the legislature. I guess it kind of shows how I've approached my relationships. I don't have any prejudices when it comes to race or ethnicity. I've had good and bad experiences with people of all backgrounds."

Chávez told of his first encounter as a state lawmaker with what appeared to be a double cross. "I was brand new in the house. A friend of the family's and a political friend of mine who served on the Corporation Commission approached me and requested that I introduce a bill to strengthen the authority of the commission to regulate the trucking industry. A couple of weeks into the session he came back to me and told me that the legislation I had introduced at his request was not necessary because he had been advised by the commission's attorneys that extension of the commission's authority over the trucking industry could be done by regulation and we did not need legislation."

Chávez refused to refer to the corporation commissioner by name, but newspaper reports of the time identified him as Dan Sedillo of Santa Fe.

"At his request, I had the trucking bill killed in committee," Chávez said. "Several months later at a meeting of the trucking industry at La Fonda, J. W. Eaves stood up to say positive things about me and my presence in the legislature. J. W. Eaves was a friend of mine, and he must have thought it would be helpful to say at that meeting that it would be wise for people to keep an eye on me because I was an up-and-comer.

"That prompted one of J. W.'s trucking friends to say, 'Representative Chávez is like most other Mexicans: You can buy them at a hundred dollars a head.'

"Defending me, J. W. responded, 'Why do you say something like that when it's not true?' Then Billy Walker, a trucker from Lea County, said that he had given the corporation commissioner who had approached me several thousand dollars to have that bill killed, and he left the impression that I was bought off by some of that money to have my own bill defeated in committee.

"Did I take a penny of that money? Absolutely not!" Chávez said. "I wouldn't have. But the implication got me real upset. The assertion stigmatized me because of my ethnic background, and it stigmatized others like me, too. In those days, if you were in the legislature and had a Hispanic surname, you were considered one of what they called the 'barefoot boys.' And some of the people who would use that term were some of our own."

The term, in its kindest interpretation of the time, referred to legislators who could be relied upon to support measures seen as favoring interests of the poor. Not all interpretations were as kind, though.

"Some lobbyists who were Hispanic would say when support for legislation was being discussed, 'Don't worry, I can take care of the barefoot boys,'" Chávez said. "I knew those characterizations were both demeaning and untrue because there were guys like Tibo Chávez and Sixto Leyva and others who were brilliant legislators. It hurt me to see people like that referred to by such derogatory labels.

"It would hurt that we'd hear the term 'barefoot boys' and nobody would say or do anything about it. I couldn't take it. Anytime I'd hear the term, I'd raise my voice against it."

As offended as he was by the trucking legislation incident, Chávez said he took out his grief on the process and not on the corporation commissioner who had requested the legislation. "I didn't make a big hullabaloo about it, but I never forgot it, I never forgot how I was used. I don't know how the money that ostensibly was paid to lobby to have my bill killed was spent. Maybe it was all given to charity but probably not. I know that [Sedillo] liked to play poker, and in those days during the legislature there were some pretty high-stakes poker games at La Fonda and the De Vargas Hotel."

The "barefoot boys" was just one among numerous colorful monikers that floated around the Capitol during the period. Diamond-Tooth Miller might have attested to that as well as to the physical nature of the fervor that accompanied some legislators on their rounds.

Diamond-Tooth Miller was the very appropriate moniker given to Senator Dean Miller of Gran Quivira. "This guy, as you might expect, was a very colorful character," Chávez said. "He got the nickname because he had a diamond attached to one of his upper front teeth. Of course, everybody and his brother would ask, 'Where did you get that diamond?' He'd say without ever changing his story, 'It was given to me during World War I by a whore in Paris, France.' He reveled in telling the story and would even tell it in front of his wife.

"If Diamond-Tooth ever wanted to start a conversation with someone, all he had to do was smile."

Miller was not smiling one day as he made his way up flights of stairs that stood between the senate chambers on the Capitol's second floor and house chambers on the fourth. It was during closing hours of the 1951 legislative session, and Miller had taken part in the senate's defeat of a bill that for the first time would have established a minimum wage in New Mexico.

"The bill was introduced by Sixto Leyva from Sandoval County," Chávez said. "It was introduced at one dollar an hour but had to be conceded at fifty cents an hour in order to pass the house. I was a strong supporter of the bill and had some personal friends ask me why I went along with cutting the minimum wage in half by the time the measure came up for a vote. I explained that we didn't have the votes for a dollar; this was a compromise that would have allowed us to get a minimum wage law in the books that we could add on to later.

"People in those days were working for thirty, thirty-five cents an hour right here within walking distance of the Capitol. Employees at Santa Fe Electric Laundry, for example, were working in a hot, soapy place for thirty-five cents an hour.

"The stairwell between the house and senate chambers ended up being a point of confrontation after the minimum wage bill was killed. Along the stairs, right outside the senate gallery, there was a window from which you could look out onto the grounds below. A house member was walking down the stairs, and Diamond-Tooth Miller was walking up from the senate. These two men happened to meet up right alongside the window. That's when the house member grabbed Miller and said something like, 'Senator, I ought to throw you out this window for having killed the minimum wage bill.'

"Diamond-Tooth Miller must have been around five feet nine and probably weighed about 150 pounds. The other guy wasn't much bigger, but you don't have to be big to be strong. Other people in the stairwell separated the two men, broke it up."

The confrontation occurred before both the house and senate adopted rules that prohibited members from questioning each other's votes.

The threat of being tossed out a window was not all that could have brought an abrupt end to Miller's tenure in the legislature. "They threatened to expel him from the senate because during the whole controversy, he boasted recklessly at one point that he was 'the best senator money could buy,'" Chávez said.

"Years later, I was attending a legislative leaders conference in Carson City, Nevada, and introduced myself to the speaker of the house for Nevada. 'Ah, Fabián Chávez from New Mexico, huh?' he said. 'Do you know Diamond-Tooth Miller?' It turns out Diamond-Tooth apparently had moved to Nevada and became sergeant at arms in Nevada's house of representatives."

Miller, indeed, held several staff positions with the Nevada house, including sergeant at arms, from 1957 through 1966.[15]

While in the New Mexico house, Chávez was credited for helping secure needed funding for completion of that period's state capitol buildings improvement program, the Governor's Residence, and the new penitentiary to be constructed south of Santa Fe. Chávez aggressively opposed having the state prison within Santa Fe city limits.

He also opposed a measure calling for eliminating the election of state district judges in favor of appointments by the governor based on recommendations of a judicial commission. The Associated Press quoted Chávez as saying: "The people are better qualified to pick the judges than are members of the New Mexico Bar Association. If this goes through, what next? Will the bankers nominate the treasurer? The accountants the auditor? Maybe pretty soon the county commissioners will be nominating the members of the Legislature."

Chávez also fought a measure that called for preventing anyone but a lawyer from being paid for preparation of deeds, mortgages, wills, and similar documents. The AP quoted Chávez: "It's an act to make the practitioners of the profession of barrister the sole advisors of humanity."

Chávez spoke in favor of a resolution asking Congress to oppose drafting eighteen-year-olds. One news report quoted Chávez, who earned five battle stars after volunteering for the army at age sixteen, as saying, "An 18-year-old is still a boy. In the last war, I saw hundreds of 18-year-olds break down and cry like babies, or become excited and take chances that resulted in their death."

Chávez also took some swipes at the press while in his first term in the legislature. The New Mexican reported: "The press of New Mexico was 'damned' from the floor of the house of representatives today. Rep. Fabian Chavez of Santa Fe told his fellow representatives that 'I recently told a reporter damn the press. I answer to nobody but God and my constituents. I let my conscience be my guide.'"

Chávez said his remarks were prompted by a reporter who had warned him, "Don't forget the power of the press." Days later Chávez wrote a letter to one of the wire services to express his respect for most who worked in the state's news media.

Chávez also took issue in 1951 with an editorial in the *Carlsbad Current-Argus* that said "legislators from some of these (northern) counties are usually hack politicians."

"It is statements such as the one in the editorial that tend to create friction between the people of the northern and southern parts of the state," the AP quoted Chávez as saying. "In the past and in the last legislature the caliber of the northern county representatives has been equal to, if not better than, that of the southeastern representatives," Chávez said.

Divisions between segments of New Mexico were sharp at times, as reflected in the 1951 Carlsbad editorial. Attacking hostile divisions, Chávez fought more than editorial writers. "Some of our schools in the east side, Little Texas we called it, were still segregated, and as someone who fought in World War II to protect equal opportunity, it turned my stomach. I remember Rep. Virgil McCollum of Carlsbad coming up to me one day in 1951 and telling me that one of the supporters of a senate bill that year to prohibit segregation in our public schools was a Taos Communist. He said someone slipped a piece of paper under his door at La Fonda and told him that Communists were behind the measure. McCollum wasn't the kind to go around scaring everybody. He took information he got seriously. It just showed the kind of opposition we were up against and the way a lot of people thought at the time."

Along with fighting for the doomed senate bill to integrate public schools, Chávez as a member of the house supported a measure that further moved Indians beyond second-class status. The resolution called for giving Indians the right to vote as well as a public referendum on the state constitutional provision that prohibited sale of liquor to them.

Chávez also was a strong advocate for a 1951 house measure that passed and for the first time allowed women to serve on New Mexico juries. "Interesting, the only letters I got were against it," Chávez said. "I got about half a dozen letters from women who said they had responsibilities at home and didn't want to be taken away from those responsibilities for something like jury duty."

As Chávez grew into his role as a state representative in New Mexico, money became an issue in his pursuit of an education at St. Michael's College. From all indications, however, he also had to acknowledge to himself that he did not consider his future to be entirely dependent on a college degree. "I had been going to school at St. Michael's from 1947 through 1950 and found out that if you were a World War II veteran with ninety acceptable hours of college studies, you could enter law school. It was my opportunity to become a lawyer.

"I had what I thought were more than enough hours, but when I went to the University of New Mexico I learned that I didn't have the ninety acceptable hours. I had been studying social sciences—history, political science, the subjects that I loved. A mathematics course that I had taken was more like general arithmetic. The dean of the law school at UNM required several subjects before I could enter. Among them were 101 and 102 basic accounting. He also recommended that I take a course in business law along with a couple of other courses that I could take as a general student at UNM.

"I enrolled at UNM and was there from 1951 and into 1952. The GI bill had been paying for my books and tuition; it paid for my meals and the dorms. Everything was fine, except for one thing: I didn't have any money in my pocket. So I decided to come back home to make enough money that would allow me to get the hours I needed to get into law school.

"I got a job as an announcer at KTRC radio station. I also got licensed to be an insurance agent with the American National Life Insurance Company out of Galveston, Texas. I was a licensed agent under Ralph 'Sabu' Gallegos. Both jobs combined gave me enough extra money to start investing in stocks. I was interested in uranium stocks and invested through the firm of Watson and Company. I'd go there constantly to watch the ticker tab tape. I was real interested, and one day Ed Watson said, 'If you have the time, why don't you learn to be a stockbroker?'"

Chávez welcomed the opportunity, fully aware that he would need money to finance future legislative races and support the household he was planning to start with Coral Jeanne Rustenbach. "To be a stockbroker meant I had to go back to the learning process," he said. "Ed Watson educated me so I could acquire the National Association of Security Dealers license and later pass a tougher exam that was required to deal with the New York Stock Exchange. I took the exam at UNM, passed it, and promptly began selling stock. After I came to make so much good money as a broker, I didn't see a need to be a lawyer. I was making more money than a lot of lawyers so I didn't go back to school."

Beginning to make good money for the first time in his life, Chávez set his sights on growth within the legislature as well, less than two years after he had first taken a seat in the Capitol. "In the state legislature, my goal was to serve in the senate, and I had enough confidence in myself that in 1952, I set out to challenge incumbent Republican Senator Reggie Espinoza. I had no opposition in the Democratic primary because nobody wanted to run against Reggie. He was very popular."

Chávez collected 2,880 votes in the Democratic primary.[16] Espinoza, of Santa Cruz, got 3,287 while running unopposed in the Republican primary.[17]

The face-off in that year's general election was closer than expected. Espinoza won, 8,539–7,160, claiming most of the city precincts.[18] Chávez ran more strongly in some of the small, rural southern precincts than he had in his 1948 house race.[19] He also showed strength around Chimayó.[20] Espinoza ran strongly near his home, but Upper Santa Cruz and Chimayó combined went for Chávez, 251–180.[21] Still, pockets of strength for Chávez were small. Espinoza, for example, claimed Cundiyó in the foothills near Chimayó, 34–21.[22] As that margin suggests, though, Chávez stayed close in most precincts.[23] It was particularly notable because Republican Ed Mechem was at the top of the ballot again and secured his second two-year term as governor.[24]

"I ran a darn good race at a time when Mechem's presence boosted other Republicans, but Reggie won," Chávez said. "It meant that I was out of the legislature after 1952."

The legislature met in regular sessions only every other year during that period. Special sessions could be called in ensuing years, but there was no special session in 1952. That meant Chávez served in only one sixty-day session as a member of the house of representatives before finding himself out of the legislature again.

"I had more time to apply to my work as a stockbroker and begin saving a little money that I knew I would need for the new family that I so wanted, even as I continued working on the Catholic Church to accept the marriage that Coral Jeanne and I were pursuing in what had become a prolonged engagement. I remained active in precinct politics, of course, and was never very far from the Capitol, especially during legislative sessions."

Chávez, in fact, went to work as office manager for the state house of representatives in 1953. Floyd Cross, who had served with Chávez in the house, had become chief clerk of the chamber and hired Chávez to help him for a year.

In the spring of 1954, Chávez and Coral Jeanne Rustenbach ended their pursuit of support from the church and were married instead by David Carmody, state supreme court justice. Chávez, with his new bride and daughter at his side, cast his eyes again on a race for a seat in the legislature.

"Reggie Espinoza wouldn't seek reelection to the senate in 1956, and Democrats scrambled to compete for a seat that we thought we could win without a Republican incumbent," Chávez said. "There were seven Democratic candidates counting me. County Democratic chairman Santos Quintana didn't support me because even though I'm a good Democrat, I didn't always go along with what the leadership wanted. Santos and I had had some disagreements. He threw his support behind Lyle Teutsch Jr., who was a prominent attorney. One of the other candidates was a blind lawyer by the name of Albert Gonzales. He was a legitimate candidate. There were two other candidates with Hispanic surnames whom Santos probably put in to draw votes away from me. Besides Teutsch, there were two other candidates with Anglo surnames who Santos probably had get in as a smoke screen to conceal what he was doing with the Hispanics.

"Because of his support from Santos Quintana, I figured Teutsch was the man to beat. I worked hard all the way from Stanley to Chimayó, and when the votes were counted, I was number one. Albert Gonzales came in second; Mr. Teutsch was third."

Chávez won, for sure, but just by 22 votes. He beat Gonzales, 1,587–1,565.[25] Teutsch got 1,236 votes.[26] Leonardo R. Quintana got 382 votes; Marcelino P. Gutiérrez, 187; Mac J. Feldhake, 129; and Roy E. Schoen, 59.[27]

Chávez once again ran strongly at home. In all divisions of Precinct 3 combined, he outpolled Gonzales, 186–84.[28] Teutsch got 104 votes in the precinct.[29]

With eighteen votes, Chávez edged out all others in Stanley.[30] Elsewhere in the southern region, though, he lost to Gonzales in Edgewood, Glorieta, and Cow Springs.[31] Up north, he lost this time in upper Santa Cruz and Chimayó and once again in Cundiyó.[32]

Chávez to that point could not claim any part of the county as being consistently strong in his favor with the exception of neighborhoods around his own. He mostly scraped out precinct wins where he could to secure election day victories.

Chávez estimated he spent three thousand dollars on the 1956 primary. "Compared to what people spend today, it was peanuts," he said. "I had established a good reputation while I was a member of the house of representatives so I had no problem soliciting contributions. Harry Bigbee once again was the major contributor to my campaign. I also got contributions from the New Mexico Liquor Dealers Association and from personal friends in the liquor business, like Louis Hymel, who was president of a major liquor wholesale company. Those liquor contributions came back to haunt me years later."

Santos Quintana apparently had no trouble backing Chávez in the 1956 general election. "Santos was a professional. He said, 'Okay, Fabián, our differences are over. Let's get out and beat some Republicans.'

"My Republican opponent was Antonio Montoya. He was originally from Sandoval County and was a distant relative of Joseph M. Montoya, who was lieutenant governor at the time. One day during the campaign, I was headed to La Fonda to have lunch with Harry Bigbee, and I ran into Gen. Patrick J. Hurley, the Republican and former secretary of war who had run unsuccessfully in 1946 against Dennis Chávez for the U.S. Senate. Remember, I had worked very hard against General Hurley in that race. He was waiting for his wife in the hotel, and he said, 'Pray tell, young man, how is your campaign for the state senate coming along?' I said, 'I think very well, General, and I hope you see your way to be able to vote for me along with your family.' He then inquired, 'Tell me one reason why I should.'

"It wasn't a time to jump into a heavy discussion of the issues, and I knew the general wasn't one of my ardent supporters. I needed to come up with something fast, something that would get him to look favorably upon me, so I said, 'I'd like your vote because I'm the lesser of two evils, general.' He just laughed.

"A week or so later, he called to my house and talked to Coral Jeanne. He said, 'Tell your husband that I've checked it out and, by heavens, he *is* the lesser of two evils. Tell him that I will support him and ask him to come by and see me in my office.'"

There were other prominent Republicans who lined up behind Chávez for the 1956 general election. "Working as a stockbroker, I met a lot of people through the brokerage firm who ended up supporting me, the late Alva Simpson, for example, contributed to my campaign. Simpson had been director of what was known as the Welfare Department in Mechem's administration. He was very successful in the uranium industry and as a stockbroker, I did a lot of business with him."

Chávez actually worked briefly as vice president and financial consultant for Pecos Land and Development Co., of which Simpson was president. The company was engaged in real estate and land development, as well as oil, gas, and mining interests.

"Everybody running for public office, if they're worth anything, will get support from members of the opposing party. I got it, and if it hurt me with others, I don't think it was much. You take pride in being able to win people over from the other side."

Chávez needed help from every corner as Mechem was back looking for a third term as governor in 1956, having been required to sit out at least one term following the conclusion of his second administration that ended in 1954. "Mechem was appealing when he came back because of the state of affairs within the Democratic Party, problems that often still had their roots in the messy 1950 gubernatorial primary between John Miles and David Chávez. I'm sure the problems within the party made my race tougher," Chávez said.

Chávez beat Montoya in the end, 8,081–7,989.[33] He narrowly won his home precinct, 782–757, indicative of the tight race.[34]

Chávez said his election was the result in part of how he had responded to his loss to Espinoza four years earlier. "I got many of Reggie's supporters in 1956 because I lost with grace in '52. I showed respect for the man and for the system that elected him," he said. "I'm convinced that's important in politics."

Even though he was in the state house of representatives for only two years, Chávez had developed a reputation in the house that followed him into the senate in 1957. "Darn if the leadership in the senate treated me in a slightly negative way because of that reputation," Chávez said. "Senator Gene Lusk of Carlsbad was majority leader of the senate when the Committee on Committees met early in my first year. I had requested a seat in the chambers close to the exit door under the balcony." Lusk was the son of Georgia Lusk, whom the Dennis Chávez faction of New Mexico Democrats supported in her bids for Congress.

"I asked for a seat near the exit door because being a Santa Fe senator, I would get live constituents to come to see me, where most of the other senators communicated with their constituents through letters or telegrams.

"Horace DeVargas of Rio Arriba County was senate president pro tem at the time, and he made the request for me before the committee. Gene Lusk said, 'No. I'm going to sit him on the opposite side from where he requested because I understand that he was a smart-ass kid in the house of representatives.'"

Chávez traced his reputation to what Rep. Rex Kipp had told him that night in El Nido in 1951. "Rex told me that as a freshman legislator, I was getting up to speak on too many issues. But he also told me that I did my homework well, that I was blessed by being articulate. He, in essence, was telling me that I was using my talents but aggravating my fellow legislators in the process. That's the only thing that came to mind years later when I heard I was being called a smart-ass kid. Prior to that time, I had never had any run-ins with Gene Lusk, and I don't recall having worked against any of his bills while I was in the house."

Not all ranking senators agreed with how the often-brash Lusk proposed to deal with Chávez. Horace DeVargas, a tall, proper man from Española with thick eyeglasses, was among them. "Horace was mad, livid," Chávez said. "He told me what had happened and that he was going to get on the floor of the senate to fight Gene Lusk on his recommendation. The minority leader was a member of the committees committee, and he agreed to go along with Horace.

"I said, 'Look fellows, the last thing I want to debate is where I sit in this chamber. That's not important in the big scheme of things.' The minority leader said, 'We understand, but we still ought to teach the majority leader a lesson so if you find the right time to do it, just give me a signal, and I'll get you the Republican votes that you need.' Horace agreed on the approach.

"Now there comes an issue that is near and dear to Gene Lusk's heart. The house passed a bill reducing the severance taxes on potash, and Lusk was in charge of getting it through the senate. Lusk came from the region that is rich in potash. The bill that was passed in the house came over with tremendous support. It was a good bill because of the competition we were getting from Canada on that particular mineral around 1957.

"I saw an opportunity to teach Senator Lusk a procedural lesson. When the bill came up in the senate for final passage, I stood up and asked that it be placed on the president's table for further study because, I said, I was getting some new information."

Democrat Joseph M. Montoya was lieutenant governor and president of the senate. Montoya, who had served two two-year terms as lieutenant governor beginning in 1947 under Thomas Mabry, served a third term under John Simms from 1955 to 1956 and began his fourth in 1957 under Republican Ed Mechem.[35] Lieutenant governors in New Mexico were elected independently of gubernatorial candidates until 1964.[36] The principal role of the state's lieutenant governors is to preside over the state senate as president.

"My motion to place the potash bill on the president's table was not debatable, but Senator Lusk, who was visibly upset, demanded a roll-call vote. As he did, I signaled to my friends on the Republican side that this is where I would need their help. Roll call was taken and the measure was tabled, 22–10.

"Three or four days later, Senator Lusk inquired whether I was ready to allow the bill to be placed on final passage, and I said, 'No, I am not.' He then made the motion that the bill be removed from the president's table and be made the next order of business. I opposed the motion and then asked for a roll-call vote, and I won again."

That set up a peace meeting that Lusk recognized had become unavoidable. It was arranged to take place in the storied building at the end of the Santa Fe Trail that wound up hosting much of the state's business—official and unofficial. "At the end of the day's legislative session, Senator Lusk asked me to join him at La Fonda for a cocktail. Once there, he said, 'Why are you doing this to me, Fabián? You know that's a darn good bill.' I said, 'Gene, I'm doing it just to teach you that it is the man that makes the senator, not the seat to which he is assigned in the chamber.' I was giving him the message that where he made me sit made no difference in my ability to get things done. He said, 'OK, let's get along and let bygones be bygones.'"

Lusk and Chávez teamed up later in their political careers, but in the years leading up to that delicate partnership that was forced upon them, Lusk undoubtedly sought vengeance. The ploy Chávez carried out with help from Republicans was the kind of insider game that perennially perplexes and annoys observers in legislative galleries and beyond. Such maneuvering is widely considered to be a waste of time that then forces lawmakers to act hastily on legislation in the waning hours of each year's session.

Chávez saw his conduct as both necessary and tactful. "There is a way within the legislative body to maintain a good sense of decorum and civility," he said. "Problems can be resolved without having to go outside the chambers. You can solve them amongst the membership if everyone maintains civility. Everything I did was proper under the rules of the senate."

Getting stung by the trucking regulation bill that he sponsored while in the house of representatives kept Chávez alert for situations that might leave him looking less than respectable. They surfaced innocently at times and from unlikely corners. "By the time I was elected to the state senate, Harry Bigbee had become a very good friend whom I respected very much. He was sharing office space with two other lawyers who were also good friends of mine, David Chávez, whom Bigbee ran against in the 1946 race for judge, and Joe Guthman, the man whose wife introduced me to Coral Jeanne.

"Harry helped me for every office that I ever ran for and with the exception of one brief incident, he never asked for anything in return. He said all he wanted from me was to be a good public officer. He would give me advice once in a while, and I knew he had major clients who had interests before the legislature.

"The one incident that could have gotten troublesome if it had involved somebody else came about when Rep. Edmundo Delgado of Santa Fe got a bill through the house to reduce the interest that could be charged by small loan companies. Edmundo came over to see me and asked that I carry the bill for him in the senate. It was an excellent bill.

"A few days later my good friend Harry Bigbee came over to see me. He represented Household Finance Corporation, and his client opposed the bill. Harry said, 'Fabián, there's this house bill, and I'd like to speak to you about it.' I told him that I not only liked the bill but that I promised to carry it in the senate. He said, 'OK,' then his conversation immediately turned to his daughter. 'Can you arrange for Nancy to page next week?' he asked. He turned what could have been a tense conversation to something sweet and familial. Compare that to how things work far too often these days."

If Chávez's role in the senate was unfolding as he had hoped, he felt that the Democratic Party that he and his family had so passionately embraced for decades appeared intent on self-destruction. It affected him and others caught in the cross fire of increasingly competing factions of the party.

CHAPTER EIGHT

Ethnic Tensions and Hara-Kiri among Party Factions

ompetition between New Mexico Democratic Party factions festered just below the surface a full decade before Fabián Chávez Jr. won election to the state senate. It was 1946, and Democrats enjoyed stirring success at the polls, but it was the prologue to a disastrous period for the party that would begin unfolding almost without restraint during the ensuing state-wide election, according to Chávez.

A heavy, prolonged snowstorm in northern New Mexico counties that pushed into election day on November 5, 1946, had state Democratic Party leaders worried after a contentious campaign that saw Democrats fighting among themselves as well as against a spirited Republican opposition.

"New Mexico looked like a Canadian border state Tuesday night as new snow continued to fall on already blocked rural roads," reported the *Albuquerque Journal.*

As much as six feet of snow accumulated in some areas. The weather was of particular concern to incumbent U.S. Senator Dennis Chávez. Chávez was seeking election to a third full term against the former U.S. secretary of war and special ambassador to China, sixty-three-year-old Patrick J. Hurley, who was substantially larger than Chávez and, with a thick, gray mane, still moved like a veteran soldier.

"The snow was heaviest in those counties where a big native vote always has favored Chávez," the *Journal* reported.

Early returns did look good for Hurley. He led in populous Bernalillo County by more than fourteen thousand votes with seventy-two of the county's eighty-five boxes counted, according to news reports. Those reports said that Hurley led in Santa Fe County by four thousand votes with more than half the precincts there counted.

Besides his own U.S. Senate race, Chávez also had his eyes set on the campaigns for the state's two seats in the U.S. House of Representatives. The state school superintendent, Georgia Lusk of Carlsbad, joined incumbent A. M. Fernández as the two Democrats competing against two Republicans. The top two vote-getters would win tickets to Washington.

Georgia Lusk had cultivated friends while studying at New Mexico State Teacher's College in Silver City and at Highlands University in Las Vegas, as well as along New Mexico's east side, her native region. A rancher and schoolteacher, she was elected Lea County superintendent in 1924 and state school superintendent in 1930 and 1942.

As U.S. senator, Chávez had thrown his considerable influence behind Lusk, who was looking to be the first woman elected to Congress from New Mexico.

Republicans had prepared to generate a heavy voter turnout, concluding that it would work against incumbent Democrats statewide. Republican state chairman Philip Hubbell told the *Albuquerque Journal* that the GOP was prepared to send wagons and carts into the snow to get stranded voters to the polls. Referring to some of his own party's strength, Democratic chairman Bryan Johnson told the paper that "native" voters would get to the polls even if they had to use sleds.

The national news media reported of millions being spent on behalf of the two major parties for the control of Congress. Although they were substantial sums for the times, they appear paltry by the standards of the early twenty-first century. "Ten organizations have poured more than two million, 600 thousand dollars into the fight for the control of Congress and were prepared today to pump additional thousands into closely fought contests," the International News Service reported a week before the election.

At home, remarkably little attention was paid to Lusk's potentially historic feat by the state's biggest newspaper. The *Albuquerque Journal* said the U.S. Senate race between Chávez and Hurley had been the focus of most attention statewide. Two days before the election, the *Journal* relegated Lusk to the jump page of a report on a Democratic rally in Santa Fe. The paper referred to incumbent U.S. Representative Fernández before referring to Lusk as someone "also seeking election as U.S. representative."

Alluding to the just-completed world war, papers quoted Lusk as saying that Democrats "will win on the home front just as our soldiers won on the battle front." The *Journal* said she credited New Mexico for recognizing what women can do and said she pledged to always welcome the voice of women while in Congress.

Alongside reporting of Lusk's bid to secure a historical breakthrough for women, Hinkel's Fashion Store in Albuquerque advertised sable-dyed China mink fur coats for $1,095. Kappa Sigma Dames publicized that it would meet for the first time in years for a "homecoming tea."

The day after the 1946 election, while results in key races were still undetermined, the *Albuquerque Journal* referred to Lusk in the fourth paragraph of its lead story. "New Mexico has never sent a woman to Congress, but signs were pointing definitely to the possibility that Mrs. Georgia Lusk, state school superintendent, may be the first U.S. representative from this state." At long last, the historic nature of Lusk's campaign was noted.

Democrats, including Lusk, claimed victory in the state's top races when all votes were counted. After giving much attention to Chávez's reelection to the Senate, the *Journal* reported that "along with the senator, the Democrats re-elected Rep. A. M. Fernandez, sent Mrs. Georgia Lusk as the state's first woman to Congress, and put in office their entire state ticket, except for corporation commissioner." Thomas J. Mabry's election as governor also got prominent news play.

Ballot boxes in Rio Arriba, San Miguel, and McKinley counties were impounded on court orders, according to news reports, establishing an early history that would follow those counties on election days for decades to come.

Fabián Chávez Jr. supported Lusk's election, but says it—or, more precisely, how others responded to it—was what led to problems that left Democrats bitterly divided for years. He makes a solid case for his contention, but the increasingly assertive presence of Senator Dennis Chávez as well as irritants from other party leaders cannot be overlooked while assessing the fate of New Mexico Democrats from the late 1940s through the 1950s.

Dennis Chávez entered his surprisingly close 1946 general election race against Hurley after a bitter primary challenge from longtime adversary John J. Dempsey, who was in his last year as governor at the time. His support for Chávez in the general election was all but nonexistent until the final days of the campaign, news reports said.

"A lot of people have been asking where the governor stands in this campaign," Dempsey is quoted by the *Albuquerque Journal* to have said at the party's November 3 rally in Santa Fe. "Well, the governor stands where he has always stood since he was able to cast his first vote—with the Democratic Party.

"That's why I am here tonight in support of Senator Chavez. That's why I am here in support of Governor Mabry and the rest of the ticket."

The *Journal* said it was Dempsey's first public address in support of that year's Democratic ticket. Dempsey had been at odds not only with Chávez but with U.S. Senator Carl Hatch, as well as former Govs. Clyde Tingley and A. T. Hannett. The newspaper reported Dempsey as saying that some expected him to bolt the party after his primary defeat. "A Democrat doesn't bolt the party," he told news reporters later.

Then, alluding to the Democrats' favored image of helping the disadvantaged and their attempts at least since Herbert Hoover to paint Republicans as uncaring, Dempsey said, "We have some needy blind now who have seeing eye dogs. But [the Republicans] wouldn't even give them a stick."

Dennis Chávez at that same rally sought to paint Republicans as insensitive to the needs of New Mexicans. The *Journal* quoted him as saying: "This campaign for a seat in the Senate from New Mexico is not a race between Dennis Chavez and Pat Hurley but a decision whether the old Sunshine State will hold her head proud or earn the reputation of a dumping ground for wealthy easterners who want to exploit her."

Chávez's reference was to the years that Hurley, a native of Oklahoma, had spent as a federal official in and around Washington, DC.

Problems for Democrats were simmering within view of anyone who cared to look, however. Dempsey contributed to them as governor. A week before the 1946 general election, news reports told of two members of the State Highway Commission who resigned, accusing Dempsey of using "dictatorial powers" in numerous areas, including the purchase of new highway equipment.

Days after the election, papers reported of Dempsey's frequent trips out of state at the expense of taxpayers. "Governor John J. Dempsey will probably go down in New Mexico gubernatorial history as the state's most widely traveled chief executive while in office," wrote reporter Gordon P. Martin from Santa Fe. "And by the same token, James B. (Jawbone) Jones will be recorded as the highest-paid lieutenant governor New Mexico has ever had, because the state records show that from the beginning of the Dempsey administration on Jan. 1, 1943, up to now, Jawbone has drawn about $9,000 for his services as acting governor while Dempsey was out of the state."

Innocuous as they appeared at the time, the election of two Democrats to lower-profile positions in 1946 also planted seeds for problems later. News reports told that former Gov. John E. Miles picked up support from late-reporting counties on election night to defeat Roswell's Jess Corn in the race for state land commissioner.[1] And David Chávez Jr., younger brother of the U.S. senator, narrowly defeated Republican M. A. Otero Jr. of Santa Fe for one of two state district judgeships contested that year.[2] Before facing Otero, Chávez had beaten Santa Fe's Harry Bigbee in the Democratic primary.[3] Bigbee had held the post for several months following an appointment by Governor Dempsey.

Fabián Chávez Jr. said Miles's narrow election as land commissioner kept him in the public eye for the bigger political plans he already had in mind. "John Miles for a number of years had been known as Mr. Democrat," Chávez said. "He was Democratic Party chairman and then was elected governor twice before he won the race for land commissioner. He was a very likeable, almost fatherly type of leader who had a way of making everybody feel good, comfortable. He came from the east side, but even the so-called natives in the north loved John Miles.

"I don't know that he had any burning desire to be commissioner of public lands, but he had his eyes set on future races, bigger races, and so he didn't want to just head back to New Mexico's east side and be forgotten."

Miles's restlessness in the land commissioner's office was apparent as candidates began lining up for races in the 1948 statewide election. "That's when Miles made his big mistake," Chávez said. "He knew he was popular

☙ **FIGURE 10.** ❧

Gov. John J. Dempsey (foreground) outside the old Governor's Mansion with Brig. Gen. Larry B. McAffe and two unidentified generals. Photo by Harold D. Walter. Courtesy Palace of the Governors (MNM/DCA), negative no. 052345.

Ethnic Tensions and Hara-Kiri among Party Factions ℘ 117

within the party so he decided to run for Congress, in effect challenging Georgia Lusk during her first attempt at reelection."

Five Democrats ran for the state's two U.S. House seats that year, but Miles's entry was widely seen as a challenge to Lusk because, news reports said, three-term incumbent Rep. A. M. Fernández was considered to be secure in his seat.

"It was a surprise to me and many others in the party that John Miles would run against Georgia, who was the first female elected to Congress

⋘ **FIGURE 11.** ⋙

Gov. John E. Miles visits with his wife's parents, Mr. and Mrs. C. Hanna.
Courtesy Palace of the Governors (MNM/DCA), negative no. 013540.

from New Mexico," Chávez said. "She had made a good name for herself as state school superintendent. Like Miles as governor, she paid a lot of attention to the north, working hard for the schools in that region. She had shown herself to be very intelligent. As a congresswoman, she was highly respected during her first term and had begun the slow process of building up seniority in Washington."

Miles's entry into the race stirred debate throughout the primary campaign of 1948. "In the five-way Democratic congressional nomination race, with two to win, John E. Miles was the most-discussed candidate," wrote Santa Fe reporter Joe Clark in his column, Capitol Slant.

Miles's newspaper advertising for the most part was low-key. He promoted himself in those ads as "experienced, friendly, able." Another described him as "a practical man."

Lusk's advertising turned to her experience in Congress as well as to her family's devotion to country. One ad read: "She's learned working procedures in Congress, hence better able to serve New Mexico interests. She gave three sons to the defense of our country in World War II. She is endorsed by Senators Chavez and Hatch because of her efficiency in Congress."

Hatch, who went on to serve as a U.S. district judge, did not seek reelection to the Senate in 1948. As the U.S. House races unfolded, the party's nomination for Hatch's Senate seat was being contested by former U.S. Rep. and Secretary of Agriculture Clinton Anderson and John Dempsey. Dempsey already had served in the U.S. House before his two terms as governor that ended amid controversy in 1946. Democratic Gov. Thomas Mabry was seeking renomination against spirited campaigns by the corporation commissioner, Eugene Alison, and Frank Gallegos. "One Good Term Deserves Another," read one Mabry ad.

Much of the campaigning in the news media was done on radio programs on either KOB or KGGM stations in Albuquerque.

Despite the big names involved in the 1948 campaigns and Miles's surprising bid for the U.S. House, voters apparently were not particularly interested. "It has been a quiet campaign, particularly in comparison to the 1946 primaries, which on the Democratic side found Senator Dennis Chavez and then-Governor John J. Dempsey shouting at each other from the House tops in their fight to get the senatorial nomination," reported the *Albuquerque Journal*. A light voter turnout was forecast.

Such forecasts and the reports of a quiet campaign came despite considerable commotion stirred in the state's newspapers by Senator Chávez's engagement in some of the races. Chávez took heat on several fronts, including his implications that Governor Mabry was less than supportive of Latino candidates. Here's one report from the *Santa Fe New Mexican*:

The Albuquerque senator has started a political storm by his current campaign for his brother-in-law for the supreme court, his former secretary for attorney general . . . and a man, who was indicted several years ago for misuse of public money, but never tried, for land commissioner.

The senator, in trying to conduct a long range campaign from Washington, is within his privileges. His trouble is lack of judgment. He is basing the campaign on racial grounds and, some may think, on the Chavez family.

The *Tucumcari Daily News* said Chávez "seems to delight in stirring up racial intolerance" every election year. It said it would like to support Chávez but found it difficult because of his approach:

Consensus over the state seems to be that Dennis Chavez has gone too far this time in trying to dictate to Anglos and Spanish Americans alike in their voting choices for various political offices.

Resentment has been felt over the state because of the humiliation Chavez forced on the state's Governor in bringing up the perennial question of racial intolerance. Governor Mabry has always "leaned over backwards" to get along with Senator Chavez whose latest move has caused such dissatisfaction among voters.

The *Las Cruces Sun-News* asserted that Chávez's approach was divisive and predicted it would backfire. "Those who know Tom Mabry know he doesn't absorb pressure very well and he doesn't scare very easily," the paper opined.

Chávez's support for candidates reached beyond the 1948 primary, as well. In a letter to Hispanic voters in northern New Mexico, news reports said, Chávez asked that Democrats support J. O. Gallegos for land commissioner in 1948 so that it might be easier to elect a Hispanic as governor in 1950. The press said that the man Chávez was hoping would become governor was his own brother, David Chávez Jr., who was serving at the time as a U.S. judge in Puerto Rico under appointment of Pres. Harry Truman.

"If we are successful, I am sure we will be able to elect a Spanish-American as governor in two years," Senator Chávez wrote, alluding to Gallegos's ongoing race for land commissioner and his brother's potential as a gubernatorial candidate in two years.

The *Roswell Record* suggested Chávez was overreaching. "Sometime or another, New Mexico's Senator Dennis Chavez is going to put a spoke in his own wheel by taking in too much territory," it said. The paper

accused Chávez of injecting racial issues into political debates to further his own missions.

"It is an instrument he uses frequently and effectively, although he claims he fights for tolerance," the *Record* said.

Incumbent U.S. Rep. A. M. Fernández, too, criticized Chávez for making race an issue in the 1948 Democratic primary.

Eight days of rain in central New Mexico ushered in the June 8 primary election. As political rhetoric peaked, so too did rising levels of the Rio Grande around Isleta Pueblo and Bosque Farms, according to news reports. Levees along the old river were reported weakening in the Middle Rio Grande District while voters prepared to go to the polls.

After votes were cast, it quickly became apparent that Anderson would easily win his primary race against Dempsey for the U.S. Senate seat Democrat Carl Hatch had held since 1934.[4] Mabry was easily renominated for governor.[5] Fernández, Lusk, and Miles were still locked in tight races for the state's two seats in the U.S. House the day after the primary. Winners still could not be declared two days after the voting. Miles led Fernández and Lusk by narrow margins as some votes were yet to be counted, papers reported.

Finally, on June 11, Miles and Fernández were declared primary winners.[6] Both went on to win in November's general election, as did Anderson and Mabry.[7]

Miles's election is what would lead to trouble before long. "Anything John Miles would run for, he would win," said Fabián Chávez Jr. "He proved that with his election to Congress, but within two years, he wanted to come back home. He flat out said he was bored with Washington, that he wasn't meant to be a congressman.

"It was a crazy turn of events. You have to work a long time to build up seniority in the House of Representatives. We tossed seniority aside when Georgia Lusk was defeated, and then we did it again two years later when Miles decided he had enough of Washington. He abandons his seat in Congress and declares he's going to run for governor again. That created a real split in the leadership of the state Democratic Party."

Lusk had enjoyed support from Senator Dennis Chávez and his faction within New Mexico's Democratic Party. Chávez and his people were stung by her 1948 primary defeat. They were angered when Miles decided he wanted to run for governor in 1950, leaving open the seat that had briefly belonged to Lusk and setting up a gubernatorial primary against David Chávez Jr., who had resigned his federal judgeship to seek the governor's office with the enthusiastic support of his brother, the U.S. senator.

There were two other men in that 1950 primary gubernatorial race: the former mayor of Roswell, Lake Frazier, and the former corporation commissioner, Ingram B. "Seven-Foot" Pickett, who by then had gone to state district court to have his nickname recognized as part of his formal name. Much of the public's attention and that of the press focused on Miles and Chávez.

It did not take long for the 1950 Democratic race for governor to become heated. "It was very bitter," said Fabián Chávez Jr. "The Chávez faction accused John Miles of being backed by special interests. Miles was flown in to Santa Fe from Washington on an airplane owned by Southern Union Gas Company so he could declare his candidacy for governor. People around Senator Chávez accused Miles of being more interested in special interests than in the people of the state. They said he should have tried to establish seniority in the U.S. House to be of service to New Mexico and that he was running for governor strictly for personal gain.

"On the John Miles side, they accused David Chávez of being the younger brother of the U.S. senator who supposedly was trying to establish a dynasty both at the national and state levels. Race or ethnicity didn't come into play, at least not overtly. It was more this talk about 'family dynasty.'

"The primary battle was so bloody that it created a major split in the state Democratic Party. I supported David Chávez, of course, but I was careful not to get caught in the buzz of the battle. Really, I tried to concentrate on my own race for the state house of representatives. I shook a lot of hands, put up posters, attended weddings and funerals. If there were more than three people gathered anyplace, I'd go there. And as I moved around, I could feel the animosity that had been created as a result of that bitter primary race for governor."

Miles was the last man standing in that primary race. He received 42,237 votes to 32,955 for Chávez.[8] Frazier got 21,376, Pickett, 6,295.[9]

"It set up a general election race against this young, attractive lawyer from Las Cruces, Ed Mechem," said Fabián Chávez Jr. The winner would succeed outgoing Gov. Thomas Mabry, who was completing his second consecutive term and thus was barred from seeking reelection.

Originally from Alamogordo, Mechem had served in the state house of representatives from 1947 to 1948.[10] He had worked previously as a land surveyor for the U.S. Reclamation Service and as an agent for the Federal Bureau of Investigation. He practiced law in both Las Cruces and Albuquerque.

"New Mexico hadn't elected a Republican governor in twenty years, but Mechem came across looking tall, strong, and refreshingly untainted on the campaign trail," Fabián Chávez Jr. said. "And he was going up against a battered Democratic Party.

"Most of Senator Chávez's faction, including me, stuck with the party. But some, still bitter about Miles, wound up supporting Mechem."

Senator Chávez's support for Miles was in doubt in some quarters until just days before the November 7 election. The *Albuquerque Journal* ran a front-page story the week before the election under a headline that read: "Chavez Pledges His Firm Support to John Miles."

Chávez was interviewed by the *Journal* in an Albuquerque Hilton hotel room rented by the state Democratic Party chairman, Ray Rodgers. The story reported, "Voicing his refutation of rumors that the 'so-called Chavez Democrats' are going to 'sit out' the Nov. 7 general election, the senator told The Journal in an interview that he intends to work as hard for Miles 'as I would expect him to work for me if I were a candidate.'"

Miles, however, might as well have had his legs tied during the race. He not only had to deal with deep wounds in his own party but was also competing against an opponent who, although soft-spoken, appeared to offer reform of old-style politics.

Old-style politics had come to connote conduct like that of the state liquor director, Tom Montoya, who since 1945 had served both Democratic governors Dempsey and Mabry. "In the last weeks of Governor Mabry's second term, Tom Montoya issued thirty-seven liquor licenses and sold some of them at a good profit for himself," said Fabián Chávez Jr. "Montoya's brother, Joseph M. Montoya, was serving as lieutenant governor at the time, and the liquor license issue created quite a storm. Governor Mabry fired Tom Montoya with one month to go in his administration."

Mechem and other Republicans had much to criticize after two decades of Democrat dominance of the governor's office.

Democrats accused Mechem of mud-slinging and digging for muck against his opponents, but he promptly drew support in key circles. "If decency in government is to endure, there must be a change in state and county officials. Keep on digging, Ed," wrote the *Las Cruces Sun-News*.

A Mechem newspaper ad asserted: "New Mexico PREFERS Good Government." It professed that record voter registrations indicated a protest vote against Democrats was in the making. It told of voluntary formation of Democrats for Mechem clubs and boasted that the personal integrity of Mechem and Republican lieutenant governor candidate Paul Larrazolo had withstood all attacks.

War, meanwhile, raged in Korea and U.S. forces were among United Nations troops from sixteen countries sent in to fight Communists.[11] "Reds Trap More U.S. Troops," read a banner headline in the *Albuquerque Journal* two days before the New Mexico election.

A newspaper ad for Mechem paid for by F. W. Moxey, secretary of the state Capitol Buildings Improvement Commission, alluded to the war while touting Mechem's background. The ad read:

> For three years (1942–1945) Ed Mechem was a Special Agent for the Federal Bureau of Investigation (FBI). Much of that time was spent in tracking down Communist espionage agents in the U.S. As a result of his rigid training and many experiences, Ed Mechem knows the aims, purpose and methods used by communists and large scale criminals. His election as governor of New Mexico would bring this valuable experience, training and know how to our state at a time when it is badly needed.

Ranking Democratic leaders met in Albuquerque two days before the election and sought desperately to mend fresh wounds. Smaller meetings had begun days earlier. Reported the *Albuquerque Journal*:

> The series of meetings actually began Thursday night, when some 30 of those who attended Sunday's meeting met at the home of

[Victor] Salazar. Also present were U.S. Senator Dennis Chavez, U.S. Senator Clinton P. Anderson, and U.S. Representative A. M. Fernandez and Wade Miles, representing his father, the party's gubernatorial nominee.

On the same weekend that Democratic heavyweights met at Salazar's home, the party held a major rally in downtown Albuquerque. "You will want to see and hear the truth from these outstanding men," read one ad promoting the assembly. Speakers included Mabry, U.S. Senator Chávez, Anderson, Miles, lieutenant governor candidate Tibo Chávez, Dempsey, Fernández, and outgoing lieutenant governor Joseph M. Montoya.

The day after the rally, organized labor ran a newspaper ad that screamed, "Vote AGAINST MECHEM." The ad said, "Don't forget that E. L. Mechem . . . was one of the sponsors of the so-called 'right-to-work' bill, which was almost put over on you in 1948. Can a leopard change his spots? Let's not give this labor baiter another chance at us."

Last-minute antics by Democrats and their supporters fell far short in the governor's race even though Democratic candidates ran strongly in most other contests. The day after the election, the Associated Press told of the vote splitting and reported that the thirty-eight-year-old Mechem appeared headed for victory. "An anti-Miles vote centered in Albuquerque and Eastside New Mexico sent Republican Edwin L. Mechem to a lead of 10,964 for governor in returns early Wednesday," the AP reported.

"The vote splitting was unprecedented in New Mexico, where a Democrat has sat in the governor's office for the last 20 years."

At midnight following the vote, Mechem was the only Republican holding a lead in a state or congressional race.

By the morning of November 9, Mechem's victory was being trumpeted. "The stinging 12,000-vote defeat administered Democrat John E. Miles was the more significant in light of the 20,000 to 35,000 vote majorities rolled up by most of the Democratic candidates for state office," the AP reported.

Though Mechem won as governor, Democrat Tibo Chávez was elected lieutenant governor, and Democrats retained control of the state legislature.[12] Dempsey won the U.S. House seat Miles vacated.[13]

As for the condition of the state Democratic Party, the AP reported:

Miles not only lost the governorship, his first defeat at the polls in 34 years of state politics, but also the post of chief of the most-powerful faction within the Democratic Party of New Mexico.
  Senator Clinton P. Anderson (D-N.M.) commented on the defeat.

He said the "Democratic party [in New Mexico] does not need rebuilding so much as it needs a new face for governor in 1952."

Others in the party also expressed the need for "new blood."

For Fabián Chávez Jr., it presented a challenge he had not expected as he began his service in the New Mexico Legislature. "We hadn't had a Republican governor since Richard Dillon in 1930," Chávez said. "Mechem came in, and that happened to be my first term in the legislature. Things were happening even before Mechem's election that I thought were a detriment to the Democratic Party. There was this perception that we had become a party of factions, each looking to be the controlling political machine.

"I could feel things eroding under our feet as a party, and it was leadership's fault. They were committing political suicide. It was hara-kiri. Lines between party factions became more pronounced. There were the so-called Chavistas who worked with Senator Dennis Chávez. There was the Clinton Anderson group and the Joseph M. Montoya group. Joe Montoya had been lieutenant governor for two terms and was already eyeing a seat for himself in Congress in the not-so-distant future. All three groups began developing

≈ **FIGURE 13.** ≈
Gov. Edwin L. Mechem is escorted into chambers of the New Mexico
house of representatives to deliver his first address to the legislature, 1951.
Courtesy Palace of the Governors (MNM/DCA), negative no. 041884.

House Speaker Calvin Horn and former Gov. John E. Miles
after his loss to Republican Edwin L. Mechem, 1951.
Courtesy Palace of the Governors (MNM/DCA), negative no. 030289.

as major factions after Mechem's election in 1950, and there was no single, recognized leader at the top. It created a vacuum that hounded us throughout the next decade."

Mechem, meanwhile, had trouble working with the state's legislature of mostly Democrats. "Gov. Edwin Mechem's legislative program took a bad beating at the hands of the Democratic-controlled Legislature," the *Albuquerque Journal* wrote after the governor's first legislative session in 1951. Less than half of Mechem's proposals got through the legislature, the paper reported.

Working to put forth the "new face for governor" that Anderson spoke of following Mechem's 1950 election, Democrats appeared most united behind John Simms Jr. of Albuquerque, who had served as speaker of the state house of representatives in 1949.

"Simms came from a prominent, highly respected family in Albuquerque," said Fabián Chávez Jr. "He had plenty of money, and he appeared to be a bright spot in the party. The Democratic Party hierarchy, as it was, decided that Simms should be the man to run in 1952 to defeat Ed Mechem. Simms said he would run but then changed his mind. That left the primary race wide open, and the factions split between Roswell's former mayor, Lake Frazier, who had been defeated in the 1950 gubernatorial primary, and Everett Grantham, a former U.S. attorney from New Mexico.

"Neither Frazier nor Grantham was a big name, and our party's factions raised their ugly heads again throughout the primary."

Grantham narrowly won the primary, 42,658–42,050.[14] Frazier contested the vote count up until just a few weeks before the general election. "It left the factions unsettled if not warring with one another, and the party was in such a bad condition when the general election came around that Mechem won a second term," Chávez said. Mechem beat Grantham, 127,116–111,034 in the 1952 general election.[15]

Chávez, meanwhile, lost his bid to defeat incumbent Republican state Senator Reginaldo Espinoza and for the most part was relegated again to watching state government from the outside in.[16]

Mechem again had trouble getting initiatives through the Democratic-controlled legislature. As Mechem prepared to return to the practice of law at the end of his second term in 1954, Simms surfaced again as the choice of state Democratic leaders for the governor's office. This time, Simms committed to the race and stayed in. He advanced after an uncontested primary and went on to trounce Republican Alvin Stockton, 110,583–83,373 in the general election.[17] Joseph M. Montoya was elected lieutenant governor.[18]

"Simms was still the Democrats' fair-haired boy, but his election ended up producing one of the worst political disasters in the history of the state," Chávez said.

"Governor Simms wound up introducing a proposal known as the Welfare Lien act. It called for placing a lien on the properties of all recipients of welfare assistance. It was an explosive issue, and it was introduced during the 1955 legislature, Simms's first session as governor."

Matias Chacón, a maverick Democrat from Rio Arriba County, was house majority leader and introduced the legislation as a courtesy to Simms.

"Matias thought it was his obligation to introduce the bill in the house because of his position as majority leader," Chávez said. "The same day he introduced it, he announced on the floor of the house that he opposed the measure."

Chacón's two-stepping did not sit well at all in Rio Arriba County, where a young Emilio Naranjo had just begun developing his forty-year grasp on local Democratic Party politics. Naranjo was a vocal advocate for the poor, and the Welfare Lien act went against all he believed in.

⤞ **FIGURE 15.** ⤝
Fabián Chávez Jr. (left) talks with children of a Santa Fe family
as part of a contest sponsored in the mid-1950s by radio station KTRC,
where Chávez worked. Gov. John Simms Jr. (far right) looks on.
Courtesy Fabián Chávez Jr. Tyler Dingee; Recorder no. 1451–23. Santa Fe, NM.

"Matias's introduction of the bill led to trouble for him back home, and it led to his defeat at the polls in 1958 because his opponents in the primary had a copy of the bill with his name on it, and they used it against him even though he had publicly said he opposed it," Chávez said.

The Welfare Lien proposal itself was defeated in the 1955 legislature, and Simms never recovered.

The state constitution required Mechem to sit out one term following his first two as governor, but he was back for the 1956 governor's race. He handily beat Simms, 131,488–120,263.[19] Montoya was reelected lieutenant governor for what would be his fourth nonconsecutive term in that office.[20]

The 1956 election brought Chávez back into the state legislature with his successful bid to succeed Republican Reginaldo Espinoza in the senate.[21]

"What Mechem's election in 1956 proved was that Democrats still hadn't gotten their act together," Chávez said. "It also proved that Mechem had developed a comfort level with the people of the state of New Mexico so that whenever there was any trouble in Santa Fe, they felt safe turning to Ed Mechem.

"Ed Mechem might have seemed safe, but he wasn't a charismatic leader. And, remember, he was still a Republican in a state with a substantial majority of Democratic voters. When things quieted down again in Santa Fe, voters elected a Democrat, John Burroughs, as governor in 1958."

The curly-haired Burroughs narrowly upset Mechem, 103,481–101,567.[22]

"John Burroughs had been a pleasant sort of legislator during his one term in the state house of representatives," Chávez said. "He owned a number of radio stations and was a very successful peanut farmer from Portales, but he really didn't have a lot of experience to be governor. And he created frequent opportunities for people to question his judgment. He had more than his share of scandals in the two short years of his administration. The biggest, perhaps, was when some of his political associates established a new company to sell asphalt to the highway department and to companies that contracted with the highway department to build highways around the state. It was a big scandal. And then there was Harold 'Fats' Leonard of Albuquerque, who accepted a position on the State Highway Commission in spite of the fact that he sold equipment to the highway department and to contractors doing highway construction for the department.

"So here comes Mechem again, who was elected to his fourth nonconsecutive term as governor in 1960."

Just as narrowly as Burroughs had defeated him two years earlier, Mechem beat Burroughs, 153,765–151,777 in 1960.[23]

"Mechem was a good man, but in my opinion, he really wasn't elected to any of those four terms; his opponents were defeated often because of their own conduct," Chávez said. "Still, good things happened under Mechem, and I can only say good things about him. He had a constituency to represent, and many in that constituency were opposed to big government. Until Gary Johnson came along in 1995, Mechem had the record for vetoing the most bills. He would say we have enough laws in the books already; we don't need anymore."

In each of his three previous terms, Mechem had served with a Democrat, either Tibo Chávez or Joseph Montoya, as lieutenant governor. But in 1960, voters elected Republican Tom Bolack of Farmington as lieutenant governor. It proved important to Mechem as he neared the end of his fourth term.

Meanwhile, Chávez and other Democrats statewide struggled to maintain a grip amid a lack of leadership at the top of their party. "Picture me as a young legislator first in the house from 1951 through 1952 and then in the senate beginning in 1957," Chávez said. "I'm dealing with nobody at the top of our party, certainly nobody with any staying power or long-term support from the public. Factions within the party couldn't get together for very long. It seemed like every other year we got a new state Democratic chairman. When we were able to elect a governor, he quickly got into trouble with the voters. It created both a vacuum and an opportunity.

"So I became what was once described as a 'legislative executive.' That is to say, for lack of leadership from the top, you create your own leader. I didn't want to just sit there and wait for somebody else to assume leadership. I began asserting myself within the state senate and within the party even though I was quite young compared to some of the other legislators who had been around for a long time. It quickly established in me the necessity to do what I thought was right irrespective of the pressures applied to me from some of the Democratic leadership.

"During the period beginning in the early 1950s, there was no detailed executive plan. There was no direction from either the Democrats or Republicans. During this period, Clinton Anderson, Joseph Montoya, and Dennis Chávez would fight with each other over who should be state Democratic chairman, who should be party treasurer, and so on. You had this murky leadership. Conditions had deteriorated from when I came back from the military. We had a well-oiled machine then. We had Victor Salazar, who called the shots and maintained unity as the so-called second-floor governor. He was able to do it even when fights would erupt between U.S. Senator Chávez and Clinton Anderson."

Occasional disputes between Chávez and Anderson erupted even into the 1960s. "Early in 1961, Senator Chávez wanted Pres. John Kennedy to appoint Chávez's brother, David, as a federal district judge in New Mexico and Anderson, New Mexico's junior U.S. senator at the time, wanted somebody else. They chose former state house speaker H. Vearle Payne as a compromise nominee," Chávez said.

Joseph M. Montoya, meanwhile, refused to be seen as anything other than a key player in the state Democratic Party. Elected lieutenant governor four times, Montoya resigned his post in April 1957 after having won a special congressional election to fill the U.S. House seat left vacant by the death of A. M. Fernández in November 1956.[24] Fernández died the day after he was elected to his eighth consecutive congressional term.[25]

"There were all sorts of rumors that Senator Dennis Chávez disliked the way that Joe Montoya operated so Joe and his group mainly sided with Clinton Anderson whenever disputes arose," said Fabián Chávez Jr. "Dennis was always keeping his eye on Joe because Joe had his eyes set on trying to defeat Dennis in a future race for U.S. senator.

"They say it affected me because Joe Montoya apparently developed a complex when he saw me asserting myself and coming up, a young Hispanic individual who's building up a reputation in New Mexico who might be

∽∾ FIGURE 16. ∽∾
Fabián Chávez Jr. (left) and former Gov. John E. Miles were cochairs
of John F. Kennedy's 1960 U.S. presidential campaign in New Mexico.
Courtesy Fabián Chávez Jr.

a threat to him later. That's where Joe was wrong, but he was never able to see it.

"I envisioned Joe being elected to the U.S. House of Representatives at some point and then later succeeding Dennis Chávez in the U.S. Senate. From the state senate, I wanted to go to the United States House of Representatives to succeed Joe Montoya after he moved on to the U.S. Senate. Way back when I was a kid, I already had pictured that some day I might be a United States senator like Dennis Chávez. But I was pragmatic enough as a politician that I knew I had to take certain steps."

Chávez was open about his ambitions and acknowledges that he "broadcast" his plans at just about every opportunity. It did not always sit well with party leaders. "It's when I started antagonizing the party hierarchy, especially Joe Montoya," he said.

"This was told to me by my brother Cuate and others in the party: Joe Montoya wanted to be the leading Hispanic politician in New Mexico, and he thought that I was a potential opponent for that recognition. As open as I was about my personal political plans, never in my mind did I have the thought of running against Joe. What I wanted to do was follow him. I saw myself as Joe Montoya's successor, not his challenger."

The new decade of the 1960s would see a continuation of the tumult that ripped at New Mexico's Democratic Party as well as major missteps by Republicans. It also ushered in the first truly stinging defeat for Fabián Chávez Jr., which happened to come amid some of his greatest accomplishments as a state legislator.

CHAPTER NINE

Majority Leader on a
Strong Presence and One Vote

If New Mexico Democrats were committing hara-kiri in the 1950s, knives were still swinging with no sign of letup even as what Fabián Chávez Jr. refers to as the golden era of legislative accomplishment began emerging near the middle of the decade. Simultaneously, Chávez's reputation as a legislator dating back to his one term in the house of representatives helped carve a course for his extraordinary future in the state Capitol.

"It had become apparent that we had no clear leadership from the top of the party so we had to become progressives in the legislature," Chávez said. "I had served one term in the house and was in my first term in the senate, but I already realized it was extremely important to know how the legislative process works so that you can make it work for you. If you didn't do it, you were eaten up by the guys who did understand the process.

"I think I signaled to others in the legislature that I understood the process when I took care of Gene Lusk following his opposition to my seating request. I think that incident gained me respect. Even Gene probably thought he better get along with this 'smart-ass kid' or I'm going to have trouble with him."

Astute maneuvering alone carries a legislator only so far, however. Accomplishments in the end determine his or her real status. "There are two things that happened during my first two sessions in the senate that helped position me for what would come later," Chávez said. "The first came when Senator Jack Danglade of Lea County introduced a constitutional proposal to establish what we know as the State Investment Council.

"At that time, I was a stockbroker. I instantly picked up on the value of that proposal because prior to the Investment Council, the state's entire investment portfolio was in the hands of the state treasurer. And, historically, all the state treasurer did was use what was under his care to lend money to cities, counties, and U.S. government securities at very low interest rates by buying their general obligation bonds or whatever bonds they floated.

"Senator Danglade explained to me that the new Investment Council would be involved in overseeing the state's permanent funds and could invest them in the equity market, invest them in the New York Stock Exchange. An equity that received our money would need a history of ten consecutive years of paying dividends."

The proposal was aimed not only at increasing oversight of state funds but at substantially broadening the investment of state funds to make more money.

"One other guy who joined me in holding hands with Jack Danglade in the passing of this measure was Senator Horace DeVargas of Rio Arriba County. Senator DeVargas was a licensed insurance agent and was also licensed to sell mutual funds so he was acquainted in this area," Chávez said. "This was brand new to the state of New Mexico, and it just intrigued the hell out of me. It was a chance to really to do something for the future of the state. It wasn't very sexy in terms of attracting public attention, but it was one of the greatest things the state ever did. We campaigned actively for its approval by the voters.

"After the State Investment Council was formed, there was a massive reorganization of all the bonds that had been issued by the state treasurer, and they were incorporated into the authority of the Investment Council. Later came the creation of the state's severance-tax fund to be overseen by the Investment Council. I pushed hard for its creation, and it was an idea that came to me from Fred Moxey. That fund now has hundreds of millions of dollars and serves to benefit all New Mexicans in times of need." Moxey was director of the New Mexico Oil and Gas Association and previously served as state tax commissioner. He also was a longtime adviser to Gov. Edwin Mechem.

The second break that allowed Chávez to noticeably assert himself in his new role as state senator came when he was appointed to the New Mexico State Judicial Systems Study Committee and was then named its chairman. "In the legislative process, things happen sometimes more by accident than by design," Chávez said. "I got involved with Jack Danglade in pushing for creation of the State Investment Council by design. He came up to me and asked for my help. It was different with the Judicial Systems Study Committee. I got onto that committee by accident.

"Majority Leader Gene Lusk and I had settled our differences, and I went up to him one day in 1959 and said, 'Gene, I want to ask a favor.' He said, 'Anything you want, Fab.' I said, 'When it comes time for appointments, I'd like to be appointed to the Legislative Council.' Gene told me, 'You've got it.'"

The Legislative Council is a committee of senators and representatives who oversee the Legislative Council Service, which Chávez helped create while a member of the house of representatives in 1951. "I considered myself one of the fathers of the Legislative Council, and I told Gene that I wanted to help it further its contribution to the legislative process."

Chávez was prepared for what he thought would be multiple years of direct involvement with the Legislative Council. "Instead, I got a mild shock on the last day of the 1959 session. The majority leader gets up and announced the appointments to the various committees from the senate side. Senator Lusk did not name me among senators to serve on the Legislative Council. I was sitting in the back of the chamber, and Gene must have felt my eyes in the back of his neck because he turned around and looked at me and motioned for me to be quiet. I had already stood up to be recognized by the president on a point of personal privilege. I wanted to know what was going on.

"Gene motioned for me to sit down so I sat down. Then he announced his appointments to the new State Judicial Systems Study Committee. He named Senator Earl Parker, Senator Earl Hartley, and Senator Fabián Chávez. I said to myself, 'What the hell just happened here?' After Senator Lusk finished with the appointments, he called for a short recess and came up to me.

"He said, 'Fabián, this is going to be an extremely important committee and a justice of the peace friend of yours, as well as others, urged me to appoint you to it.' I said, 'Who's the justice of the peace?' He said, 'Your friend Gilbert López.'"

Chávez described López as one of his "closest and dearest friends." López was chief clerk of the house of representatives when Chávez returned from World War II. Chávez briefly did volunteer work for López in the Capitol.

Rep. Albert Lebeck of McKinley County introduced the bill that created the State Judicial Systems Study Committee.[1] It was to include members from the senate as well as from the house and initially was intended to study what had become an increasingly controversial and corrupt justice-of-the-peace system statewide. "Route 66 went from Gallup to Tucumcari. There were a growing number of complaints about how police patrolled that major highway and about how some of the JPs were dealing with traffic citations," Chávez said. "There were hundreds of complaints, and some of them were almost too hard to believe. As Representative Lebeck's bill made its way through the legislative process, people decided they wanted to study the state's entire judicial system, not just the JPs."

Chávez recognized the important impact the committee could have. He thought Senator Hartley would be the logical choice to chair the committee and had called before the panel's first meeting to propose that he take the chairmanship. "He was an attorney. Senator Parker wasn't an attorney. Senator Hartley also was chairman of the Senate Judiciary Committee so I called him and told him I'd like to nominate him to be our chairman. I already had called other committee members, and they agreed that this was the approach to take.

"But Senator Hartley had other ideas. He told me, 'No Fabián, you are the logical man to be chairman. You live in Santa Fe; we have to be staffed by the Legislative Council Service, which is in Santa Fe; the state law library is located in Santa Fe so it's logical that you be the chairman.' I said, 'But Earl I'm not a lawyer.' And he said, 'That's to your advantage because we who are lawyers are de facto officials of the courts and somewhat reluctant to ask the tough questions that are going to have to be asked of the judges as the committee does its work.' Being a layman became a distinct advantage, and that's why I was elected chairman of the committee."

It would turn out to be an extraordinarily high-profile position for Chávez, one that brought him tremendous attention from around the state as well as considerable scorn from within his own Democratic Party. The colorful reputation that Chávez had developed as a legislator dating back to the early 1950s left him with a steady footing, nonetheless. His was a record of which Democrat and Republican legislators alike had to take note, whether they agreed with his missions or not, and it propelled him into his second term in the senate.

Chávez openly tells of the inspiration he drew from conditions of the times. He had used his introduction to civil rights legislation in 1949 while an aide to Senator Tibo Chávez to press for civil rights as occasions arose once he himself was elected to the legislature. "I stood with people like Senator Chávez and Sixto Leyva in the house to improve the standing of New Mexicans who didn't always have a strong voice in the legislature," Fabián Chávez Jr. said. "I think of the bill in 1951 that for the first time would have integrated our public schools. Remember, that's the senate bill that was being pushed by Communists, according to Rep. Virgil McCollum of Carlsbad. Virgil was a World War II vet and a prisoner who was forced into the Bataan Death March. I always regarded him as a patriot, but so many people in the early '50s got caught up in Joe McCarthy's red scare and walked around believing that there were Communists around every corner."

Indeed, it was the fear of Communism that killed the 1951 school integration bill. A February 1951 headline in the *Santa Fe New Mexican* read: "Anti-Segregation Bill Iced by Red-Tinged Hint." The story under the headline reported: "The senate today prepared to dig further in charges that 'Communist influences' were backing a bill to prohibit racial segregation in public schools. The bill took a setback yesterday when it was voted back into the judiciary committee. Some senators believe it may never emerge from that committee again."

The bill was returned to the judiciary committee after Española Senator Horace DeVargas, who was chairman of the Senate Education Committee, had tried to force a vote on the floor. The *New Mexican* reported at the end of the session two weeks later, "The measure went down in defeat after charges were voiced that it was backed by 'Communist influences.'"

Chávez sought in vain to dispel that perception and was similarly vocal while supporting the 1951 measure that called for lifting the ban on liquor sales to Indians. "Representative Willard Stolworthy of Farmington stood in opposition to the legislation, saying that Indians by nature are savages," Chávez said. "I took great offense to that, as did many others in the Capitol. I had grown up alongside Indians all my life and was repulsed by comments like that, some of which were expressed openly and others that were spoken in private."

The 1951 legislature adjourned after having approved a $63-million budget for the next year. Six months later an editorial in the *New Mexican* told of new cracks in ethnic discrimination, specifically school segregation that had so agitated lawmakers only months earlier. It was progress that money could not buy. "The high school at Carlsbad, deep in the heart of Little Texas, has admitted Negro children for the first time in memory," the editorial read. "Nine Negro youngsters were enrolled for the current term. Segregation in the lower grades remains in practice but may be doomed if the high school action is an indication of things to come."

The editorial noted that segregation remained firmly in place in other east side school systems "in blunt contradiction" of what New Mexico seems to stand for. "Here, more than anywhere else in the country, there is a successful blending of cultures and races. The few ulcerous spots of exception seem to belong somewhere else," the paper said.

Chávez said Carlsbad's school superintendent had signaled to him that such changes were coming. "My gosh, these kinds of gains were so late in arriving, yet I took some pride in knowing that our legislature prodded them along years before our U.S. Supreme Court took up the issue of school desegregation in 1954."

Chávez had reason for pride, but even after the welcome advances were recorded at Carlsbad High School, he got a very public reminder that the march for civil rights often meant there would be one step back for every step forward. The reminder came in 1952 from the school that was to become New Mexico State University. "I heard from this young married couple in Santa Fe that had been accepted at New Mexico A&M in Las Cruces and had even been approved for married couple housing on campus," Chávez said. "They contacted me after they had gotten the blow of their young lives."

The call for help came from Reginald and Bonnie Barrow. College officials, upon learning more about them, told the couple they would have to live off campus because of their "Negroid extraction," according to a report in the *New Mexican*.

"The Barrows, both born of parents having white and Negro ancestry, have been told by a college official that the institution 'shall be happy to try to help you locate satisfactory quarters in Las Cruces' off campus," the *New Mexican* reported on August 3, 1952.

Barrow, sixteen, and his wife Bonnie, nineteen, said they would not accept housing off campus. They wanted the apartment-trailer on which they already had paid a deposit.

A&M Pres. John Branson said the university's board of regents would have to deliberate the matter at its next meeting, according to news reports. "The institution can hardly be said to have a policy. We've had two or three similar cases before, and Negroes were welcomed on the campus, but were told they'd probably be happier living in Las Cruces . . . It's because people are what they are. The community up to now has hardly been ready for a move as drastic as that is," he said of blacks being granted housing on campus.

Gov. Edwin Mechem, who lived in Las Cruces before his election, declined to intervene in the case, newspapers reported. "I don't want to interfere in the matter. The control and management of the institution is under the Board of Regents, and they make the policy," he said.

Chávez, though, refused to keep his hands off the case. "Jesse Richardson was chairman of the board of regents and was a state representative from Doña Ana County. He also was a friend of mine," Chávez said. "I called Richardson right away and asked him what the hell was going on down there. He says, 'Well, Fabián, you have to understand that we're only forty miles from the Texas border.' That was his answer to me.

"My reply was, 'Damn Texas.' And, frankly, my language was a bit more colorful than that. 'This is a New Mexico state institution supported by

New Mexico taxpayers, and they shouldn't be treating this couple that way,'" I said. "The couple and I exposed their story through the press and we got a lot of attention for their plight."

It all occurred at a time when blacks were gaining increased attention in the newspapers nationwide. Republican Dwight Eisenhower and Democrat Adlai Stevenson were competing for the U.S. presidency, and political

᪥ **FIGURE 17.** ᪥
U.S. presidential candidate Adlai Stevenson (left) with Fabián Chávez Jr.
and vice presidential candidate Estes Kefauver at the 1956 Fiesta de Santa Fe.
Courtesy Fabián Chávez Jr.

observers were predicting black voters could determine the winner. Both candidates shaped campaign strategies to attract black voters. The popular Drew Pearson column reported that Eisenhower had even said "he might appoint a qualified Negro to his cabinet." Some black leaders, like U.S. Rep. Adam Clayton Powell Jr. of New York, criticized the gestures as insincere.

On sports pages, blacks got occasional attention for extraordinary accomplishments as well as for what had become ordinary efforts. "Negro boxers sweep Olympic fights in Helsinki," read one headline. Another read, "Leroy 'Satchel' Paige wins one for St. Louis."

The A&M board of regents met in Santa Fe twelve days after the Barrow story broke and unanimously approved a policy that said distinctions among students would not be made based on race, creed, or color, according to newspapers. The Barrows obtained campus housing. "The ground won should never be lost," the *New Mexican* wrote in an editorial. Even the *Carlsbad Current-Argus* weighed in from a community where segregation was slow to take hold. "All citizens are entitled to equal treatment at state institutions, regardless of race or creed," it said in its own editorial.

Chávez pledged during the 1952 incident that he would propose in the next legislative session a measure that banned segregation in all New Mexico's public institutions. It was a pledge that Chávez could not keep because of his failed attempt that year to unseat state Senator Reginaldo Espinoza. Nonetheless, the U.S. Supreme Court in 1954 ruled in *Brown v. Board of Education of Topeka* that segregation in public schools—in any state—was unconstitutional.[2]

In New Mexico, the antidiscrimination banner was picked up in 1955 by Chávez confederate Rep. Albert Amador of Rio Arriba. He successfully sponsored a bill that prohibited discrimination in public accommodations, resorts, and amusements. The new law, however, did not provide penalties for violations.[3]

"Too often, despite the Supreme Court ruling and the 1955 state law, discrimination continued in practice," Chávez said. "It was still evident in the schools, and it was very evident in our restaurants, motels, movie theaters, swimming pools. I wanted it stopped.

"Elected to the senate in 1956, my first session as a senator was in 1957. That year I asked the Council Service to draft a bill that would have provided penalties for all violations. I felt so strongly about it that I initially wanted to make each violation a fourth-degree felony."

Chávez's efforts died on the vine, but the first-term senator drew a lot of attention within the Capitol for pressing the controversial issue in delicate times. Not long after, the issue was revived with a different outcome while Chávez's standing within the Capitol solidified further. "There was talk within the party about this fellow whom Gene Lusk just a few years earlier had referred to as a 'smart-ass kid,'" Chávez said. "Ever since working with Rep. Sixto Leyva in 1951 on the bill that would have established our state's first minimum-wage law, I guess, I had begun making a reputation for myself as a legislator who aggressively stood up for the rights of the disadvantaged and disenfranchised. Even getting a minimum wage was civil rights legislation. All you had to do was stick your head into the laundries, the restaurants, the hotels to see who was working as maids, cooks, janitors, laborers. More than 90 percent were Hispanics who were working for less than fifty cents an hour. It was true around the state.

"Minimum wage laws after that first year were introduced in just about every session of the legislature, and even after we secured a minimum wage, I kept working hard for pay increases as time went on. Sometimes we succeeded, sometimes we didn't, but we were always ready to try.

"As a state senator, I was also a champion of worker's compensation to improve conditions in the workplace and to ensure that workers injured on the job weren't simply forgotten. I also led the fight in many cases against the so-called right-to-work laws, which were meant to destroy trade unionism. I felt that collective bargaining is the only real tool that poor working people have when it comes to improving their lot as workers. I fought efforts to take that right away. That's civil rights legislation, and I had a lot of help in such work from labor lawyers like Edwin Felter and Lorenzo Chávez. In the civil rights cases that involved overt segregation, I relied a lot on Marcel Pick from the Anti-Defamation League and Hobart LaGrone, who was the state representative for the NAACP."

Indeed, Chávez was building a reputation as one of the legislature's most liberal members. Bobby Mayfield, who represented Doña Ana County in the state house of representatives during the 1960s and later competed against Chávez in a Democratic primary race for governor, said Chávez had assembled a strong reputation in the area of civil rights. "He probably had more to do with civil rights legislation than any other single legislator that I knew about," Mayfield said. "He sure was ahead of his time as far as civil rights legislation was concerned.

"Fabián was a Democrat through and through. He was very, very partisan, but Fabián also had a good, broad view of what the state of New Mexico was all about," Mayfield said. "I think at the time that I was around Fabián that maybe he knew as much about state government in total as anybody I knew. He had a tremendous working knowledge of all branches of state government, and he was a consummate politician. He knew how to ring the bells in large part because he was raised in politics in Santa Fe."

Floyd Darrow, who represented Bernalillo County as a Democrat in the house of representatives from 1951 to 1955, said Chávez's reputation as a "silver-tongued orator" mostly served him well while building his record as a civil rights champion, even if he had to endure some teasing along the way. "We named him that because Fabián in his enthusiasm decided that he knew everything about anything that came up for discussion, and he made sure that he had something to say about it," Darrow said from his home in Kansas.

The more Chávez talked, the more his work piled up. "He did what he said he was going to do. That's true," said Darrow, who along with his brothers and father owned Darrow Ice Cream Company in Albuquerque.

"One day Fabián came into the ice cream company and asked me if he could borrow a hundred dollars," Darrow said. "He said he could leave me a pocket watch for security. I said he didn't have to do that, but he left the watch anyway. About a year later he came back and said he wanted his pocket watch back. And, yeah, he paid back the hundred dollars."

Chávez said he sought such loans on occasion while still taking classes at the University of New Mexico.

Keeping his commitments in multiple areas enhanced Chávez's standing as a leader almost since he first took a seat in the Capitol. One such commitment came unexpectedly during his first term in the senate, much as had his involvement with the State Judicial Standards Committee. "Los Alamos County had just recently been created, and Harold Agnew represented the new district in the state senate," Chávez said. "On the first day of the 1957 session, he introduced a bill to abolish the New Mexico Liquor Fair Trade Law, also known as the Alcoholic Beverage Minimum Markup Law. It was supposedly intended to protect the little liquor dealers from being swallowed up by the big liquor dealers and ensure that consumers got a fair price in the end. I had supported the law while in the house and again in the senate because I thought it was serving its purpose.

"Senator Agnew's bill was referred to the Senate Public Affairs Committee, where I was a member. Senator Agnew made a very interesting presentation before the committee when his bill came up. He brought in full-page ads from the *El Paso Times* and the *Denver Post* that essentially showed our law wasn't working. Outlets in both El Paso and Denver advertised the sale of various alcoholic beverages for less than, ostensibly, the wholesalers in New Mexico had to pay for them. Our law wasn't protecting the retailers; it was enriching the wholesalers, and consumers often were footing the bill.

"I cast my vote in the committee for the maintenance of the law as it existed at the time but realized that something had to be done. After the committee meeting, as I walked from the meeting room back to the senate chamber, Senator Agnew grabbed me by the arm and said, 'Fabián, you know better than that. This is a bad law, and I'm surprised you voted the way you did.' I said, 'Harold, you made an excellent presentation, and you certainly opened my mind for further study, but we cannot repeal this law solely based on the sale of cheaper alcoholic beverages.' I told him that, in fact, several churches supported a bill that would make it even more expensive to buy liquor and so it was important that we make a study so that our actions would be based on more than just cheap liquor."

Chávez for years had received donations from the liquor industry, so Agnew, at least initially, had reason to suspect Chávez's explanation, and suspect it he did, to put it mildly. Chávez in time overcame Agnew's doubts, though. The legislature at that time still met in regular session only every other year, and in the session following the defeat of Agnew's bill, Chávez revived the issue. "I kept my promise to Harold, and in 1959 I went to the Legislative Council Service and asked them to make a thorough study of the liquor pricing issue. They were kind enough to assign Dick Folmar, the council's deputy director, to do the study."

Folmar said he was not quite sure at first what his charge was. "Fabián came to me and said that he and other senators wanted a collection of the whole picture for the liquor industry, particularly in terms of pricing. He said he wanted me to acquire information on pricing in New Mexico and in other states as well.

"After his initial request, I might have checked with him a couple of times to see if this is where he wanted to go," Folmar said. "Other than that, we were turned loose to see how it came out. Fabián said, 'I have a feeling how it's going to come out, but I want something that I can show to other senators, something I can show in debate.'"

Chávez said he instructed researchers to go where the facts led them. "I told them I wanted the truth because something is very wrong when you see the kind of information that Senator Agnew made available."

Agnew, meanwhile, left the senate for new developments in his professional career. Long-affiliated with the national laboratory in Los Alamos, Agnew had worked on development of the atomic bomb and upon his departure from the New Mexico Legislature, went to work as an adviser to NATO's supreme allied commander in Europe, while Chávez and other incumbent state senators campaigned for new terms through the fall of 1960.

Chávez was unopposed in that year's Democratic primary. He defeated Republican Thomas McKenna by 1,249 votes out of 8,711 cast in the November general election. "McKenna was an attorney, an Irish Catholic in very good standing with the church, and religion came into play as the general election went along," Chávez said. Local religious leaders, it turns out, were unhappy with Chávez for his role in defeating a measure that they had supported the year before the election.

Chávez in 1959 had been instrumental in killing legislation that was advanced as an antipornography bill and sponsored by his good friend, Jack Campbell of Roswell, in the house of representatives. "It passed the house and when it got to the senate, I knew I had to oppose it because it was a censorship bill; it was too broad," Chávez said. "I had learned that the Michigan Supreme Court had declared a similar bill there to be unconstitutional. The court said the measure burned down the house to kill a mouse, and I used that same argument on the floor of the senate to get Jack Campbell's bill defeated. Jack's intentions were good, but the bill was written in such a way that there was no real way to define pornography.

"Archbishop Edwin Byrne endorsed the bill. Some local Catholic schools wrote letters in support of it, trying to get me to vote for it. And just a couple of months before the general election, Thomas McKenna publicly got a special, extraordinary designation by the church. On top of that, his supporters kept referring to him as 'a good Catholic' as they went around campaigning for him. Some of them placed fliers on cars parked outside the church, which was a mistake because people don't like that sort of thing going on while they're at church."

Newspaper columnist Will Harrison had predicted that Campbell's measure would sail through the senate, alluding to the makeup of the chamber. "Harrison predicted that the Baptists and the Catholics in the senate would get together to pass the bill," Chávez said. "And since people generally equated Hispanics with Catholics, it was assumed that Hispanic senators would support the bill. In the end, they opposed it unanimously.

"Members of the press in those days were allowed to sit at a table within the senate chamber itself. Will Harrison was one who sat at the table. When the bill was defeated, Senator Palemón Martínez of Taos got up and said, 'For the distinguished newspaper columnist sitting up there, you implied that all Catholics and people with Hispanic surnames would vote for the bill. Well, they voted against it. And I need to correct you on one other thing: I'm not Catholic. I'm Presbyterian.'"

Chávez asked for a meeting with Archbishop Byrne following the election to personally explain why he had opposed Campbell's bill. "We met in his chamber off Cathedral Place in Santa Fe. He offered me a glass of wine, and we sat down and visited."

Having gained the understanding of the archbishop along with the support of most of his constituents, Chávez was headed into a second term in the state senate. Maurice Trimmer, who had arrived in Santa Fe in 1958 to cover the Capitol for United Press International, said he was among those

in the press corps who were glad to see Chávez return even while working to maintain impartiality in their reporting. "Fabián was great. He was
a reporter's dream," Trimmer said. "He was very bright, articulate, and he
had a great sense of humor. I knew that if I went to him with any question,
he'd give me an honest answer.

"I went to [Gov.] Ed Mechem to ask about Fabián. He said Fabián stood
out among legislators. Mechem was a Republican, Fabián was a Democrat,
but he was very professional and could work with people on the other side."

Soon after the November 1960 election, Chávez and other Democratic
senators got a letter from one of their peers. "The letter was from Senator
Ike Morgan of Portales," Chávez said. "He had been in the senate for eight
years, and he informed us in his letter that he had been encouraged by fellow senators to run for majority floor leader, that he had decided to run for
the position and that he would appreciate our support."

Morgan's letter crossed paths with specific plans that Chávez had, until
then, kept to himself.

"I countered with a letter to all senators," Chávez said. "I told them that
I felt I had the knowledge to be a good majority leader. I said I had not been
encouraged to run by any of my fellow senators and, in fact, was partially
dissuaded by my wife. I learned later that a number of senators got a kick
from that particular line.

"I wasn't as experienced as Senator Morgan, but I knew I was a good
parliamentarian, and I had a sense that I could run a very good senate. I
had experienced what happens when you let things run away from you
while both in the house and the senate so I had come to appreciate the value
of decorum and civility. My feeling as I sought the leadership position was
the worst my fellow senators could say was 'no.'"

Gene Lusk had served as majority leader but opted against reelection to
the senate in 1960. That prompted at least a little maneuvering behind the
scenes. "Senator Al Montoya, brother of Joseph Montoya, had approached
Tibo Chávez to run for majority leader, but Tibo said no, that he was going
to support me and that he wanted the others to support me, too. By the
others, he meant the other Hispanics," Chávez said. "I wasn't surprised by
Al's move because the Montoyas already were envisioning me as a threat to
their goals."

Chávez followed up on his letter of solicitation by traveling across the
state and personally asking senators for their support. In the process, he
let it be known that he was supporting William Wheatley of Clayton to
become senate president pro tem because he was the chamber's most senior
member. "I volunteered my vote prior to my visiting with Senator Wheatley
to ask that he support me for majority leader. He frankly told me that he

already had committed to vote for Senator Morgan. I then said, 'Fine, keep your commitment, however if on the first ballot we end up tied, would you consider me in the second ballot?' Senator Wheatley said, 'I can do better than that. If it goes to a second ballot, you have my vote.' I made the same request to all senators about being considered in case the first ballot wound up in a tie. They'd just laugh. Senator Wheatley pledged himself."

An unexpected turn of events during that period ended up boosting Chávez's chances in the contest for majority leader. Senator Jack Danglade of Lea County died of cancer, and the Lea County Commission appointed Harold "Mud" Runnels as his successor. "Runnels read my letter requesting help, and he got a laugh from the line that said nobody had encouraged me to run and that my wife had tried to talk me out of running," Chávez said.

"Runnels had asked around about me, and the next time he was in Santa Fe, he asked if we could have dinner. We went to El Nido and had some very deep discussions about how the senate functions. He asked me all sorts of questions about rules of the senate, and he asked for advice on which committees he should try to sit on to best serve his constituents. When it was all over, he said, 'I'll probably be the only guy from the east side who votes for you in the race for majority leader, but you can count on my vote.' I think he knew that senators from the east side had already committed to Ike Morgan.

"I knew the count going into the election. Out of the twenty-four Democratic senators, I knew I had twelve votes once Runnels came to my side. Sure enough, it was twelve to twelve on the first ballot. At that point, Senator Morgan asked for a thirty-minute recess before we cast another vote. I said, 'No, let's not waste our time just yet. Let's try one more ballot before any kind of a break.' The presiding officer called for an immediate vote, and with Senator Wheatley's help, I won, thirteen to eleven."

The victory came even while Chávez already was sensing less than enthusiastic support from two of the state's leading Democrats, Senator Clinton Anderson and Joseph M. Montoya, who at the time was serving in the U.S. House. Santa Fe columnist Will Harrison said at the time that both Montoya and Anderson pressed for Chávez's election as state senate majority leader, however.

"Revenue Commissioner Bob Valdez, political mayordomo of the statehouse, and U.S. Rep. Joe M. Montoya were up front in the drive for Chavez," Harrison wrote. "And the defeated Morgan people think they were also hurt by State Chairman Seaborn Collins and Dick Pino of Senator Anderson's group."

At thirty-seven Chávez, the stockbroker, became the youngest New Mexico senator ever elected to the power-laden position of majority leader. He also apparently was the first Hispanic to hold the post.[4] Hispanics had served as minority floor leader and minority whip in the senate, even president pro tempore. The pro tempore post traditionally had been reserved for the most senior members of the chamber. Hispanics—most recently Tibo Chávez and Joseph M. Montoya—also had presided over the senate as lieutenant governors, having been chosen by a predominantly Hispanic electorate, not by members of the senate.

Despite the comment Senator Tibo Chávez purportedly made in his conversation with Al Montoya, Fabián Chávez Jr. said the 1961 senate election for majority leader did not pit Anglos against Hispanics. "I didn't experience any kind of friction like that at all," he said.

Chávez in the majority leader's race got votes from eight senators with Hispanic surnames, five with Anglo surnames. It probably was a greater accomplishment than what he appeared willing to acknowledge. "I was pretty blissfully unaware of any tensions that might have existed between Anglos and Hispanics at that time," said Maralyn Budke, who began working as a legislative staff member in 1958 as a University of New Mexico student intern. A Republican, Budke arrived at UNM from Amarillo, Texas. She went on to serve as director of the New Mexico Legislative Finance Committee for fourteen years and was roundly respected as a ranking aide to two Republican governors.

"I remember being surprised and horrified when we began talking about such things," Budke said of ethnic tensions. "I thought, 'Gee, why did I never notice that Hispanics thought they were being discriminated against?' But looking back, the powerful members of the senate in the early days were all Anglos until Fabián became floor leader. I really didn't know the inside politics of the senate well enough to say why."

Bobby Mayfield expressed similar conclusions from his law office in Las Cruces. "Fabián had a lot of natural leadership, but for a long time leadership positions in the legislature were held by a lot of east side New Mexicans and southern New Mexicans. If you look at the committee chairmanships, the house speakers, the majority leaders, and so forth, there was a lot of power centered in eastern and southern New Mexico.

"The power structure in those days was in the southern half and eastern part of the state. It required ability, but Fabián also had to have a lot of respect from his colleagues in the senate to overcome that geographical bias that he had against him when he was elected majority leader."

Frankly, Mayfield said, it was more than just a geographical bias that Chávez had to beat. "Quite a bit, quite a bit broke along ethnic lines," Mayfield said. "I think it's another tribute to Fabián. I think it had a lot to do with the observation that everybody made: that Fabián knew so much about state government. That's what helped him along."

It was in the early 1960s that Chávez, Mayfield, and other strong-willed legislators were fortifying their hold on much of government. "We had a falling together of people in the 1960s, and it had a lot to do with what got done in state government. There was a group of legislators that worked so closely together, Republicans and Democrats, for the good of the state," Mayfield said.

As majority leader, Chávez would be called upon to tend to the orderly conduct of business in the senate as well as to legislation growing out of major issues that had been dropped on his plate during his first term in the chamber. Successive governors—one Republican and one Democrat—would also turn to him to sponsor other legislation deemed critical for the state.

"It's what I dreamed of as a kid," said Chávez. "Other kids would play on the ground with marbles or toy trucks. I'd play alone, going through all the parliamentary motions of the legislature that I learned while visiting the Capitol when my dad was buildings superintendent. I would introduce bills. I would kill bills. And, in my mind, I would direct the process through which others would tend to the business of the legislature, the business of our state. I had it all memorized years before I was even elected to my first term in the house. Now, I was senate majority leader, and I recognized that people had placed a lot of confidence in me. What was my first thought? Simple: I wanted to let people know that their trust was well placed."

CHAPTER TEN

Reapportionment and Death
of a Political Pillar

By 1960, New Mexico's population had grown to 951,023, increasing by a remarkable 40 percent during the previous decade and reflecting growth that was evident through much of the Southwest.[1]

Accompanying the growth were major changes that took effect around the midsixties that affected how voters of New Mexico elected members of the state legislature as well as their delegates to Congress. Not only was the state house of representatives reapportioned to reflect population shifts, population density was also used to determine state senate districts for the first time.[2] Until then, each county had one senator. That meant that the most populous counties—Bernalillo, Santa Fe, Doña Ana—had the same representation as the smaller counties, like Harding, Hidalgo, and Catron.

Under the old system, state representatives were elected at large, often making the election of minorities difficult. "There were nine members of the house from Bernalillo County, and none was Hispanic. There were no Navajo legislators at all," said David Cargo, who as an Albuquerque attorney in 1961 filed a reapportionment lawsuit demanding change. As Cargo's lawsuit unfolded, it tracked with a Tennessee case, *Baker v. Carr*, which in 1962 drew a decision from the U.S. Supreme Court. The high court ruled that federal courts have authority to decide lawsuits challenging the fairness of apportionment.[3] The Supreme Court later ruled that election districts should have approximately equal populations.[4] It all disrupted entrenched political systems like that in New Mexico, which not only protected incumbency but in many cases also locked out minorities.

"In the New Mexico senate we had what became known as senility row," Cargo said. "Some were members of the John Birch Society, and for a long time, they controlled everything."

The election of legislators by district, instead of at large, produced immediate changes. "Right out of the box, in 1964 we elected Navajo legislators. In Bernalillo County almost half the representatives were Hispanic," Cargo said.

The change in the state senate meant that Bernalillo County, for example, went from one senator to ten in 1966.[5] "By sheer numbers, it gave bigger counties more power in the legislature but not always as much as you might think," said Fabián Chávez Jr. "About half of Bernalillo County's senators came from the heights and half from the valley so you had this competition between them."

As major structural changes in the New Mexico Legislature began unfolding, the state's congressional delegation took a major blow that sent leaders of both parties scrambling. U.S. Senator Dennis Chávez, the pillar of New Mexico politics who had worked with four U.S. presidents, died of cancer in November 1962. Ill for years, his death was anticipated with a controversial procedural move in the 1961 session of the state legislature.

"My good friend Mack Easley, who had been speaker of the house, sponsored a bill that would have provided for a special statewide election to fill a vacancy in the U.S. Senate," Fabián Chávez Jr. said. That was the process already used for filling a vacancy in the U.S. House.[6] Then–Lt. Gov. Joseph M. Montoya won such a special election in 1957 following the death of longtime U.S. Rep. A. M. Fernández.[7] Thomas G. Morris, who had represented Tucumcari in the state house of representatives, was elected in 1958 after U.S. Rep. John Dempsey died in office.[8]

New Mexico's vacancies in the U.S. Senate were to be filled by gubernatorial appointment, however.

"Joseph Montoya's people were pushing the bill that called for the change to a special election. They denied it, but there was no question about it," Chávez said. "Republican Ed Mechem had just been elected to his fourth term as governor, and he's the one who would fill the U.S. Senate vacancy should Dennis Chávez die in office, and it was expected that he would because he had become increasingly ill. The cancer had robbed him of his strength and even the voice that he had used for so long to champion the causes of minorities and the poor. It was thought that Mechem, of course, would appoint a Republican, and Joe Montoya's people were among those in the Democratic Party who didn't like that idea. I think that from his recently acquired position as U.S. representative, Joe saw himself being chosen in a special election to succeed Dennis Chávez.

"I worked against the bill, using the argument that it was immoral to try to pass legislation in anticipation of a man's death," Chávez said. "The bill was defeated, and I strongly suspect that my role in killing it didn't endear me to Joe Montoya or his faction. The factions were always in play back then. Joe Montoya, Clinton Anderson, Dennis Chávez. Factions, factions, factions."

Dennis Chávez, despite the heavy criticism he took from many in the news media in the 1940s for vocally promoting Hispanic interests, had become a true political power in New Mexico as well as Washington. He chaired or sat on Senate committees that controlled two-thirds of the federal budget in the mid-1950s, according to information compiled by the Center for Regional Studies at the University of New Mexico.[9] He fortified funding for science laboratories in the state,[10] and he was principally involved in the campaign that led to as much as 98 percent of U.S. Hispanic voters supporting Democrat John F. Kennedy in the 1960 presidential election.[11]

Chávez was one of our country's first national politicians to stand up repeatedly for civil rights, said Tobías Durán, director of the Center for Regional Studies at UNM. Referring largely to civil rights issues, former Pres. Harry Truman said Chávez "always was on the right side of the right cause when it mattered most."[12] Vice Pres. Lyndon Johnson, long close to Chávez, spoke at the senator's funeral in Albuquerque.[13]

"His death was a big blow to politics in New Mexico, no doubt about it," said Fabián Chávez Jr. "He was Mister Democrat in the minds of many, but I think just about everybody recognized that he would be succeeded by a Republican because of our Republican governor at the time. It was only logical."

A big surprise—and more than a little resentment—surfaced nonetheless as state Republican leaders opted to have Mechem resign as governor so that his successor, Republican Lt. Gov. Tom Bolack, could appoint him to succeed Dennis Chávez. Democrats had served as lieutenant governor during each of Mechem's previous three terms as governor. Bolack's election in 1960 gave New Mexico Republicans what they needed to maneuver and get one of their own into the U.S. Senate for the first time since Chávez had succeeded Bronson Cutting in 1935.

"Knowing Ed Mechem, he was probably humble enough to have suggested someone else for the U.S. Senate," said Fabián Chávez Jr. "But, remember, Republicans called upon Mechem throughout the Democrats' hara-kiri years. Mechem was elected governor four times, and the Republicans really didn't have any other strong personalities with a good chance of retaining the Senate seat two years later when it would be opened up for a statewide election. Mechem was by far the strongest choice to fill the vacancy."

Cargo, who in 1962 was elected to the state house of representatives from Bernalillo County, concurred. "Jack Redman thought he was going to get it," Cargo said. "Jack was a physician in Albuquerque, and he had run unsuccessfully for Congress twice."

Redman's latest congressional race was in 1962 against incumbent Joseph M. Montoya. He lost to Montoya, 128,651–116,262.[14]

"Heck, New Mexico Republicans hadn't had anybody real strong since Bronson Cutting," Cargo said. "In the '50s and early '60s, Mechem and Tom Bolack were the only Republicans who could get elected state-wide. Mechem, really, was the only one who stood a chance to be elected to that Senate seat in 1964. Albert Mitchell was New Mexico's Republican national committeeman and was a very powerful guy. I imagine he pressured Mechem to take it."

Mechem's appointment to the U.S. Senate set up the 1964 race between Mechem and Joseph M. Montoya, who had served in the U.S. House of Representatives since 1957 and had been elected lieutenant governor four times; the last was in 1956 to serve during Mechem's third gubernatorial term.

Montoya beat Mechem with 55 percent of the vote and began what would be twelve full years in the U.S. Senate.[15] He further solidified his faction's standing in the state Democratic Party. Bolack served as governor for a month in 1962 after appointing Mechem to the Senate.[16]

There was considerable mutual respect between Mechem and Fabián Chávez Jr., but Chávez supported Montoya in the 1964 election. "In spite of whatever he thought of me, I always supported Joe because of his congressional voting record," said Chávez. "If I had been sitting in Congress for the twenty years that Joe was there, I would have cast votes the same way Joe did about 90 percent of the time. He was a liberal Democrat, and so am I.

"Personally, though, I didn't like him too much. He had a personal arrogance about him, and he conveyed this image that he was the número uno Hispanic leader in the state, and we all had to do things his way. One time when a number of us were at La Fonda having drinks, I ordered my favorite, Scotch and water. I said, 'Make sure it's Johnny Walker Red.' To make the other guys laugh, Joe said, 'Serving good Scotch to a Mexican is like serving champagne to a pig.' He was one of those so-called Hispanic leaders that tolerated that braggadocio: Don't worry, I'll get the votes of the barefoot boys.

"Still, you have to measure a person serving in a congressional or legislative body by how he votes on key issues in that body, not on his personality. I supported Joe Montoya. He might be the bastard when it came to personality but as far as I was concerned, he was a good legislator."

Democrat Clinton P. Anderson was in the early years of his third term as New Mexico's other U.S. senator while the extraordinary occurrences unfolded around the state's accompanying Senate seat. Suddenly the state's senior senator, Anderson's political clout increased along with that of Montoya as he moved from the House to the Senate.

Both men each sought to use their clout as major changes unfolded in how the state elected its members to the U.S. House. Beginning in 1960, U.S. House members from New Mexico were elected from separate ballot positions, but voters statewide still cast ballots for each of the two posts.[17] It was not until 1968 that congressional apportionment requirements caught up with New Mexico, and the state for the first time elected representatives from two U.S. House districts, north and south. The legislature drew the districts, and Democrats still controlled the legislature, so they determined where the boundary was drawn.

Democratic Party leaders, including U.S. Senators Anderson and Montoya, decided the districts to which their two incumbent House members were assigned.

Thomas Morris of Tucumcari was assigned to the northern district. E. S. Johnny Walker was assigned to the new southern district. Walker had moved from Albuquerque to Silver City in his early years but took up residence in Santa Fe as state land commissioner before being elected to Congress in 1964. Then, in an attempt to make sense of the new districting process, he felt compelled to move south again, this time to Las Cruces.

"Party leaders thought it was the best way to protect both of their incumbents, but stupidity is the best way to describe their actions," said Fabián Chávez Jr. "Morris was a soft-spoken state legislator from Tucumcari when the party nominated him as a compromise candidate to run for the U.S. House when John Dempsey died in office in 1958. He was a good man, but he hadn't proven himself to be a strong leader, like former house speaker Calvin Horn, who was considered for the position by party leaders."

Horn had influential support, but it was not enough to put him over the top. "John Burrows was for Calvin Horn because Calvin had agreed to put forty thousand dollars to help Democrats in the general election that fall," Morris said. "It was attractive to Burrows, I imagine, because he was the party's nominee for governor that year." Joseph M. Montoya also supported Horn, Chávez said.

"I'm not sure what I had going for me in 1958 because I didn't have any money and I came from a county that didn't have very much input," Morris said. "What I had was a neighbor who happened to be in a key position who was honest and straightforward."

Morris referred to Henry Priddy, an old friend who lived across the street from him in Tucumcari. Priddy was one of ten members of the Democratic Party's executive committee at the time. The committee had one member from each judicial district, and it was that panel that voted to select the party's nominee for special elections. "Henry came to me and said he wanted me to run for Congress, and he said I wasn't looking at things the way they are. He said, 'How many people have ever had for certain 10 percent of the vote before they announced their candidacy?' He says, 'That's at least what you've got.'"

In fact, Morris in 1958 had more than just his influential Tucumcari neighbor in his corner. "Clinton Anderson anointed Tom Morris at a party caucus," said James "Bud" Mulcock. "There's no doubt that Morris got the nomination because of Clinton Anderson." While driving Anderson one day following Morris' selection, Mulcock said Anderson told him Morris recognized his indebtedness to the senator.

"Senator Anderson told me that Tom Morris promised people at the party's convention that if he went to the House, he would never leave it to run for the Senate. I thought it was too limiting a statement, and I asked Senator Anderson why Morris would say something like that. The senator said, 'Tom Morris said what I told him to say.'"

Chávez, who had yearned to get to Congress, lacked that kind of inside help years later when it came time to draw congressional districts in New Mexico for the first time. Meanwhile, Morris had developed clout and had expanded his support since he first took his seat in Congress. "Tom Morris had been in the House for ten years. I had proven myself to be one of our party's strongest young leaders and in the process had made it clear that I assigned a lot of importance to the political seniority system," Chávez said. "I could have beaten Morris in a northern district race in 1968; that's where my strength was. I was a known and proven candidate in the north. But our party's senior leaders knew that I wouldn't challenge Morris because of his seniority in Congress that was working to New Mexico's benefit.

"Johnny Walker had been in Congress for only two terms, and I would have beaten him, too, in a northern district race. Had he been assigned to the northern congressional district, I would have challenged him because New Mexico wouldn't have lost much seniority with him gone. But Walker had the support of Joe Montoya, and he was encouraged to move from Santa Fe to Las Cruces so that he could run in the southern district.

"That meant I was locked out. I could see how our party's leaders were lining up against me. Joe Montoya felt like he needed to look over his shoulder to see where I was. Al Montoya in Santa Fe stayed in contact with his brother, Joe, about such things. And the Clinton Andersons didn't exactly support Fabián Chávez Jr. If I had been more cold-blooded, I would have said damn the seniority system, and I would have beaten Tom Morris. But I put the bigger picture ahead of my own personal interests."

Viewing developments from the Republican side, Cargo said what he saw did not make sense at all. Cargo had risen rapidly within Republican Party ranks and was finishing his first term as governor in 1968. "When Democrats assigned candidates to the House districts, they should have done it the other way around," he said.

Morris said he probably could have kept New Mexico's House seats from being districted at all years before he and Walker were pressed to jockey for northern and southern district posts. "Rep. Manny Celler of New York was chairman of the House Judiciary Committee and was handling the legislation on redistricting. He told me, 'New Mexico has never been districted. If you want to leave it that way, I'll leave it that way.'"

It is not clear what came from that purported offer. According to news reports, though, both Morris and Walker opposed the federal legislation adopted in 1965 that required all states to elect U.S. representatives from equally divided districts intended to implement the U.S. Supreme Court's one-man, one-vote rule.

The *Albuquerque Journal* reported in March 1965, "Only last week Rep. E. S. Johnny Walker took a major hand in causing the New Mexico House of Representatives to reverse itself and kill a bill in Santa Fe which would have broken the state into two congressional districts."

Cargo, who sponsored that legislation to force districting in New Mexico no matter what Congress did, recalls that U.S. Senators Clinton Anderson and Joseph Montoya also made a hasty trip into New Mexico to defeat the bill.

Meanwhile, maneuvering continued at the federal level. Morris, reported the *Albuquerque Journal,* had worked unsuccessfully with several leaders of the U.S. House to exclude New Mexico and Hawaii from provisions barring at large elections.

"Both Morris and Walker expressed the hope that the Senate will amend the bill to exclude [New Mexico and Hawaii]," Paul Wieck of the *Journal* reported.

There was no such change, but Anderson said he had hoped that redistricting in New Mexico could have been delayed until after the 1970 census, which he thought would show the state was eligible for three U.S. representatives. In truth, New Mexico did not gain a third representative until after the 1980 census.[18]

Suddenly required to draw U.S. House districts in the mid-1960s, New Mexico found itself in for considerable commotion. "It set the wheels in motion and sent a lot of ambitious people in the state legislature scrambling to draw the boundary so that they might have a chance to get to Congress either right away or in future years," Morris said. "When the line was finally drawn to leave me in the northern district, I didn't try to get it changed, which was probably a mistake. Johnny Walker said he didn't think he'd stand a chance if he ran from the north. He said we'd both stand a chance if he ran from the south and I ran from the north, the way the line had been drawn. And I think he was right."

Although Morris agreed Walker's best chances were in the new southern district, he thought that he, too, could have run strongly in the south.

For the first election under the new congressional districts, Morris drew three opponents in the 1968 Democratic primary and beat them all handily.[19] Morris captured nearly thirty-eight thousand votes.[20] His closest competitor, state Senator Sterling Black of Los Alamos, got just more than nine thousand.[21]

Down south, Walker drew primary opposition only from state Senator Harold Runnels of Hobbs. Walker won by two thousand votes.[22]

Meanwhile, in the 1968 Republican primary, insurance dealer Manuel Luján Jr. of Albuquerque easily outran five competitors for the opportunity to challenge Morris in the November general election.[23] Ed Foreman, who served in the Texas Legislature from 1963 to 1964, was unopposed in the Republican run up to challenge Walker in November.[24]

Luján beat Morris, 88,517–78,117.[25] Foreman edged out Walker, 71,857–69,858.[26]

"The Democratic Party had set itself up for failure," Chávez said. "Our leaders didn't want me to run against Walker so they sent him to the south, where they figured he would win because of his roots in Silver City. They positioned Morris in the north because they knew I respected his seniority and wouldn't challenge him. They thought they had two safe seats. Instead, we lost them both. It was stupidity at its best.

"I followed religiously the preaching of the Democratic Party. I would have thought that the older Democrats would have looked at me and said, 'Here is a young man who understands our party and could have a long future representing our interests in the Congress.' Instead, they locked me out, and much of it probably had to do with some of the issues I took on as senate majority leader. I was a good Democrat, and I did represent their interests. But I also knew that there was important work that had to be done not for Democrats or Republicans, but for New Mexicans. In the senate, I wouldn't let the party or anyone else pull me away from such work."

Morris, along with doubting how the new congressional districts were drawn, said that neither his campaign nor that of Walker really got off the ground in 1968. "Walker replaced Joe Montoya in the U.S. House when Montoya moved up to the Senate to succeed Dennis Chávez," said Morris. "He wasn't a very good campaigner, and even though he had lived in Silver City, the people in the new southern district didn't seem to take to him when he went back down there.

"In my race, well, Manuel Luján ran a very good campaign. He was well respected, and his family was well liked. They also were well financed. During that campaign, my mother-in-law was sick with cancer. She died two weeks before the election. My heart wasn't into campaigning and raising money. Right after her death, I looked at our campaign, and I realized I was going to lose the election.

"I think Joe Montoya tried to help me in that election. He was always a very straight guy with me. Clinton Anderson, I don't know. Anderson was always a strange one to me. He was always suspicious and never was straightforward the way Dennis Chávez was. Senator Chávez was my kind of a gentleman. Clinton Anderson always thought I had great ambitions to succeed him in the Senate, but I did not."

Clearly, Morris had his own problems while trying to sort through New Mexico's Democratic Party politics in the 1960s. He further suggested that Fabián Chávez Jr. might have had an even tougher time trying to make sense of his surroundings. "The people in the upper positions were not behind Fabián, no they weren't," Morris said. "Fabián always worked hard, and he was loyal to the party, but I don't think Senator Anderson and Joe Montoya especially liked him."

CHAPTER ELEVEN

Keen Strategy and a Walk
Give Birth to a Medical School

The New Mexico state senate for years had been controlled by conservative political veterans, so in a sense, the election of young, liberal Fabián Chávez Jr. as the chamber's majority floor leader in 1961 was part of the political tumult that characterized the decade. Rancher Bruce King of Stanley could not help but notice the political climate as he stepped into the legislature for the first time as a Democratic state house member in 1959.

"People like Bill Wheatley and Ike Smalley, they were Democrats, but they ran a real conservative operation in the senate," King said.

Democrat Bobby Mayfield of Doña Ana County, who served in the house through the sixties, said much of state government was not getting funded adequately because of "the conservative, real conservative" fiscal atmosphere that prevailed at the time in the senate.

"Fabián was a liberal, but he wasn't anticonservative," King said. "In fact, the conservatives had a lot of respect for Fabián. He had great knowledge of the political system and always tried to be fair. He presented the facts as they were and always tried to help the people. He was a Democrat, but what he promoted more than anything was good government."

That approach was evident in 1960 and 1961 after newly elected Republican Lt. Gov. Tom Bolack asked Chávez to help him prepare to preside over the senate, which is the lieutenant governor's principal responsibility. "Tom called me from Farmington and said he was coming to Santa Fe. He said he wanted to visit with me and said it was important," Chávez said.

"He admitted that he had no experience presiding over the senate and said some of his friends suggested he contact me to see if I would help. I said, 'Sure, of course I will.' We locked ourselves up several times in the old senate chamber and went through several procedural motions to show him how it operated.

"I also advised him that if there was any question from the floor of any of his rulings, as the presiding officer he could yield questions to me as majority leader. There were several occasions where some of our Democratic friends tried to embarrass the lieutenant governor by throwing what you'd call rule curves, which he promptly shoved over to me, and I took care of them."

It did not always sit well with Chávez's fellow Democrats. "I got criticized by some of them, and my answer to them was simple: My job as majority leader was to maintain decorum and civility in the operation of the chamber. In order to do that, we had to work cooperatively with the presiding officer. I could not see and would not tolerate all this hanky-panky from the floor because it would create a degree of confusion in the operation of the senate. I wouldn't stand for it, otherwise you have nothing but a mess."

Republican Edwin Mechem, who served as governor eight of the twelve years from 1951 to 1962, had considerable respect for Chávez, the man who tutored his lieutenant governor and then protected him against partisan assaults. "I think Fabián knows more about state government than anybody else in the state . . . Interesting character," Mechem told former Gov. Jack Campbell's biographer, Maurice Trimmer. Mechem also appreciated Chávez's inclination to promote civility over political posturing. The *Albuquerque Journal*'s Ed Minteer quoted Chávez to have said that he did not support the time-honored practice of introducing legislation simply to force a Mechem veto and arm Democrats with political ammunition.

As governor, Mechem turned to Chávez to sponsor some of his key legislation, like the safe mining act, because of the respect and authority Chávez held in the legislature. "We were never personal friends, but Ed and I developed a high degree of respect for each other," Chávez said. "He was like a comfortable pair of old shoes. He put you at ease. He was the kind of guy you could talk to, a guy you could reason with."

Along with turning to Chávez for help in the legislature, Mechem called upon Chávez in 1962 to help him put the state's best ceremonial foot forward during New Mexico's golden anniversary. "He said he was naming me chairman because my family appreciated history and because I knew how to get things done," Chávez said. "It was quite a celebration. I led a procession that included all five living governors."

If Mechem admired him, Chávez also was regarded highly by the man who was elected governor immediately after Mechem: Jack Campbell. Campbell worked with Chávez both as speaker of the house of representatives and later as governor. Chávez was "one of the most competent legislative operatives to ever serve in that [legislative] branch of government," Campbell told his biographer. "His election as majority leader for the 1961 session was similar to mine as speaker in that we both won by one vote. During the 1961 session we kept in constant contact by telephone to coordinate legislative strategy and prevent parliamentary entanglements."

Although Chávez was an unabashed liberal legislator and Campbell was a conservative east sider, Chávez said he and Campbell both were "idealistic pragmatists."

"You come in with these ideals, and then as a pragmatist, you ask what it is you have to do to get there," Chávez said. "In doing so, you have to work with other people to educate, twist arms, whatever it takes."

It was the approach Chávez employed in 1961 when he and Los Alamos Democratic Senator Sterling Black took up business left unfinished since the 1957 legislative session. "Ever since the incident involving the two black college students in Las Cruces, I was determined to get a law passed that truly discouraged discrimination," Chávez said. "We got the law in 1955 that spoke against discrimination but did not provide penalties. Then in 1957, I had a bill drafted that would have made discrimination a fourth-degree felony, but it became apparent to me that the mood of the legislature was such that I wouldn't get anywhere with that bill.

"So, as majority leader in the senate in 1961, I cosponsored a bill with Senators Sterling Black and Ike Smalley to provide penalties for discrimination. I still wanted to make it a fourth-degree felony, but Gene Lusk, who had left the legislature and was lobbying for several interests, came up to me and said I couldn't get my bill passed unless I made it a misdemeanor for every count. He explained that I could still inundate offenders with multiple counts for each violation. For example if there were five people seated at a table and they were refused service simply because they were black, the case could be treated as having five counts and not just one. That way, we could secure substantial penalties when it was appropriate.

"Gene told me that a lot of senators could support that approach. They just opposed making violations a felony."

The bill drew considerable interest around the state. "In debating the bill on the floor of the senate, I was very careful not to point fingers at senators or their constituents from the southeast, for example," Chávez said. "I didn't even mention the discrimination that I had seen with my own eyes in that region's public accommodations like restaurants, theaters, barber shops, beauty shops, where there were signs that said no Mexicans or Negros allowed."

Chávez said it was important that the historic debate over civil rights be rooted in civility and decorum. "Rather than summon negative images, I talked about how we, the populace of our great country, believe in equal opportunity and fair treatment. I told how we needed to stand by the principles on which our country was founded and how all of us fought together during World War II to protect those principles. I told them how during the war, they slept while I guarded over them and how I slept while they watched over me."

Chávez recalled one assembly of the senate when the gallery was packed with mostly blacks while the antidiscrimination bill was being debated. "Senator Harold Runnels supported the bill, but I remember him looking up at the gallery that day and telling me later that he saw nothing but eyes and teeth. He was helping to create very important change in our society, but he was still a product of his environment. Remember, this was three years before landmark U.S. civil rights legislation signed into law by Pres. Lyndon Johnson in 1964.

"The 1961 bill in our state legislature was written to make violations a misdemeanor, but I also made it clear that fines could grow to more than one thousand dollars, depending on how many people had their rights violated in a single incident.

"That did it. The law passed, and Governor Mechem signed it. Over time, I had learned to cover all the bases all the way through. I would not spend all this time working to pass a bill if it was going to get vetoed at the end. That's a waste of time. So I worked with the governors early in the process."

Mechem's signature on Chávez's civil rights legislation did not end abuse overnight, of course. "When I got married in 1967, we went up to Carlsbad Caverns and White's City during the middle of a week in June," said Manny Aragón, a longtime state legislator from Albuquerque. "I pulled into a motel that had a completely vacant parking lot, but when I asked for a room, I was told they were full. It was a two-story motel. There must have been two hundred rooms in that thing, and it was the middle of the week, but I was told it was full."

Aragón, a young athletic teen growing up in Albuquerque's South Valley while Chávez directed the state senate through issues big and small, was impressed by Chávez's skills and demeanor. "I was probably a freshman in high school when my mom took me to Santa Fe to see legislators working in both the house and the senate," Aragón said. "I remember sitting in the senate and being impressed by Fabián's eloquence. His mannerisms on the senate floor were very impressive. He was well dressed and well groomed, and I remember he had these real thick glasses. He kind of reminded me of Everett Dirksen, the prominent U.S. senator from Illinois at the time, because he had this strong voice, he was very articulate, and because of those black-rimmed glasses. The big difference, of course, was that Senator Dirksen was never so well groomed.

"I looked at my mom and told her I wanted to be in Fabián's position one day."

Indeed, Aragón was elected state senate majority leader decades later.[1] His passion while speaking for minorities on the floor of the senate was at least as intense as Chávez's, though his tactics were more polarizing. Far more controversial than Chávez, Aragón worked tirelessly for civil rights during thirty years in the senate, but he thinks few, if any, were more successful than Chávez with the issue.

"You look at Fabián's entire family, and they were all promoting civil rights, equality, and justice," Aragón said. "I don't know of another family that influenced New Mexico to that extent. Fabián has to be in the top five of legislators ever to serve New Mexico, maybe even number one. I don't think Fabián ever got a college degree, but to spar with him and his vocabulary wasn't much fun. He must have been very well read. With his knowledge, wit, and hearty laugh, he was a hell of an opponent if he went against you and because of his presence, probably the leader of all the allies when he was with you."

Evident in his fight for civil rights, Chávez's knowledge of government, tenacity, and persuasive skills were all applied in what became one of his proudest accomplishments. "New Mexico suddenly was growing at a rapid rate. Our latest census showed it. But we were still a rural state with a severe lack of the basic services that determine quality of life. Good medical care, for instance, was very hard to come by for many of our citizens, mostly because of a shortage of doctors.

"To study medicine, New Mexicans had to leave the state because there was no medical school here. Once they left, too many didn't come back."

Jake Spidle Jr., a longtime history professor at the University of New Mexico, alluded to the problem. "From the early 1940s to the mid-1960s, the medical schools of neighboring or nearby states played the dominant role in supplying physicians to New Mexico," Spidle wrote in *Doctors of Medicine in New Mexico*.[2] Colorado, Texas, and Oklahoma were among biggest contributors.[3]

Spidle wrote, however, that "ten years of experience showed that the New Mexico residents who went off to school . . . were much more likely to set up their practices there than to return to New Mexico."[4]

It made access to doctors difficult if not impossible. Spidle recorded that in 1960, De Baca and Sandoval counties each had only one medical doctor.[5] Catron, Guadalupe, and Mora had two. Socorro, Torrance, and Hidalgo had three. Harding had none.[6]

In 1960, the ratio of doctors to residents was 1 to 3,101 in McKinley County; 1 to 2,991 in De Baca; 1 to 2,650 in Taos; and 1 to 2,419 in Rio Arriba.[7]

New Mexicans had been able to take advantage of a student-exchange program the Western Interstate Commission for Higher Education (WICHE) coordinated that gave special status to students from states without medical schools within medical schools of states that did.[8] By the late 1950s, the five western states with medical schools found increasing demand and had to reduce the number of spaces allotted for exchange students.[9] A WICHE staff report, meanwhile, warned of dire shortages of physicians in the West by the 1970s.[10]

By 1959, University of New Mexico Pres. Tom Popejoy, who had helped organize WICHE in 1951, began working against stiff odds to establish a medical school at UNM. Popejoy developed crucial support for his plan on the UNM campus, then turned his attention to the legislature. "He realized that the cost of the project was certain to be a major concern to many around the state," Spidle wrote.[11] "Virtually no one questioned the desirability and utility of a medical school, but many questioned the capacity of the state to support one."[12]

The house speaker, Jack Campbell, was among the first legislators approached. "Tom Popejoy was not only a top administrator but a damned good politician," said Chávez. "He worked intimately with legislators. He didn't send spokesmen or representatives. He did it personally.

"Jack Campbell supported the proposed UNM medical school, but he knew he had a couple of members from Doña Ana County who would fight him tooth and nail in the house over the issue. See, New Mexico State University in Las Cruces thought it would lose money from the legislature if a new, expensive medical school was established at UNM. So Jack suggested that it get started in the senate side, and he encouraged people to get me to sponsor the bill."

Chávez said he had never given much thought to a medical school at UNM. "I was up to my neck being majority leader of the senate, setting up the calendars for each day, fighting off a proposed right-to-work law, and overseeing major reform of the courts, as well as reform of the liquor industry. I had a full plate when they approached me with the proposal for a UNM medical school.

"It was Tom Popejoy, Ralph López, and W. C. Kruger who came to see me. I had worked with Dr. López on what became known as the López Plan, which helped get many New Mexicans trained to be dentists. I also had worked with Willard Kruger, who was a very good architect and a very active Democrat who got a lot of state contracts because of it. Ralph López and Willard Kruger were very good friends of mine, even drinking buddies, you could say. Tom Popejoy came with them to ask me to sponsor the bill for a UNM medical school.

"I told them 'Oh my God, guys. You're talking about big money here.' Those were times when we didn't have billions of dollars in state investments. Colorado at the time was floating a $20-million bond issue simply to continue supporting their existing medical school. I said, 'Let me think about this. The money situation is going to be tough.'"

Chávez's response could not have surprised either of the men. Chávez in 1960 publicly said the state's universities and colleges needed stricter control of their budgets and called for a reordering of spending priorities on campuses. Early in 1961, the *Albuquerque Tribune* reported that Chávez called for an investigation into appropriations and expenditures at the University of New Mexico in the wake of a dispute involving Popejoy, the university's regents, and a faculty member who had been pressured into retirement.

"Little did I know that after my meeting with President Popejoy and the other two men regarding the proposed medical sciences school my darling wife would be involved. I got home at the end of the day, and Coral Jeanne said, 'Honey, what do you have against a medical school?' She said, 'Willard Kruger and Dr. Ralph López called me and asked that I talk to you about it because it's a good thing.' I told her I had to study the proposal very carefully because it was going to involve a lot of money."

Chávez's examination of the proposal led to a meeting with Popejoy at Chávez's stockbrokerage office at La Fonda in Santa Fe.

"We met so that President Popejoy could give me his best pitch and so that together we could discuss the hurdles that we would have to face," Chávez said. "The main thing we had to do was turn thinking away from an expensive four-year medical school and get people thinking about a far less expensive two-year basic science school.

"Before our meeting was done, we decided that Popejoy would write a letter to me that would include key questions related to the proposal and the president's responses to those questions. The letter would be addressed to me and also mailed to each member of the legislature's joint Appropriations and Finance Committee. We rigged that letter, in effect, to begin getting over the hurdles. It was a legislative tactic, and it worked. Successful tactics are a very important part of the legislative process, and the presentation of this issue included several, beginning with Jack Campbell's suggestion that it all get started in the senate because it was the best way to deal with opposition that he knew he would face in the house."

Paula Tackett, the longtime employee of the Legislative Council Service who eventually became its director, said Chávez was one of the best tacticians she has known.

In his letter dated February 13, 1961, Popejoy told how New Mexicans' access to medical schools already was declining in western states and beyond because states with medical schools increasingly were "taking care of their own first." "Population pressure has virtually closed the medical school door to out-of-staters," he wrote.

To address concerns about soaring costs associated with four-year medical schools, Popejoy told how Dartmouth, North Dakota, and South Dakota had had two-year basic science schools since the early 1900s and had seen no need to expand. He then listed six universities that had waited between 17 and 117 years before expanding from two-year basic science schools to four-year medical schools.

"In short, two-year schools of basic medical sciences have not readily converted to regular four-year medical schools," Popejoy wrote. "The shift to a four-year program has taken place only when the state's population and resources have permitted—and not before."

Popejoy explained in his letter that the proposal was to have New Mexicans get their first two years of basic medical science education in New Mexico, transfer to a western university for their last two years, and then take three years or more to complete internships and residency training.

"No time should be lost," Popejoy wrote. "Thirty-six New Mexicans have applied to western medical schools for the fall of 1961. This is a 30 percent increase in applicants in one year. We can expect more qualified candidates each year, and they will compete for fewer and fewer available spaces.

"In the past, the University of Colorado Medical School has taken the bulk of our students. However, Dean Robert Glaser has stated that his school cannot guarantee any quota for New Mexico students, and that 'we are not apt to accept more than six to eight students per year from New Mexico in the next four or five years.' *Such a number will not begin to satisfy New Mexico's needs.* Plainly, we cannot any longer safely count on our neighboring states to educate New Mexico youth in medicine."

Finally, Popejoy said in his letter that the Kellogg Foundation would make available a grant of more than $1 million, half of which could be used for capital outlay, for the first five years of a basic medical sciences school.

"In the light of all the evidence, we believe there is every reason to start the two-year program of basic medical sciences *now*," Popejoy wrote in his letter to Chávez.

Chávez said opposition to the proposal could be found statewide but was focused largely around New Mexico State University and Doña Ana

County. "I told President Popejoy that once he wrote the letter, I would have the tools I need to concentrate attention on creation of a basic medical sciences school and, hopefully, erase some of the opposition.

"I got the letter, then went to work building support. And that led me to another important legislative tactic. I decided not to introduce a bill to create the basic medical science school, but to insert a line item for funding in the 1961 general appropriations act. If I had introduced a bill, it would have meant that the measure would have had to be assigned to several committees in both the senate and then the house, and it would have had to come up for debate on the floor of each chamber. Inserting a simple line item into the appropriations act after it came from the house to the senate let us get away from most of that. And the tactic worked."

Chávez turned to his old, powerful ally, Senator Gordon Melody of San Miguel County, to ensure that his plan unfolded successfully. "Melody was chairman of the Senate Finance Committee, and I asked him to insert the simple line item requesting money once the appropriations act arrived in the senate." Chávez said. "Tom Popejoy initially wanted at least fifty thousand dollars but later agreed that twenty-five thousand would be enough to get things started. It would show a commitment from the state, and it would be enough to get that grant of a million-plus dollars from the Kellogg Foundation. It was an amendment to the act that already had been approved by the house so that meant it would have to return to the house and the speaker, Jack Campbell, for simple concurrence along with the other amendments made to the act in the senate.

"Here's the real cute thing: despite everything that Tom Popejoy and I had done to get people thinking about a basic medical sciences school and away from a medical school, the line item that Gordon Melody inserted into the appropriations act read 'medical school.'

"Was it a simple mistake? Yeah, I think so. The discussion early on was all about a medical school and that's what stuck in Gordon's mind. It was a slip on his part, but when the amended appropriations act passed in the senate, the line item for twenty-five thousand dollars read 'medical school' at UNM."

The house of representatives took up the amended appropriations act, and the sides were already drawn on the Popejoy-Chávez initiative. Rep. Bobby Mayfield, a Las Cruces Democrat, and the speaker, Jack Campbell, had taken an informal count of votes.

Mayfield, a former air force pilot and farmer at the time, was on the House Appropriations Committee and close to ranking administrators at New Mexico State University. "I was getting a lot of pressure from my people here in Doña Ana County to oppose the UNM appropriation,"

Mayfield said. "Dr. Roger Corbett was president at New Mexico State, and Bill O'Donnell was vice president. They were pressuring me quite a bit to defeat the bill because they could see in years to come that if there was a medical school at UNM, it would require that a lot more state funds go to UNM that might otherwise come to New Mexico State.

"I studied it hard and came to believe that we really needed a medical school in Albuquerque. All this lobbying was going on, and I kind of counted the votes on the House Appropriations Committee ahead of time and could see it was going to be real close. The chairman of the committee was John Mershon, and he was against the appropriation. I figured out that if I stayed in the committee room when the vote was taken and I had to vote against the bill because of my ties to my constituencies and to New Mexico State University, the bill was going to fail.

"So I did something that I did only one time during my ten years in Santa Fe: I took a walk. I didn't stick around to take a vote in the appropriations committee, and as a consequence the bill passed."

Mayfield said he took some heat from some quarters. "But it was worth it," he said. "I don't walk out on votes. But I took a walk on this one strictly because I felt so strongly about the issue. I never had any second thoughts. No, no. It was the right thing to do, and we have a great medical school up in Albuquerque today."

Although criticized by some, Mayfield said the key players never confronted him after his walk. "John Mershon never mentioned it. He never talked to me about it." Nor did Corbett or O'Donnell at NMSU. "They were two big, fine people, great leaders at NMSU. They knew how I felt. They had an alternative plan when this thing was being considered. They told me that if there was going to be an appropriation for a medical school at UNM, they thought the legislature should consider establishing a school of veterinary medicine at New Mexico State—which we didn't need. But that's just the politics of the university."

Mayfield said Chávez was grateful, without question. Mayfield was right. "It was another one of those legislative tactics employed on behalf of this legislation. If you ever see a legislative tactic taken for a great cause, that was it," Chávez said of Mayfield's walk.

Mayfield recalled it all in a March 2001 letter to Chávez, which was prompted by a newspaper article recounting the origins of the UNM medical school. "Today's legislators and educators have no idea what a big step was taken in New Mexico's progress when that preliminary medical school legislation was passed," Mayfield wrote. "I can't think of a piece of legislation passed in the sixties that has been more far-reaching than the establishment of our medical school and now, the hospital attached to it."

In the letter, Mayfield alluded to Corbett's and O'Donnell's opposition to the appropriation and their desire to see a veterinary school created at NMSU in trade. "I could not tell Dr. Corbett and Bill how strongly I felt they were wrong on both issues," he wrote.

He also referred to what might be called his nonvote in 1961. "I've always thought that was one of the best 'votes' I ever made."

Soon after the twenty-five thousand was approved in 1961, serious talk about expansion began. "Only a few months into the second year of operation of the two-year basic medical sciences school, discussion began concerning its expansion into a full four-year institution," wrote Spidle.[13] "It was more than just the growing anxiety of students facing the necessity for transferring [out of state]. Faculty, too, quickly recognized the inherent limitations of the two-year concept."[14]

Now serving as governor, Jack Campbell in 1965 urged Popejoy to ask that the legislature fund a four-year medical school. Campbell also turned to someone else for help. "In January 1966 Jack called me in and said, 'Fabián, the time has come for us to go to a full-fledged medical school, and I want you to lobby for me because you know more about it than anybody.'"

Chávez had left the legislature in 1964. It was the same year that the first classes of the new two-year medical sciences school were held in a former mortuary and converted 7UP bottling plant.[15] Though out of the legislature, Chávez was eager to see the two-year school at UNM expanded. "I studied information that Governor Campbell provided and saw that the U.S. Congress was appropriating hundreds of millions of dollars for medical schools because of the great shortage of doctors," he said. "I retraced my steps with Gordon Melody and other key people in the legislature and took advantage of my friendships with legislators on both sides of the political aisle. Then I turned to a tactic to get a joint meeting of the Senate Finance Committee and the House Appropriations Committee in one room. That way I wouldn't have to go through both chambers. I told the committee that New Mexico could get between $20 million and $30 million for a four-year medical school if we created it, and if the money didn't come to us, it was going to go to somebody else."

The joint committee and later the full legislature adopted the idea but not before getting over some bumps along the way. "We were still in committee, and Rep. John Mershon brought out the 1961 letter that Tom Popejoy had written to me while we worked to advance the idea of a two-year school. He read from it, stressing the parts that told how other universities had gone decades with two-year medical science schools without finding a need to expand to full-fledged medical schools and alluding to our assertion that a two-year school likely would serve New Mexico's needs for a long time.

"'What do you say about that, now?' he inquired sternly. I didn't see it coming, and I had to respond quickly. I said, 'Representative Mershon, if the legislature knew absolutely what the future held for us on certain issues, it wouldn't have to meet every other year. Millions of dollars are now available to us from the federal government. We can take it or leave it.' We took it."

The University of New Mexico's School of Medicine had its first graduating class in 1968.[16] Years later, Chávez's three doctors—cardiologist H. William Adkison, pulmonalogist Charles Riley, and general practitioner Gerzain H. Chávez—were all graduates of the UNM Medical School. "If that's a conflict of interest, it's the kind of conflict I can live with," Chávez said.

In 2001, the school honored Chávez by creating the Senator Fabián Chávez Endowed Chair for Population Health Research. "What I would like to do is have the honor of 'holding that chair' for you," Mayfield wrote to Chávez.

Other major education issues occupied Chávez during his term as senate majority leader as well. "I am pleased to have played a substantial role

⊰ **FIGURE 18.** ⊱
Fabián Chávez Jr. (left) worked closely with Gov. Jack M. Campbell
to create the UNM Medical School. Courtesy Fabián Chávez Jr.
MILO Photographer 1503. Santa Fe, NM.

in creating the Technical Vocational Institute, now Central New Mexico Community College, in Albuquerque, as well as in the creation of two junior colleges that then led to other junior colleges around the state," Chávez said. "In both cases, as in so much that I did, these were issues that were dropped in my lap by others who had good ideas but needed help in turning them into reality.

"In the case of Albuquerque's TVI, two state representatives from Albuquerque, Jerry Brasher and Willis Smith, successfully passed legislation in the house to establish the Technical Vocational Institute. They couldn't get their senator from Bernalillo County to carry their bill in our chamber, so they brought it to me. It struck me immediately as good legislation, and I was able to carry it successfully through the senate. It became a model for the rest of the state and became the beginning of technical-vocational institutes in the state.

"Meanwhile, Senator Harold Runnels introduced legislation for creation of junior colleges, but it would apply only to Lea County and San Juan County. To create the colleges, you would need to get local voters to approve imposition of new taxes, and Runnels didn't want to fight that battle statewide. Even while limiting the legislation to two counties, Harold ran into stiff opposition from the oil and gas industry. That industry would bear a major burden of the new taxes in both counties if Harold's bill passed."

Runnels approached Chávez for help, and the two recognized they would get support in promoting the initiative from influential Hobbs insurance agent Jack Daniels. "People in the southeast corner and in the northwest corner of the state had come to feel neglected. They said they felt like orphans, while the Rio Grande corridor seemed to get all the attention," Chávez said.

"Well, this legislation gave them the opportunity to bring something substantial to their regions, and in the end they agreed to tax themselves to get it done. Jack Daniels, even though he did a lot of business with the oil and gas industry, lobbied hard for the legislation and also worked to win local support. He played a very important role, and because we worked so well together, he became one of my reliable supporters. Whenever he'd see me, almost to the day he died, he'd say, 'I sure appreciate what you did for us down there.'

"But I can't stress it enough: This, again, was one of those situations where things are brought to you by somebody else and you end up a hero. This was all part of that golden era of accomplishment for the legislature that I talk about. Even in the middle of political turmoil sometimes, we got so much done from the late '50s to the mid-1960s, and it was with relatively meager budgets. It's as if our strong will overcame our lack of money."

CHAPTER TWELVE

Judicial Reform Springs
from Nest of Corrupt JP System

If Fabián Chávez Jr. had spent all his time as state senate majority leader working to create medical schools and community colleges, he might not have had so much trouble with New Mexico's two most influential political leaders of the 1960s. U.S. Senators Clinton Anderson and Joseph M. Montoya declined to embrace Chávez at critical times as the decade unfolded.

They had multiple reasons. Principal among them was Chávez's zeal while majority leader for reforming two major systems that impacted the lives of almost every New Mexican and that, in their own way, had sustained Democratic Party interests for years, even while soiling the state's reputation.

Both issues—judicial system reform and liquor merchandizing—had fallen on Chávez's lap during his first term in the state senate. He picked them both up promptly after his election as majority leader. Chávez was repeatedly urged to back off his reform-minded pursuits, but this only made him push harder. He was working not for the party, he said, but for New Mexicans. He was confident that in the end, his work would reflect well on the party and that his efforts would be appreciated. He was in for a few surprises.

Without question, the nastiest strands of the state's judiciary in the 1960s could be found in practices of many justices of the peace from Farmington to Hobbs. Their conduct evolved from what was known as the JP fee system and was as dreaded as it was corrupt. With relatively few exceptions, it guaranteed that people who appeared before a justice of the peace in New Mexico would be found guilty. If the defendant were found innocent, the justice of the peace might not get paid for handling the case.

One JP in the late 1950s acknowledged he could not recall dismissing a single case out of 570 over which he had presided.[1]

Stephen Stoddard, a former state senator and JP in Los Alamos from 1956 to 1962, found conditions ridiculous. "In order to get a fee, you had to find the defendant guilty. That's kind of crazy," said Stoddard. "If a guy was in it for the money, there wouldn't be anybody who would get acquitted in his court."

To boost their earnings, many JPs actively encouraged police officers to cite traffic offenders and other accused lawbreakers into their courts in return for kickbacks or other favors. "On old Route 66, which is now I-40, there was a fellow who had a deal going on with the police: Everything that got cited east of Albuquerque would go to him, and the JP would get money back to the police," said Eugene F. Romero, former Santa Fe county magistrate. "This particular JP was making about thirty thousand dollars a year. At that time, that kind of money was unheard of."

Here is what state legislators were told in January 1961: "When the JP system reaches to the police, many odd and unhappy things begin to happen. No matter how brilliant the policeman's star of law enforcement may be, the mud of the JP system begins to splatter it."[2]

That evaluation was part of the first lengthy report compiled by the State Judicial System Study Committee on which Fabián Chávez Jr. was unexpectedly appointed to serve and that, with just as much surprise, he was asked to chair on the last day of the 1959 legislative session.

"We all had heard complaints about the JP system long before the committee was even created," Chávez said. "Once I assumed chairmanship of the new committee, I began digging and remember saying, 'My God, what a disgrace!' And once we got started, people throughout the state and even some from out of state said: Ah, somebody is finally checking into what these JPs do in the name of justice."

The justice of the peace system had its roots in New Mexico's territorial days and when attempts were made legislatively to try to improve it, they often went disregarded. Conclusions drawn as part of the committee's first official report were damning. "The justice of the peace system in New Mexico is administered in a manner that varies between the incompetent and the ridiculous. The administration is often accompanied by law violation by the JPs themselves, much of the law violation being unintentional but some of it being both premeditated and willful."[3]

One JP who was asked how the system could be improved said frankly, "I know of a lot of justices of the peace that aren't qualified as justices of the peace. They can't even sign their name and can't read or write."[4]

Another said, "I can read, and the only thing is that I can't explain very well."[5]

An elderly JP told committee members, "I am healthy, all right, but my memory is kind of going off, you know, as so is my tongue. I can hardly speak as well as I used to."[6]

The committee report said, "Any member of the public realizes, almost immediately, that the JP (with rare exceptions) has no preparations for his office.[7]

"The JP, with few rare exceptions, is almost certain not to have a college degree . . . It is probable that he did not even graduate from high school."[8]

Among occupational backgrounds of New Mexico's JPs going into the 1960s: curio-store operator, gas station operator, feedstore owner, school bus driver, truck driver, barber, garage mechanic, Indian trader, coal miner, and rock layer.[9]

Living rooms in the homes of JPs commonly served as courtrooms.[10] Kitchens, basements, abandoned schoolhouses, the rear of a curio shop, and the booth of a café did as well.[11] "I received over a hundred cases that I tried in a café booth," one JP said. "The patrolman would bring them in the café and fine them before all the people during the noon hour."[12]

Stoddard told of another JP who apparently did not mind mixing justice with his meals. "We had a judge who was trying people here over a plate of eggs in his home," Stoddard said.

Testimony to Chávez's committee from a coal-mining JP went like this:

Q. "You hold court right there at the coal mine?"
A. "No, I don't hold court. They just come in there and they ask me how much the fine will be and I get their citation or whatever they have . . ."
Q. "And they give you the money right there?"
A. "Yes . . ."
Q. "You're assessing a fine and costs. Did you ever say in the coal mine, 'The Court will come to order?'"
A. "No, sir. Nothing official."[13]

One state policeman testified that superior officers ordered him to take traffic violators to one particular JP even after he protested that the man was not fit to hear cases, reportedly handling at least one case while shirtless.[14]

Other testimony told of a JP who "ran a wrecker and was a mechanic and had a grocery store besides, and when (the police) brought a violator in, he usually came in from under his car and he was usually all greasy and dirty and had nothing but a table in there, and in no way did it look like a court of justice."[15]

Hams, turkeys, and cash payouts from JPs to police officers were not at all unusual, particularly during the holidays, according to testimony Chávez's committee received.[16] One officer told of a JP who offered him a dollar for every person he cited into the JP's court.[17]

Another JP, asked to tell what he knew of ongoing graft, said rumors abounded. "I've heard so much of it, it don't smell good anymore," he said.[18]

One JP was asked about gifts of gun handles to state policemen:

Q. "Did you ever give them a set of silver and turquoise gun handles?"
A. "No, sir, I never have. I have given them a set of Mexican silver and gold but not turquoise."[19]

JPs were to submit fines they collected to the counties in which they worked or to villages in cases where JPs were serving as village officials. Record keeping was often shoddy, however, and governments had little way of knowing if what they got was what they truly had coming. "They never look to see if all the cases are accounted for," one JP said of his county commissioners. They only looked at the bottom line, he said.[20]

After admitting to the legislative committee that he had not paid his county all it was due, one JP faced criminal action for shortages of approximately ten thousand dollars.[21] Another JP turned in four thousand dollars to his county after acknowledging to the committee that he probably owed several thousand.[22]

Beyond the fines assessed, JPs at the time collected five dollars in court costs for each case where the defendant was found guilty. It was money the JPs kept for themselves. If defendants were judged not guilty, counties were supposed to pay the JPs their fees. Just as JPs did not always submit to their counties all money collected from fines, however, some counties withheld payments of court costs to JPs.[23]

Chávez's committee told of a New Mexico attorney general who said, "We run into that all over the state where the [JPs] tell us the county commissioners say, 'If you don't get your costs, it's too bad because we don't have the money to pay you.'"[24]

"The end result of this administrative practice by many counties is to increase pressure on the JPs to find traffic violators and others automatically guilty," the committee reported.[25]

Chávez said many JPs found appearance bonds to be particularly helpful in boosting their incomes. "People cited for speeding would come in and plead not guilty. The JP would then set a court date for several days, maybe weeks, later, and by then the person who had been cited would conclude it wasn't worth going back in to face a so-called judge who might be found busy working as a mechanic or a coal miner. So the JP would stay with the appearance bond, which he might or might not have listed on the official record—if an official record had been opened in the first place.

"Some of these JPs were making twenty to forty thousand dollars a year, even more, in 1960. That was good money for those times, especially if it was money that you made on the side while you generated other income by driving a school bus or running a café."

Each political precinct in New Mexico by law was allowed to have a JP, and there were several hundred when Chávez's legislative committee went to work. Almost all the JPs were Democrats, many of whom were politically influential in their precincts and to whom the Democratic Party turned every election to help maintain the party's dominance, according to Chávez. More than foot soldiers, they were leaders of foot soldiers who kept the party on top. "It's what gave them their power," said Romero, former Santa Fe magistrate.

Some in the Democratic Party hierarchy did not want Chávez pressing in a way that would disrupt such grassroots support. "Joe Montoya's people, like his brother Tom and others, contacted me and wanted me to back off," Chávez said. "Their position was that reform would hurt good Democrats."

Stoddard, a Republican, was familiar with such arguments. "Fabián was upsetting a long-standing system," he said. "It was one of the most important things that Fabián ever did. I don't have any idea why the judicial system would have put up with it for so long. They couldn't have been ignorant of it, I don't think."

Maurice Trimmer, a United Press International reporter at the time, recalled that JPs were engaged in "a freewheeling system without much supervision" that had become "a kind of point of humor."

Eugene Romero himself came upon a situation with a Santa Fe JP who, because of insufficient supervision, left Romero wondering whether to laugh or cry. Romero owned a car lot at the time and sold a car to a Santa Fe man who then turned it over to his son. The son wrecked the car the first night he had it, and his father drove it back to Romero's lot the following day to complain that he had been sold a car without being told that it had body damage.

"We went to court before a JP who was friends with the father, and the JP said I had to give the man his money back," Romero said. "I had a lawyer with me, and we fought the JP's ruling. I didn't have to give back the money because I had made an honest sale. Damage to the car occurred after the sale."

Despite such occurrences, Chávez's determination to reform the JP system had less than universal support, Trimmer said. "It was controversial because, yes, a lot of the JPs were Democrats who supported the party, and not everybody was thrilled about going after them."

Paula Tackett, longtime director of the state Legislative Council Service and daughter of a former state district judge, said the JP system had grown so foul that it needed someone like Chávez to step in. "I remember my aunt had come to pick me up at Girl Scout camp, and she had a Texas license plate on her car. She got stopped for speeding. It was like highway robbery the way she was treated, simply because she had a Texas license plate. It had the sort of scummy feeling that the JPs got what they could get. It was so biased. It was not a very savory system."

The system had its backers, though, even if some of the most influential among them worked only from behind the scenes. "Early on when he began insisting on reform, Fabián was out there in left field by himself," said Richard Folmar, who had just begun working at the Legislative Council Service when Chávez's committee was assembled. "The JP system was almost sacred. You couldn't touch them. You couldn't beat them. Well, Fabián beat them. Even though some in the legislature said the system had worked just fine for a long time, I think most legislators knew this was a rotten system. They just couldn't speak out because they knew the political power of some of these JPs."

It was a judicial system that smelled foul not only in New Mexico but well beyond the Rio Grande. In far too many places outside New Mexico, the stench went on with little attention from government officials even as Chávez and his committee worked for reforms in this state. Late in 2006, the *New York Times* told of "justice courts" throughout the Empire State where judges are truck drivers, sewer workers, or laborers "with scant grasp of the most basic legal principles.

"In the public imagination, they are quaint holdovers from a bygone era, handling nothing weightier than traffic tickets and small claims. They get a roll of the eyes from lawyers who amuse one another with tales of incompetent small-town justices," the *Times* reported after studying the small courts for a year. "The examination found overwhelming evidence that decade after decade and up to this day, people have often been denied fundamental legal rights. Defendants have been jailed illegally. Others have been subjected to racial and sexual bigotry so explicit it seems to come from some other place and time."

Years into the new millennium, there still were about thirty states that relied on such courts, which were rooted in an era when lawyers were scarce, according to the *Times* report.

Assigned to chair New Mexico's State Judicial System Study Committee at the end of the 1959 legislative session, Chávez began putting committee members to work in 1960, even though the legislature did not convene again until 1961. Committee members worked for five years not only compiling information to justify reform but also lobbying fellow lawmakers and others in the community to build the support that would be needed to pass controversial legislation.

It was the 1965 session before the committee's recommendations were presented to the full legislature. By then, Chávez had stepped out of the legislature, choosing to pursue other political options. The house majority leader, David Norvell, a Curry County Democrat, had served as vice chair of the judicial reform committee and succeeded Chávez as chairman. He shared Chávez's view that the panel was dealing with pressing matters, particularly in its review of the JP system.

"As a practicing lawyer, I observed it up close and saw that the system was not designed for fairness and accountability," Norvell said.

Even while freshly out of the legislature, Chávez remained one of the most vocal proponents of the judicial reform committee's work. It was Chávez, while working from outside the legislature, who drafted key revisions to judicial reform legislation after early proposals were rejected. Chávez's revisions were sponsored by Senator Al Montoya, brother of U.S. Senator Joseph M. Montoya and close friend of Democratic Doña Ana County Senator Jerry Apodaca, who served on the committee and eventually succeeded Norvell as chairman.

A final decision on the legislation did not come until the 1965 legislature's closing day, and even then, it did not come easily, according to news reports. The legislature adopted a resolution to put before state voters a constitutional amendment to completely abolish the JP system within five years. A magistrate system would be created in its place. Magistrates would be paid as "provided by law." Collection of fees would be prohibited.[26]

The legislature also agreed to send to voters a proposed constitutional amendment to create a state court of appeals of at least three judges that would serve as an intermediate appeals court between district courts and the state supreme court.[27] The move was intended to help reduce mounting demands on the supreme court that had developed over years, seemingly with little concern and even less attention.[28]

In a third move, legislators sent to voters a proposed constitutional amendment to create a state Judicial Standards Commission that would hear charges of misconduct, malfeasance, or misfeasance of judges.[29] The committee would make recommendations to the supreme court, which then could discipline, suspend, remove from office, or order the retirement of a judge or magistrate. The committee would be composed of two judges, two attorneys, and five citizens who could not be attorneys.

Senator C. Fincher Neal, an Eddy County Democrat, argued only days before adjournment that the legislature was trying to do too much at once and suggested that action on the JP system be delayed. "We're trying to get the whole ball of wax here, and we don't know what we're going to do with the peace justices," the *Albuquerque Journal* quoted Neal to have said.

Valencia County Democratic Senator Tibo Chávez, who chaired the Senate Rules Committee, was quoted by the same paper to have pressed for adoption of the entire legislative package. "In view of the late date, we feel this is the only practical solution," said Chávez, a longtime legislative ally of Fabián Chávez Jr.

In the end, only Senators Aubrey Dunn (D-Otero) and Cirilio Maestas (D-Mora) voted against the JP amendment. The JP amendment passed the house of representatives on a 40–23 vote, newspapers reported.

New Mexico voters in a September 1965 special election handily approved creation of the state court of appeals as well as the creation of the Judicial Standards Commission.[30] They overwhelmingly approved abolition of the JP system and creation of the magistrate courts in the 1966 general election. The vote on that issue was 81,055–26,317.[31]

"It's not easy to pass constitutional amendments," said Norvell. "That one passed with strong opposition from justices of the peace around the state who had a lot of political influence."

Indeed, there was more than a little behind-the-scenes maneuvering as judicial reform proposals came to a head. "David Carmody was chief justice of the state supreme court when the legislature approved the three measures, and he got Gene Lusk and Dean Zinn to lobby me so that I would support placing the issue of the appeals court on a special election ballot separate from the general election when voters would decide the fate of the JPs," Chávez said. "They didn't have any problem lobbying me because I already had determined that I would push for abolishment of the JPs during the regular election. Fewer people vote in special elections, and I figured that the vested interests supporting the JPs would get like-minded voters out and would have a better chance of winning in a special election. In a general election, I knew that the bigger number of voters would include droves of people who had been wronged in JP courts and wouldn't hesitate to get rid of them."

Carmody at first had called for expanding the state supreme court to deal with the backlog of cases that had accumulated over years. Carmody and other supreme court justices might have been reluctant to give up their dominance over appellate cases, but news reports told how Carmody won support for his approach from the national Institute of Judicial Administration and from state Rep. Richard "Deacon" Arledge. Arledge introduced legislation to expand New Mexico's supreme court from five to seven members. "Arledge was a former district judge who had ambitions to be appointed to one of the new supreme court positions that he wanted created," Chávez said.

"The backlog of cases in the supreme court began building earlier in the 1950s, and what's amazing is that something wasn't done long before the judicial review committee was formed," Chávez said.

The *Santa Fe New Mexican* reported that by late 1965, before the appeals court was impaneled, it took thirty to thirty-six months for decisions appealed

～≈ FIGURE 19. ≈～
The 1960 New Mexico Supreme Court (from left): Irwin Moise,
James C. Compton, James B. McGhee, David Carmody, and David Chávez Jr.
Courtesy Palace of the Governors (MNM/DCA), negative no. 074114.

from district court to clear through the supreme court. Information about the backlog was included in a 1992 article written by Thomas Donnelly and Pamela Minzner, both appeals court judges at the time, for the *New Mexico Law Review*.

"Once we got started trying to address the problem, Justice Carmody was the most active of the justices seeking solutions, but his solutions were the wrong ones," Chávez said, recalling his time as committee chairman. "He advocated immediate relief by simply expanding the supreme court. That would have made it possible for more panels to be created within the court to review cases that then would have to be taken to the full court for review. But that approach would have offered only a temporary solution for maybe ten years.

"Justice Carmody had spoken to me to win my support. I told him, 'I'm not a judge. I'm not a lawyer. I'm just a man with common sense.' It did not make common sense to me to simply expand the supreme court. I worked against the proposal to expand the state supreme court, and I killed it.

"Instead, I found more logical reasoning in the Constitution of the United States of America. It says there shall be a Supreme Court of the United States and such other courts as created by law. I took that argument to the state legislature, and we agreed to press for creation of our own court of appeals to deal with cases even before they got to our state supreme court. We started with a small number of judges but left it open so that more could be added as our population grew and caseloads mounted. There was very little opposition to the idea once it started rolling."

Donnelly, a Santa Fe lawyer who served as a state district judge as well as a judge on the New Mexico Court of Appeals, helped document work Chávez did as chairman of the judicial reform committee. "Fabián played an incredible role in sort of deflecting what Chief Justice Carmody wanted," Donnelly said. "What we ended up with was sort of patterned after the federal circuit court of appeals. Our state court of appeals actually disposes of a large volume of cases and leaves the supreme court free to examine in detail some of the larger, more high-profile cases.

"Fabián was the primary mover and shaker instrumental in creating the appeals court," Donnelly said. "His efforts in improving the judiciary during his terms in the state senate were instrumental in bringing about much-needed reform in the courts from top to bottom."

As governor at the time, Democrat Jack Campbell appointed the first four judges to serve on the new court of appeals. "It was a good geographical representation of the state," Donnelly said of Campbell's selections: Joe Wood of Farmington, Waldo Spiess of Las Vegas and later Albuquerque, LaFel Oman of Las Cruces, and E. T. Hensley of Portales.

The backlog of appellate cases that had accumulated when the new court was impaneled was so great that the supreme court, through special designation, had the appeals court judges review many of the backlogged cases rather than simply wait for new cases to come up, Donnelly and Minzner wrote.[32]

The first judges were installed in April 1966 at an annual salary of $18,500.[33]

Carmody, after initially opposing creation of a court of appeals, wound up asking voters to approve the proposed constitutional amendment that would create it. On that issue, at last, Chávez and Carmody were on the same side. But beginning with their dispute over Carmody's early inclination to expand the supreme court, bad blood had developed between Chávez and Carmody, the same man who had presided over Chávez's wedding a decade earlier.

"What happened between him and me almost became personal," Chávez said. "A new justice of the peace organization had been created, and during the campaign leading up to the special election, it held a meeting in the auditorium of the State Land Office to listen to an address by the chief justice. I went to that meeting and sat way in the back so as not to attract attention. I knew I wouldn't be the most popular man in that crowd.

"Justice Carmody made a very strong plea to the JPs to help in the creation of the court of appeals. In that same presentation, he pointed out that those who are proposing the abolishment of the JP system don't know the history of that good system, which evolved from the English law.

"The very next day, I went to the press and said that I expected such a stupid presentation to be made by persons who did not understand our judicial system but not from a member of the New Mexico Supreme Court. I openly blasted Justice Carmody. Two other supreme court justices called me in to calm me down and told me they would take care of Justice Carmody."

Tension between Chávez and Carmody also grew from their dispute over two state district judges Chávez, while chairing the judicial review committee, believed should be removed from the bench. "The supreme court had authority to discipline errant judges, but it didn't really have time to tend to such matters because of its tremendous backlog of cases," Chávez said. "The legislature also had the authority to impeach bad judges, but the process was long, tedious, and expensive. We needed something else, and it all came to a head as we examined the conduct of a district judge in Alamogordo and another one in Doña Ana County.

"The two judges were not fit for their jobs, and I asked the supreme court to get rid of them. Nothing was going to be done, so I said that as chairman of the Judicial System Study Committee, I was willing to consider impeachment. Justice Carmody told me I wouldn't dare. The next day, I asked the press to leave because the committee was going to consider proceedings for impeachment of some judges. That's all it took. The supreme court convinced the two judges it would be in their best interest to resign.

"I found out that California already had established a Judicial Standards Commission so I met with the chairman of the California senate's standing committee on the judiciary in San Francisco. He gave me the whole lowdown on how they did it. He said make sure the majority of members are laypeople; nothing but lawyers would make a propensity for lawyers to be more protective of their fraternal organization."

Since its creation, the state Judicial Standards Commission has acted on cases involving judges from around the state, including politically powerful jurists as well as whimsical, derelict, and sexually abusive judges. In 2006, the *Albuquerque Journal* reported of a Doña Ana County magistrate winning a second term unopposed in that year's election only to be barred from judicial office the following day, as the state Judicial Standards Commission recommended. The magistrate had tested positive for cocaine and stood accused of other misconduct.

For state district courts in low-income counties like Las Vegas, Taos, and Rio Arriba, some of the most important work of the Judicial Systems Study Committee came in the creation of central court financing. "Financing for the district courts was based on a one-mill property tax collection from the county where those courts operated," Chávez said. "Some counties, like those with oil and gas, collected sufficient money for their courts, even surpluses. Poor counties, however, could be left completely stymied. They'd run out of money for their courts. Taos, Mora, Torrance: There were a lot of them. They just didn't have the tax base, and they were not receiving the same level of administration of justice that the richer counties were getting. The contrast between the poor and the rich was abominable."

Chávez said a judge assigned to Socorro, Torrance, Sierra, and Catron counties appeared before the committee and promptly offered that he was breaking the law simply to meet his court's daily expenses. "He said he was borrowing from his district's court trust fund and transferring the money into an account used to meet routine obligations. He said it was the only way work could get done."

Two other counties were guilty of their own infractions. "In Taos County, the judge directed the sheriff and local police to cite traffic violators into district court instead of to the JPs," Chávez said. "The district court clerk had these mimeographed forms for the cited persons to look at when they came in. It said they could be fined three hundred dollars and assessed another three hundred in court costs. But it said that the three-hundred-dollar fine would be suspended if they simply agreed to pay the three-hundred-dollar court costs. That's what would happen if they signed the form.

"All money from fines collected would go to the state education fund. Court costs would stay at the county. In essence, violators were pleading guilty to a court clerk, which was illegal. And they were doing the same thing in Doña Ana County. This is the kind of crap that was going on."

Chávez thought the state needed to make the same financial commitment to its courts that it had made to its two other branches of government. "The third arm of government was starving to death," he said. "The answer was to create central court financing, which we did through simple legislation, and now our courts get their money like everybody else: from the state's general fund. Common sense dictated the answer to that one."

Even if common sense won out in most instances involving judicial reform, victories did not always come easily. Jerry Apodaca told of one committee hearing where heated debate nearly turned to fisticuffs in 1967, while Norvell was still chairman and the panel sorted through details of the new magistrate system.

"There was this attorney named Pablo Marshall from Socorro County. He was Hispanic, and he was a short, little guy—shorter than me," Apodaca said. "He was testifying before our committee and proposed that all the new magistrates that were to replace the JPs should be attorneys. Some, like Pablo, wanted all the magistrates to be attorneys. Others didn't want such a requirement at all. We were calling for Albuquerque magistrates alone to be attorneys.

"I was directing all these questions to Pablo Marshall, and after we had gone on for a while, he prefaced one of his responses to me with the comment: 'Well, in your little mind . . . ' Needless to say, that really pissed me off. It was around noon. Dave Norvell was presiding, and he immediately called a recess for lunch so things could cool down. Pablo came up to talk to me before I left. I told him, 'Unless you want me to knock the shit out of you, please walk away.' Pablo kept trying to talk, and I told him, 'Please walk away now unless you want me to knock the shit out of you.'

"It was a controversial process, but in the final analysis what came out of the committee was very well accepted. As it applied to the JPs, it was a major, major change for New Mexico. The system had become so corrupt. There were no term limits, so JPs could be there forever—and in some cases they were."

Even though Chávez was out of the legislature when lawmakers finally voted on reforms, he was the main force behind the changes, according to Apodaca. "Fabián carried this whole thing through its infancy. We were just recipients of a lot of work that had been done before he left. He followed the whole process through. He had the political savvy and the political muscle to move it along."

Chávez said he later asked many judges why it took them so long to reform what had become a very troubled system in so many areas. "I wanted to know: Why did it take a layman like me to come in and press for the changes that had made their lives and the lives of so many New Mexicans so difficult? I still don't have the answer. I came to the conclusion that it was just because they didn't know what the heck they were doing."

CHAPTER THIRTEEN

Entrenched Liquor Industry
Battles Change

Los Alamos' first state senator, Democrat Harold Agnew, did not place much stock in the 1957 pledge he got from Fabián Chávez Jr. after Agnew's bill to repeal the state's minimum markup law on liquor was defeated in that year's legislative session.

Chávez commended Agnew for making a good argument on the bill that New Mexico's liquor industry vehemently opposed, but he voted against Agnew's bill nonetheless. He told Agnew that more information was needed for the measure to win broad support and pledged to help collect that information. He started the process beginning with the legislature's next session in 1959.

"The issue was a straightforward thing," Agnew said. "You were either for it or against it." Agnew did not buy Chávez's explanation. "I think Fabián had a commitment with the liquor industry. I think he had a commitment with [George] Maloof and those guys," he said, referring to the state's top liquor wholesale dealers.

The *Santa Fe New Mexican*, in fact, reported just weeks before the 1963 legislative session when the liquor markup issue finally came to a head that Chávez "once was one of the votes on which the liquor groups could count."

Chávez himself told of having regularly received campaign donations from the liquor industry. "I know it led to misperceptions and that it angered people in the industry later when I took them on," he said.

Chávez, with considerable help from Richard Folmar, deputy director of the state Legislative Council Service, and others, intently studied various aspects of pricing, marketing, and regulation before Chávez in the 1963 legislative session introduced three bills intended to reform the state's liquor industry.

It was like shooting a flaming arrow into a haystack. All hell broke loose.

Agnew said Chávez might well have recognized the need to repeal the liquor minimum markup law but was probably pressed more by politics and personal interest to change positions on the issue after his 1957 vote against Agnew's bill. "I really think one of the reasons he switched was because he had ambitions for higher office, and clearly, I think, repealing the old law was something that the public was in favor of. It was the thing to do."

Maybe. The powerful liquor industry and many in the state Democratic Party—from its top leaders to its precinct captains—were firmly opposed to Chávez's initiatives, however.

Agnew said he was pleased to see Chávez's reversal of position. "I just thought, fine. He's a free man again. He isn't indebted to anyone."

The *Santa Fe New Mexican* reported that the state's minimum markup law had its origin in 1939, written by James Woolsey, an attorney who went on to become a vice president of one of the nation's largest liquor distillers. The law set markups at both the wholesale and retail levels.

At the wholesale level, the law required a minimum markup of 17.5 percent on whisky, 25 percent on wine, and 20 percent on beer.[1] The required markup at the retail level was 38.8 percent on whisky and wine and 25 percent on beer.[2]

The maximum markup for wholesalers was about 25 percent; for retailers, about 50 percent.[3]

The U.S. Supreme Court and several state courts had declared parts of fair-trade laws elsewhere unconstitutional, but news reports said New Mexico's statute had never been tested.

There were fourteen wholesalers in New Mexico in 1963. News reports of the period concurred that five controlled as much as 95 percent of the business: George Maloof, Richard Zanotti, Louis Hymel, Primo Corrazi, and Carlo Bachechi. Chávez said there were 1,300 to 1,400 liquor retailers across the state.

"The law was intended to protect the retailer, particularly the small retailer," Chávez said. "It was supposed to guarantee a profit to the wholesalers but also prevent those same wholesalers from making too much profit at the expense of the retailers. I supported the law for years, but then Senator Agnew made a very interesting presentation in 1957. He brought in full-page ads from the *El Paso Times* and the *Denver Post* where major retail outlets in both El Paso and Denver advertised the sale of various alcoholic beverages for less than, ostensibly, the wholesalers in New Mexico had to pay for them.

It didn't make any sense. Somebody was cooking the numbers. Wholesalers were manipulating the pricing in our state. The old law wasn't helping at the retail level at all. Many retailers were making only small profits even though their prices to the consumers were among the highest in the nation."

Chávez said information the Legislative Council Service compiled showed that prices of a dozen popular brands of Scotch, bourbon, and blended whiskies were 85 to 90 percent higher in New Mexico than in Arizona, Colorado, Kansas, Oklahoma, Texas, and Utah.[4] "I found out I could get my favorite brand of Scotch cheaper from Anchorage, Alaska, than I could in Santa Fe," Chávez said.

Another problem had developed along the way. "Retailers were required by law to pay wholesalers within thirty days of their purchases," Chávez said. "Many couldn't, especially the small retailers. So, often, wholesalers would sign a note on the side, lending the retailer the money that was owed. That allowed the wholesaler to continue selling to the retailer, but it also was against federal law. Those small retailers often had to raise their prices to consumers even higher than the bigger chains just to pay off their debts to wholesalers and stay in business."

As that problem became entrenched, it gave rise to yet another one, one that led to Chávez himself breaking the law repeatedly before he was elected to the senate. "My father-in-law at Capital Pharmacy had a liquor license and used to keep a few bottles of liquor on the shelf and sold them mostly as a convenience for his regular customers, who usually went into the pharmacy to make purchases other than liquor.

"I used to get bottles of Scotch, vodka, and so on from Pay-Less Liquor on West San Francisco Street. Pay-Less bought in great quantities so it was able to keep its retail prices lower than the little guys. I could buy liquor at retail prices at Pay-Less, take the bottles to Morry, my father-in-law, and he could sell them at his retail price and still make a small profit.

"We broke the law in two ways: One, Pay-Less sold to another retailer, and two, Morry bought from another retailer even though he was supposed to buy only from a wholesaler. Pay-Less, ostensibly, didn't know that they were selling to another retailer. But the guy who ran the liquor division at Pay-Less knew who I was, and when you go in there and buy in the quantity that I bought, they had to know I wasn't buying for home. He must have known I was buying it for Morry. I knew I was breaking the law when I did it as a favor to my father-in-law, but it was a ridiculous law. And I even used that story while debating the legislation that I took before the legislature in 1963."

Chávez introduced three liquor reform bills that year. One was to repeal the guaranteed minimum markup at the wholesale level. Another called for replacing the state liquor director with a five-member board appointed by the governor. The third would provide liquor licenses to hotels, motels, and restaurants under strict regulation but without regard to a community's population ratio.

Chávez and other supporters of the bills argued they would lower prices and make the liquor business more competitive; devalue the price of liquor licenses, which had soared; and increase the state's oversight of the liquor industry.

"People who qualified for a liquor license were getting it from the state for fifty dollars, but by the early 1960s those licenses that were in well-placed locations were being resold at a great profit, sometimes for fifty thousand, sixty thousand dollars, and more," Chávez said.

"And it was all because liquor licenses were issued based on a county's population. Probably every county was maxed out, no more new licenses could be issued so existing licenses took on great value. But it also discouraged new development. Hotels or restaurants, for example, might be reluctant to come into a community if they knew they wouldn't be able to get a liquor license.

"Up until 1951, my first legislative session, there was no population formula for liquor licenses. The formula came about because Tom Montoya, who was state liquor director at the time and brother of Joseph M. Montoya, issued all those pocket licenses as he was leaving office and made a substantial profit for himself. His friends who got the licenses also made out very well. So when the legislature next convened, it passed the population formula law that effectively froze the issuance of new licenses."

As Chávez sought to ease restrictions on licenses, he faced mounting rumors that he had taken money from hotels and others that would benefit from his proposal. "I figured it was the liquor dealers spreading the rumors. I was never under any circumstances bought off in any way, shape, or form. I simply wouldn't do it.

"As I pressed for reform, my opponents said the soaring prices for liquor licenses simply represented the free marketplace. As for the high prices on liquor, they said high prices deterred drinking and therefore meant less drunkenness in the state."

Chávez introduced his bills on the second day of the 1963 legislative session and braced for a strong battle. Senator Sterling Black, a Los Alamos Democrat, was cosponsor. "I knew George Maloof would be the guy who would orchestrate the opposition. He was a brilliant businessman and politician. I had great respect for the guy. He had a personal touch about him. He was very bright and a good overall citizen. We'd be fighting the wholesalers as well as the retailers, who were aggressively represented by Pancho

Padilla. He was president of the New Mexico Liquor Dealers Association and a former member of the house of representatives. George Maloof would be directing it all like a symphony."

The entire liquor industry, in fact, had developed quite a reputation around the state Capitol. "The liquor industry has demonstrated that it is in favor of keeping things just as they are, and it has never lost a fight in the legislature in the 24 years that the liquor law has been in the books," wrote Santa Fe columnist Will Harrison.

There was other opposition beyond the industry, though, major opposition. "Joe Montoya's people, his brother Tom, and others who took care of his interests contacted me. They wanted me to back off," Chávez said. "Their position was that my legislation would hurt good Democrats. Liquor people were contributors to the party, and they were what Joe Montoya's people considered to be an important part of the state Democratic organization."

The liquor industry, said former state Rep. Bobby Mayfield, pushed its weight around and knew how to win votes. "The liquor industry then was a pretty strong force," he said.

Long before he introduced his bills, Chávez had been getting information about New Mexico's archaic liquor laws as it became available through Folmar, whom Chávez had enlisted to help guide his reform efforts. Information included that which documented the substantially lower prices paid for liquor by consumers in other states, inflated values of liquor licenses, and even the issue of constitutionality of fair-trade laws.

"Dick's work was so thorough that at least one member of the liquor industry tried to get him fired from the Council Service," Chávez said of Folmar. "We collected information about liquor laws in all fifty states, and several states interested in their own reform asked us to share our final report with them."

Information was coming in even as Chávez worked as chairman of the committee that was charging into reform of the state's judicial system. It came in, too, as Chávez helped lead efforts to fund a medical sciences school at the University of New Mexico and secure funding for new technical vocational institutes and junior colleges. It arrived as Chávez worked for landmark civil rights legislation. He sought to balance it all while tending to the routine, yet demanding, duties of establishing each day's senate calendar and ensuring it was tended to in orderly fashion.

"I remember getting home late one night and when I got into bed, my wife very delicately asked me why I was taking on so much in so many critical areas all at once. I told her I didn't know. I told her that's just the way things presented themselves. But it reminded me that I needed to stay sharp when it came to compartmentalizing the issues before me."

Chávez seemed to have the wind at his back when he introduced his three liquor reform bills as the 1963 legislative session got under way.

"Senator Chavez started out as the underdog. Right now he seems to have the upper hand and support is mounting," the *Santa Fe New Mexican* wrote in its At the Capitol column in January 1963. "Numerous newspapers over the state have endorsed his bills. Two newspapers in Albuquerque are running articles on the bad practices connected with the industry there."

This report came from Fred Buckles of the *Albuquerque Journal*: "Sen. Fabian Chavez, D-Santa Fe, is receiving strong favorable reaction to his bill removing the mandatory markup on wholesale liquor" and most approving responses are from Albuquerque.

"The so-called 'fair-trade' law requiring these markups is about as far from fair trade as you could get and still remain on the same planet," the *Albuquerque Tribune* said in an editorial in January 1963. The paper said Chávez's legislation offered "a great opportunity to strike a blow for free enterprise."

The *Santa Fe New Mexican* sought to rally early support against what it predicted would be a stiff challenge from the liquor industry. "We have high hopes for Chavez' success. He will be working for justice and for the public interest," the paper wrote.

Testimony went on for hours when Chávez's legislation got its first hearing before the Senate Public Affairs Committee on January 23, 1963. "A crowd of more than 200 persons packed the Senate Chamber yesterday afternoon for the hearing, and dozens were turned away," wrote Bill Feather.

Most of the heated debate was focused on Chávez's proposed repeal of the markup law. His bill to allow motels, hotels, and restaurants to be issued new liquor licenses without regard for population ratio also came under sharp attack as well.

As part of the debate, Chávez told how the population ratio requirement was set in law after Tom Montoya's mass issuance of liquor licenses on his way out of office as liquor director in 1950. It created new problems, he said. "We killed a rat and created a Frankenstein," he told reporters at the time.

Chávez's bills were doomed to fail, however, largely because of tough opposition from the liquor industry but also because of competing interests and pressure influential people in their districts applied to customary Chávez allies.

Opponents even got Chávez's stepfather-in-law, the man Chávez bought liquor for from the Santa Fe Pay-Less store, to testify in committee against the legislation. "I remember Morry turning to me during his testimony and saying, 'You're wrong, son.' I said, 'No, you're wrong, papa.' And I was telling that to a man who I loved dearly.

"In that committee hearing, it was pretty much me against the world," Chávez said.

The senate by a vote of 18–14 defeated the measure to repeal the wholesale liquor markup law two weeks after it had been introduced. The vote came after a ninety-minute floor debate, according to the *New Mexican*. Neither of Chávez's two other liquor reform bills got out of the legislature, either. "Sterling Black, cosponsor of the legislation, made compelling arguments during the floor debate. But as in so many other issues that come up for debate in the house or the senate of any legislature, minds are already made up before the floor debate even begins," Chávez said.

Senator Fincher Neal (D-Eddy) and Al Montoya (D-Sandoval) were among the most vocal opponents of Chávez's markup repeal bill. Neal called Chávez's legislation "glamour" bills, suggesting they meant little. As for public support that got behind Chávez, Neal told the *Albuquerque Journal* that Chávez "has done a masterful job in selling his crusade to the press."

Neal's hometown paper, the *Carlsbad Current Argus*, said in an editorial two days later that Neal and the other seventeen senators who voted against repeal of the markup law should "review their stand and look again at the public interest rather than let the liquor industry continue its stranglehold on our lawmakers."

Chávez said he went into the senate vote believing he had it won. "I had my laundry sheet, the piece of paper with all the senators' names on it, and had marked how I thought they were going to vote after having visited with them one by one during previous days," Chávez said. "As majority leader, I could time when I wanted the issue to come up on the floor. I brought it up when I thought I had the votes, but a few key votes had changed in the hours leading up to the debate on the floor." Chávez's count was wrong, and he wound up losing largely because some of his customary allies in the end could not stand with him on this issue. "The powers that be got to some of my fellow senators. Cirilio Maestas was a young first-term senator from Mora County, and he had committed to me but came up to me later and said he was going to have to vote against the markup bill because he had been threatened by his county Democratic chairman. The chairman told him he would have him defeated in the next election if he voted with me.

"My very close, dearest friend, Tibo Chávez, voted against me. I had worked with Tibo going back to 1949 when I was his aide and helped him with the Fair Employment Practices Act. He was a good man and a great senator, but my legislation was seen as a threat by many of his constituents who, despite all the information that Dick Folmar had collected for me, still felt that the old liquor markup law was good for small retailers. He told me, 'Valencia County has more liquor licenses than any other county in the state, and they are all uniformly against it. I can't help you on this one.'

"And then there was Gordon Melody, a good friend and a longtime senate leader. He sat right next to me in the chamber and said, 'Pal, I'm sorry I can't help you this time, and you know why.' Gordon couldn't help because he had a franchise for some of these big billboard signs along the highways in northern New Mexico, and many were rented from him by people in the liquor industry.

"These guys loved me and respected me, but it was political suicide for them to support me on that legislation."

Even though Chávez found it easy to explain his defeat, it was a difficult loss for him nonetheless. He and Folmar had devoted a lot of time and energy to the issue. Little if any legislation examined that year had been exposed to so much research. Beyond that, Chávez repeatedly had engaged in contentious debate, often against former supporters in the liquor industry and even against a cherished family member.

"In a sense, it was so-called glamour legislation," Chávez said. "It was sexy and got a lot of public attention because it dealt with liquor, which is always an attention grabber whether you intend it to be or not. We sought to make some changes for the betterment of our state, which by no means were insignificant, but it wasn't the same as our civil rights legislation, or creation of a new medical school, or complete reform of the state's judicial system. My friends stood with me in those battles. Still, I have to confess that I left some blood on the canvas while fighting for liquor reform. And I didn't regret it. I remember telling George Maloof that I wasn't against liquor; I was in favor of good laws."

Following his bitter defeat, Chávez could not help but think of former Los Alamos Senator Harold Agnew, who in 1957 had made the quickly dispatched pitch for liquor reform. "There was no way we could pass that legislation solely on the argument of cheap liquor, as Senator Agnew had wanted. You couldn't say, let's do away with our law so that we could benefit from cheap liquor like people in neighboring states. Information on pricing was important to have, but we needed more. George Maloof was bringing in people from various churches to argue against making liquor cheaper, some even wanted to increase the price.

"I had to present it in such a way that we would reveal we had a capricious law that was based on false premises and was using small-business people as a front for the special interests behind it. It was a good strategy, but I failed to get enough people to recognize what was occurring. One guy threatened to shoot me because he thought I was trying to ruin his business. I didn't learn about the threat until after the fact, when the chief clerk of the senate asked the state police to watch me. My wife and I would go out to dinner at El Nido, and a state policeman was at our side. It was that way through the end of the session."

Thinking his liquor fight was over that cold day in January 1963, Chávez knew even after the sun fell that his obligations were not done yet. The traditional "100 bill party," an assembly to mark the introduction of the hundredth bill in the house of representatives, was being held that night at La Fonda. It is an annual gathering of lawmakers, lobbyists, and others who figure prominently in legislative sessions.

"I got home that night and was drained from everything that had gone on during the day, not just the debate and vote on the liquor bill," Chávez said. "I told my wife that I didn't feel up for the party and that I'd rather stay home. She said she didn't feel like going either, but she told me that I probably ought to go at least for a little while. She said people would think I was a sore loser because of that day's vote on the liquor bill and that it was an impression that I didn't want to leave with people. 'No, no. Shower and shave,' she told me. So, I followed her instructions, as I usually did, and drove to La Fonda."

Chávez walked into the hotel's large New Mexico Room after nine and soon made his way to the open bar. "I asked for a Scotch and water and while I was waiting for my drink, someone walked up behind me and put his arm around my shoulder and said, 'I'll buy you a drink, cabrón.' I turn around and see that it's Pancho Padilla. He clearly had been drinking."

Frank "Pancho" Padilla Jr. was a bear of a man from Albuquerque's South Valley who had grown accustomed to pushing his weight around. Articulate in both English and Spanish, he could be both smart and foolish. Very few outside the legislature knew the intricacies of the legislative process as well as he. He basked in attention while serving as one of the liquor industry's principal lobbyists.

"I brushed his hand off of my shoulder and said, 'I already have a drink,'" Chávez said. "Visibly upset now, he grabbed my coat and whirled me around then said, 'You think you're a big shot. I own you, and I own the legislature.' It was all in Spanish.

"Pretty soon other people, including people from the press, started moving toward the commotion that had developed. Pancho had been pulled away from me temporarily by Rep. Bob Martin from Silver City, but Pancho soon started coming back toward me. I figured I better switch him to English so that reporters and others could understand what he was saying and what he was trying to do. I got him talking English, and he essentially repeated what he said moments earlier. He said, 'I elected U.S. Senator Dennis Chávez. I elected Senator Clinton P. Anderson, and I own the legislature. I bought you a thousand times.'

"Pancho was a nice guy and a smart guy, except if he had been drinking. I liked him, really, and knew that when he was lobbying the legislature he was under the direction of other people, especially George Maloof. That night, during the incident at La Fonda, he had been drinking and was on his own. I told him, 'You don't own the legislature, and you don't own me.'"

Reports of the incident were splashed in the papers during following days. They told that Padilla purportedly had confronted at least one other lawmaker, first-term Republican house member David Cargo of Albuquerque. Cargo had introduced a bill to curb lobbying and had talked of wanting a bill to place stricter controls on issuance of liquor licenses.

Cargo told reporters he had an incident with Padilla before his confrontation with Chávez. He said Padilla grabbed him by the shoulder and spun him around. "You can't introduce bills on lobbying and on liquor because I own the legislature and I run it," Padilla reportedly told Cargo. "He was hopping mad," Cargo was quoted to have said. "I told him to go to hell and that I could introduce anything I wanted to."

Padilla initially denied the accusations. Associated Press reporter Harold Williams said at the time, though, that he heard Padilla boast about owning the legislature. He said he saw Padilla grab Chávez's lapels and shake him and that other legislators, including Rep. Foster Evans of Los Alamos, separated them.

Rep. Bobby Mayfield of Doña Ana County said later on the floor of the house that he had heard Padilla boast to Chávez about his influence and that he had seen Padilla verbally and physically assault members of both chambers. Mayfield introduced a resolution in the house calling for Padilla to be banned from legislative chambers for the remainder of the session.

"I was pretty upset, so I went to Clay Buchanan at the Legislative Council the next morning," Mayfield said. "Clay was director of the council. Although he never voiced his personal opinion about things, it became evident that Clay was not fond of Pancho Padilla's tactics. I asked Clay if there was any way we could keep Pancho out of the Capitol during the legislative session. He said we probably couldn't keep him out of the Capitol but that we probably could pass a resolution that would prohibit him from coming into the legislative halls. I asked Clay to draw me up a resolution, and he was more than happy to do it. He had a big smile on his face."

Others were not as certain that Mayfield was on the right path because of the influence Padilla enjoyed through the powerful liquor industry. "Senator Gordon Melody was the other power in the senate besides Fabián," Mayfield said. "Senator Melody came to me and said, 'Don't make a mistake. You might have a future in the legislature, and you don't want to ruin it in the beginning.' That didn't worry me a bit."

Mayfield introduced his resolution the following day. The *Albuquerque Journal* reported that a similar measure was introduced in the senate by I. M. Smalley of Deming. Senator Joe Skeen of Picacho, who doubled as state Republican Party chairman, seconded Smalley's motion for adoption. Both resolutions passed unanimously two days after the incidents at La Fonda, the *Journal* reported.

The paper said that as the resolutions were being considered, Padilla publicly apologized and announced that, irrespective of the resolutions, he would be leaving town in the morning.

It was an embarrassment to more than Padilla and the liquor retailers he represented. The stain spread throughout the industry. "Pancho went way back with the liquor industry," Chávez said. "He was the right-hand man of Tom Montoya back in the Mabry gubernatorial administration when Montoya was state liquor director. Pancho would go around the state back then, supposedly making sure that all the liquor people were following the law, but he probably spent at least as much time making sure that they all voted straight Democrat.

"To understand Pancho, you have to look at him from several angles. One was the business angle. Probably the biggest supporter of his organization was not the little retailers but, from behind the scenes, the big wholesalers. The little retailers didn't pay much to be a member of the retailers association, maybe fifty bucks, a hundred bucks a year. You had to be blind not to see George Maloof orchestrating everything and everyone, including Pancho.

"The other angle for looking at Pancho was the political side. The liquor retailers' organization without question had been turned into a tool of the Democratic Party. And from that angle, you had Pancho, who was very, very close to Joe Montoya. And Joe, by 1963, was sitting in the U.S. House of Representatives and kept an eye on everything that went on in the state. He sought to control as much as he could."

The confrontation at La Fonda was among old allies turned adversaries. "It's just too bad that the incident even happened," Chávez said. "I'll always remember that proverb that Senator Dennis Chávez had hanging in his office: 'Those whom the gods would destroy, they would first make mad.' That's what happened with Pancho that night. He lost his cool. I always remembered to keep my cool. If a mistake was to be made, let it come from the other guy."

In their arrogance that stemmed from their political influence, people in the liquor industry were prone to mistakes. "Over a period of years, the liquor industry had contributed to my campaigns and so they thought that if they contributed to us, they owned us," Chávez said. "In situations like that, you hope that a bill comes up where you can show that you're a good legislator and not someone who is beholden to others. If I got nothing else out of that bitter battle over liquor reform, I at least was able to prove my independence. That helped me in some quarters; it hurt me in others. But I would do it all over again."

The New Mexico Supreme Court in 1966 found that the so-called fair-trade contract and markup provisions of the Liquor Control Act are "manifestly unreasonable legislation, are not an appropriate exercise of the state's police power, and are in violation of . . . the New Mexico Constitution."[5]

Among the five judges who heard the case was David Chávez Jr., the Santa Fe attorney who, beginning with his role in having Fabián Chávez Jr. committed to the Springer boys' school, developed a long association with the former state senate leader who pressed for liquor reform.

The lawsuit was filed by Drink Inc., a corporation whose members included Albuquerque lawyer George Hannett, a relative of former New Mexico Gov. Arthur T. Hannett. "George loved what I was doing, taking on the liquor industry. He and others with him helped me a lot with the research as they prepared to challenge the liquor law in court.

"They lost their legal argument initially, but on appeal, the supreme court found that they had made their case. In military terms, we lost the battle in the legislature, but we won the war in the courts," Chávez said.

CHAPTER FOURTEEN

Bucking Power Brokers
in Race for Congress

Some of the state legislature's most pressing business was still tugging at Fabián Chávez Jr. early in 1964, even as he was intently engaged in activity charted to propel him to new political heights before the year was done.

It was February 24, a Monday, and not a particularly good day at all for Chávez. The legislature was in the final hours of a special session Gov. Jack Campbell had called, and the state budget for the following year had yet to be adopted. It was apparent that a second special session, to be convened Tuesday immediately after the first one was adjourned, would be needed before all the work on the $147.8-million budget could be completed.

The house speaker, Bruce King of Stanley, predicted at the time that no more than a day or two would be needed for the second special session.

Legislators historically had left votes on some of their most important work for the final hours of a session. In 1964, they thought they had one more day than what they actually were allowed by the state constitution. The attorney general, Earl Hartley, told them so. It meant lawmakers ended up with more work than time.

Chávez had taken an even-more staggering blow just as the new week began while most other New Mexicans were asleep in bed. About fourteen hundred state Democrats had convened in Santa Fe for their much-anticipated preprimary convention on Saturday, and by Sunday's first hours, the convention had dealt Chávez a defeat that for the first time exposed the intense opposition building against him within important elements of the political party he grew up worshipping.

Dismayed and wounded, Chávez arrived at the Capitol on Monday and before noon was confronted in a restroom by a news reporter who said he had heard a rumor about Chávez having spent time as a youth at the reform school for boys in Springer.

"It's not a rumor," Chávez told the reporter simply, then walked away and back into the senate chambers where he addressed the issue directly, telling how his father had enlisted help of political acquaintances to have him committed to the Springer school when he was twelve.

Chávez's senate colleagues, who were just settling back into their seats following a brief recess, were surprised by the turn of events. "In a highly emotional scene," the *Santa Fe New Mexican* said later, "New Mexico senators rallied around their distressed floor leader after a report on his being sent to the Springer boys' school in his youth. Several senators arose quickly to defend the shaken floor leader after he had spoken."

Veteran Senator I. M. Smalley, a Deming Democrat, called Chávez the best floor leader he had known in the senate. "There have been times the Senate stood behind Fabian Chavez simply because of his integrity," Smalley was quoted as saying. News reports said a vote of confidence was proposed and seconded by the man Chávez had defeated in 1961 in the race for majority leader, R. C. Morgan of Roosevelt County, and by senate Republican leader Joe Skeen of Lincoln County.

Democratic Senator Fincher Neal of Eddy County, who helped lead the fight against Chávez's liquor reform legislation the previous year, said the entire senate was hurt that reference to Chávez's stay in Springer as a pre-teen was made in an apparent attempt to wound him politically, reported the *New Mexican*.

Republican Edwin Mechem, who was serving as a U.S. senator after having been elected governor four times, sent Chávez a note following the flare-up over Springer that said simply, "Don't let the bastards get you down."

Chávez never determined who raised the Springer issue, but he was certain it was done to wound him in his unfolding effort to succeed Joseph M. Montoya in the U.S. House of Representatives. From his seat in the House, Montoya in 1964 was challenging Mechem for the U.S. Senate seat to which Mechem had himself appointed two years earlier upon the death of Dennis Chávez. That would leave the U.S. House seat Montoya had held for eight years vacant at the end of 1964. Chávez had long considered himself to be Montoya's natural successor, even though he knew he would not have Montoya's support.

Two other big-name Democrats were also interested. Four-term state land commissioner E. S. Johnny Walker filed for the race as did longtime

Albuquerque businessman and lawmaker Calvin Horn, who served as state house speaker in 1951 when Chávez began his first year in the legislature. Horn in 1958 had worked hard to win the nod of party leaders to whom fell the task of filling the vacancy in the U.S. House John Dempsey's death created. The nod, in 1958, surprisingly, went to little-known Tom Morris, a native of Brownwood, Texas, who had settled in Tucumcari after graduating from the University of New Mexico.

"I regretted having to leave the state legislature, but the U.S. House seat opened up, and I figured it was my time," Chávez said. "I had gotten a lot of public exposure because of my fights for judicial reform and liquor reform, so rather than seek election to a third term in the state senate in 1964, I chose to run for Congress."

Preprimary conventions were dominated by party bosses, and Walker had been preparing for the February 1964 convention for months. Perhaps more than Chávez, he enjoyed high name recognition around the state and turned to the kind of politics he knew best. "He could not speak formally. But he was very good in a crowd, handshaking, backslapping, and that kind of thing," said James "Bud" Mulcock, who went to work for Walker after meeting him at a political rally in the autumn of 1963. The rally had been organized to prepare for the convention still several months away.

Walker had run successfully for land commissioner four times and in the 1950s had even challenged Dennis Chávez for his U.S. Senate seat.

Walker, along with pal Murray Morgan of Alamogordo, had alternated possession of the state land commissioner's post for more than a decade leading into 1964. Santos Quintana, the longtime chairman of Santa Fe County Democrats, was an aide to Walker in the land office, where Quintana's political muscle was never far from the surface.

"He never supported me in the primaries when I ran for the legislature," Chávez said. "He'd support me once I got to the general elections, but I was never his first choice among Democratic candidates. He ran his political operations out of the land office throughout the time that he worked for Johnny Walker."

Morgan was one of numerous friends Walker had made while serving in the military during World War II. "Walker tried to get into the military several times, but they kept rejecting him because he had very, very poor eyesight," said Mulcock. "They finally accepted him and put him in a unit that was predominantly New Mexicans. He was the first sergeant of that unit and absolutely beloved by his troops."

The main reason for that affection appeared to have been rooted in Walker's willingness to get around the rules in support of his men. "He was a schemer. Everybody else was eating K-rations, and Walker's men were eating steaks," Mulcock said. "Walker was such a rebel, he'd get busted about every six months and loose his rank as first sergeant, and Murray Morgan would take it over. But the guys didn't like Murray like they liked Walker, so they would plot and scheme to get Walker back in as first sergeant so that he could get them steaks, or wine, or whatever they thought he could get his hands on. Walker was a consummate loyalist to people who were loyal to him.

"Those military men later became Walker's core of political support. There was Hot Cakes Smith in Truth or Consequences, Speedy Archuleta from Santa Fe, B. A. Cook from Portales. There were about seventy of them scattered around the state."

Walker worked as an aide in Washington, DC, under the patronage of Democrat U.S. Rep. John Dempsey before being elected to the New Mexico house of representatives twice and then, in 1952, to his first two-year term as land commissioner. His bid to dislodge Dennis Chávez from his post in the U.S. Senate in 1958 fell flat. Walker lost by a margin of nearly two to one.[1]

"Walker loved to tell how John Miles asked him to come over after that election and told him, 'Now, son, you got your ass beat, but you can't get mad. Don't give the sons of bitches that voted against you a reason to vote against you again.' So that sort of became Walker's mantra from then on," Mulcock said. "He generally tried to keep people happy, and when he came back in as land commissioner two years later, he didn't target those who had voted against him and had gone with Dennis Chávez."

By the time of the Democrats' 1964 preprimary convention, Walker had run in five statewide races and had won four of them. He was originally from Albuquerque, where he was known as Elzer. Later, he was called Stephen while working as an aide in Washington. "The time came when he began looking to get into politics. He figured Silver City was the place to go so he went down there, opened a bar, and changed his name to E. S. Johnny Walker," said Mulcock.

Walker went into the February 1964 preprimary convention confident that he had enough support to win the party's endorsement over Fabián Chávez Jr. and Calvin Horn. "But we were surprised by Fabián's strength in Albuquerque. We couldn't get the votes we thought we were going to get because of Fabián's strength in Bernalillo County," Mulcock said.

"It was a new group in Albuquerque. They got the name of 'grass rooters,' and they were led by Henry Kiker Jr. Fabián was the first big-eyed liberal to make a statewide race in New Mexico, and he attracted people like Henry Kiker and Bert and Imogene Lindsay. Fabián didn't start that group. They were there, maybe because of the John F. Kennedy influence, and Fabián happened to come along in 1964."

Kiker was Bernalillo County Democratic chairman at the time. He was the son of a former state supreme court justice and a successful Albuquerque lawyer in his own right. "He had a brilliant mind and was one to take a broad view of world affairs," Chávez said. "He liked my voting record in the legislature. He liked what I was doing to reform the courts and how I was working to reform liquor laws. He liked my work on the medical school, so he went all out for me."

In fact, Kiker was the only county Democratic chair who supported Chávez going into the preprimary convention. Walker had most of the others.

Horn was confident enough about his own support, which included U.S. Rep Joseph M. Montoya and emerging strong man Emilio Naranjo, Rio Arriba County chairman.

Chávez considered U.S. Senator Clinton Anderson to be behind Walker at the convention, but Mulcock suggested that was not so. "Clinton Anderson developed a reputation as a kingmaker, but if one observed the senator, he very rarely anointed a candidate at the front end. Everybody would strive for his endorsement because it would pretty much ensure their election. But Anderson usually would wait and watch a campaign develop before he committed to anyone. Anderson could push candidates over the top, but he almost never put any of them into the race."

Maybe so, but Chávez knew early on he did not have Anderson's support. "He called me into his office in Albuquerque well before the convention and tried to talk me out of running," Chávez said. "It was a kind of father-son type of conversation. He said I was doing a real good job as state senate majority leader and that I should stay in that position a while longer. 'Stay in there, son. Your time will come,' he said. He suggested I was too young to move up to Congress. But I told him that at forty-two I was about the same age that he, Joe Montoya, and Dennis Chávez were when they first went to Washington."

Convention delegates had all three men—Chávez, Walker, and Horn—to choose from once the gavel hit the table that February weekend. Or at least that was the appearance. "You know how those things worked," said Mulcock. "Some of those county chairmen didn't poll their delegations. They'd stand up and give their delegate counts [on their own]."

Chávez said the intent of the opposition was to keep him from winning enough delegates to get on the party's ballot altogether. "The whole idea was to cut me out at the convention. People were going around talking to county chairs and trying to convince them to withhold votes for me. Santiago Campos from Guadalupe County was one of those approached, and he wouldn't go along. He made sure I got votes from a third of his county's delegation."

Campos was a young lawyer aligned with Harry Bigbee, the Santa Fe attorney and former judge who had long supported Chávez.

Henry Kiker Jr. delivered the nominating speech for Chávez at the convention. "His remarks stood out from all the rest," Chávez said. "He was the kind of man who had the potential to be governor or U.S. senator, and I told him so. I told him that if he filed for either office, I would give his nominating speech."

Party rules required that candidates get at least 20 percent of the convention delegate votes to be placed on the primary ballot. The *New Mexican* reported that all three candidates qualified on the convention's first tally, but none had the 50-plus percent needed to stand out as the convention's nominee.

The fight went on for four hours. After the fifth ballot, Chávez released his delegates to end the gridlock, according to the *New Mexican*. Chávez was convinced that even without the momentum of being the convention's nominee, he could secure enough of the rank-and-file Democratic vote to win the party's primary election in May.

Press accounts reported that it was Chávez's freeing of delegates that allowed Walker to get 50.35 percent of the convention's votes on the sixth ballot. Mulcock said something else also figured into the results, however.

"Calvin Horn had bought Emilio Naranjo prior to the preprimary convention, probably with something like money for the [Rio Arriba] campaign," Mulcock said. He said, though, that Walker had struck a deal with Naranjo even before Horn thought he had locked up support in Rio Arriba County through its party chairman. "Walker told Emilio that he had enough votes to win the preprimary convention and that he could go ahead and support Calvin in the convention, then slate Walker in the primary."

Again, the purported deal in its most basic form: Naranjo could take Horn's money for local campaigning and would support Horn at the convention, but then go with Walker after he became the convention's nominee heading into the primary.

The hung vote after several ballots at the convention required a change of plans, Mulcock said. "After the first several ballots, Emilio was told Walker was going to need his help, after all, at the convention."

Mulcock said he was 100 percent certain that the pact between Walker and Naranjo had been struck and that Naranjo was subsequently asked to help Walker at the convention out of necessity. "Emilio's help was needed. Fabián's people were on a mission. They were the first 'true believers' that I was acquainted with in New Mexico. They were the more doctrinaire liberals who were comfortable with neither Johnny Walker nor Calvin Horn. I don't know how many of Fabián's delegates went over to Walker even after they were released."

Naranjo denied Mulcock's account. "I'm the kind of person who once I make up my mind, there are no new deals at all," Naranjo said. "I've never sold myself to anyone."

Chávez's struggle from the position of underdog led to unexpected turns. "Fabian was abandoned [at the convention] in such native counties as Rio Arriba and San Miguel. As the torrid congressional battle wore on, some natives appeared to be taking offense to the way Fabian was being chopped up," the *New Mexican* reported in its column, At the Capitol. Among those rankled, the column reported, was none other than Frank "Pancho" Padilla Jr., the same man who had battled Chávez verbally and physically during the previous year's liquor reform battle in the legislature. Padilla, who had supported Horn, suddenly threw his support behind Chávez, according to the *New Mexican*.

"That's old Pancho Padilla, born and raised in tiny Puerto de Luna," said Chávez. "Yes, we had had our differences, but he got mad because he thought people were working against me at the convention simply because I was Hispanic. It was his ethnic pride that came out in him."

Horn, who was second in convention balloting, soon was out of the race altogether, and Chávez turned all his attention to defeating Walker in the primary. "Calvin figured that if he stayed in, it would guarantee my victory," Chávez said. "If he had stayed in, the race would have been between two Anglos and one Hispanic, and that would give me an advantage. Who do you think pulled Calvin Horn out? Joe Montoya. He didn't want me in Congress even if it meant that a Montoya was going against a Chávez in favor of a Walker."

Mulcock agreed that it would have been Chávez's race to win if Horn had stayed in. "Fabián inarguably would have won because Calvin had pockets of strength that migrated to Walker. Calvin was a very well known, big-name Baptist who had connections with the oil and gas industry. Joe Montoya might have asked Calvin to pull out, but if he did, it probably was on the basis of, 'Hey, man, you have no chance.'"

Chávez, suddenly in a two-man race, immediately looked to build on the solid support he had within Bernalillo County. "I knew I had Henry Kiker and all the people he knew across the state to help me," Chávez said. "I knew that in some counties where I didn't get much delegate support at the convention, I could win those counties irrespective of the positions taken by the county chairs. I was looking at Santa Fe, Rio Arriba, Socorro, San Miguel, Valencia, and even Grant County, which was Johnny Walker's home base. I knew I could win there because organized labor would support me and organized labor was big there."

As Chávez worked these and other counties, though, he ran into evidence of high-powered opposition. "Henry Kiker had invited recently elected Congressman Henry González from Texas to a campaign rally organized for me in Albuquerque," Chávez said. "I had met Henry González when he was a state senator in Texas and I was a state senator in New Mexico. González agreed to attend the rally only to call back later and tell Henry Kiker that he had to cancel because Congressman Joe Montoya had told him that he should not get involved in a Democratic primary race here. This was the same Joe Montoya who, whenever he ran for office in a primary election, would invite every prominent Hispanic official in the country to campaign for him."

Not surprisingly, Chávez had two of the most influential constituencies within the New Mexico Democratic Party working very hard against him.

~&~ FIGURE 20. ~&~

Fabián Chávez Jr. addresses a 1964 Democratic rally in Santa Fe. Courtesy Fabián Chávez Jr. Picture no. 2–33 by Henry B. Balink. Balink's Studio. Santa Fe, NM.

"The JPs and the liquor guys around the state were the most loyal Walker supporters in that race," said Mulcock. "But it wasn't necessarily because of an association with Walker. It was a dislike of Fabián."

With Horn out of the race and Senator Anderson now aligned with the convention's nominee, Chávez did what he could to get his underdog message out at campaign rallies and through free news coverage. He had little money, perhaps five thousand dollars, according to Chávez. Walker was in better shape, but he, too, was far from loaded with cash.

"It was all personal campaigns then, rallies, that kind of thing," Mulcock said. "I bet we didn't have thirty thousand dollars to spend. Nash Hancock, an auto dealer in Santa Fe who was friends with Walker, loaned Walker a 1962 Plymouth. That Plymouth was campaign headquarters. It was the media center. It's where we operated from."

The two-year-old car also served Chávez's needs on more than one occasion. "Walker and Fabián were good friends," said Mulcock. "I bet there were half a dozen times that we traveled together in that car. Walker had no animus toward Fabián. I don't remember ever taking Fabián to a rally, but he rode back with us several times from Albuquerque and perhaps once from Ruidoso."

Mulcock, along with tending to other duties, was Walker's driver and recalls that both Walker and Chávez on occasion would open a small bottle or flask for a hard drink on the way home from political gatherings. Mulcock thought each man's choice of drink was ironic. "Neither one was a heavy drinker, but I remember Fabián would pour himself some Johnny Walker Red Scotch and Walker would drink Chivas. Fabián and I would laugh about that years later."

Chávez agreed that there was little rancor in that 1964 primary race. "We were running for the office. We weren't running against each other. The closest thing to negative came in Carlsbad, when I challenged him to debate me and he said, 'I'm no damn fool. I'm not going to debate Fabián.' He was quoted the next day in the *Carlsbad Current Argus*."

Chávez, said Mulcock, was probably one of the top five debaters ever in the state.

Low on cash, Chávez said he received substantial in-kind contributions. "I was endorsed by the labor union, COPE, only to have Joe Montoya come later and tell them not to get involved in a primary race. COPE told Joe I had been a good supporter, and they stuck with me. I'd cut my own radio ads in English and Spanish, and COPE placed them in radio stations around the state.

"On several occasions, Henry Kiker bought plane tickets for him and me on commercial airlines that we would ride to Hobbs, Alamogordo, and Las Cruces."

According to Mulcock, Chávez's lack of campaign funds led to problems that fueled speculation about his integrity. "We'd get phone calls where people would tell us things like, 'When you get into Clayton, come by because I have a check of Fabián's that has come back.' Fabián would write personal checks for cash, and he wouldn't have sufficient funds." If the intent of people who called with word of bounced checks was to give Walker ammunition to discredit Chávez, Walker did not follow through, according to Mulcock. He said Walker never publicly mentioned the bad checks. Still, said Mulcock, "There was a significant cloud over Fabián's integrity at that time.

"It was seen in things like the old Pancho Padilla incident at La Fonda where Pancho told Fabián, 'I bought and sold you a thousand times.' I think stories like that frightened Senator Anderson about Fabián's trustworthiness."

If they did, Anderson was selective about what he heard because Padilla not only claimed to own Chávez, he made remarks that same evening about being responsible for Anderson's ascension in New Mexico politics.

"Even after my intense battle to reform the liquor industry, I knew there were people who thought I was indebted to the industry because of their contributions to my early campaigns," Chávez said. "It probably didn't help when Pancho surprised everyone and announced he was supporting me over Walker. But even after he did that, all you had to do was look at all the people in the liquor industry who were aggressively working for Walker.

"I grew up recognizing that my reputation, in the end, is what really matters. I fought back rumors about being on the take, and some of it probably was fueled by the fact that I was a poor boy on the campaign, hitching a ride whenever I had to, having a check bounce once in a while when I couldn't get back home soon enough to get money into the bank to cover costs that I incurred at the tail end of a campaign trip. But the whole issue makes me think back to two dear people in my family. My brother, Cuate, was more than a brother to me; he was a good friend, and he was very knowledgeable about politics. Once, after I turned down a five-thousand-dollar contribution from a state highway commissioner in the Clovis District, Cuate told me I was a fool. The contribution sought to commit me to a particular personnel decision, but I wouldn't go along. Cuate knew I wanted to be a good public official. But to do that, he said, I first had to get elected. To get elected, I needed money, he reminded me. On the other hand, I'll never forget what my father taught me at a very early age. He used to tell me it was more important to get people to respect me than to like me. He'd say people won't like you if they don't respect you.

"Things like what my father taught me can get lost on the campaign trail, especially when rumors have been planted in people's minds before you get a chance to talk with them. I knew all along what my values were: Simply, you don't steal or sell yourself out. You don't do it in the name of Jesus. You don't do it for your mother. You simply don't do it."

Walker, because he already had run in five statewide races, had a distinct advantage over Chávez, who going back to 1948 had run only in Santa Fe County. Add that to Walker's support from the state's two U.S. senators, all but one of the county Democratic chairmen, plus the enthusiastic help from hundreds of JPs as well as the liquor industry, and Walker had reason for optimism going into the May primary election.

Mulcock said optimism was tempered by tough political realities of the times. Both Chávez and Walker claimed Santa Fe as home although Walker had come by way of Albuquerque and Silver City. "We had the Santa Fe County chairman behind us, but I think we got killed in Santa Fe County because of Fabián's brother, Cuate," Mulcock said. "Cuate was municipal judge in Santa Fe, and if you were an identifiable Johnny Walker supporter, you had an X on your back. Cuate let it be known through the street talk common in a small town that if you were supporting Walker, you better not appear in his court."

It was an ironic story to hear, given Chávez's high-profile and successful battle to dismantle the state's politically corrupt system of JPs, who were now probably unanimous in their opposition to Chávez.

Chávez, too, was optimistic going into the election, even though he was aware that he had not run overpowering races against opponents for legislative seats in his home base of Santa Fe County.

When ballots were totaled, Walker had 55,440 votes, Chávez, 53,225.[2] It was easily the closest of statewide races Democrats contested that year. Tom Morris, the state's incumbent congressman from Tucumcari, ran unopposed and collected 70,669 votes.[3] Joseph M. Montoya, who was unopposed in his bid to challenge Republican Edwin Mechem for the U.S. Senate in that year's general election, got 83,253 votes.[4]

Walker's nomination followed by his general election campaign marked the first time dating back to 1943 that New Mexico Democrats had two Anglos competing against Republicans for the U.S. House. The party bosses, largely through the preprimary conventions, had been careful to balance contests for the two seats with one Anglo and one Hispanic, Mulcock said.

Bernalillo County, as expected, was strong for Chávez in the primary race. He beat Walker there, 12,677–8,762.[5] Counties where Chávez thought he could beat Walker despite Walker's endorsement by county chairmen mostly came through, as Chávez had hoped. Santa Fe County went for Chávez, 5,079–1,815.[6] Among other victories were those in Rio Arriba, 3,388–2,107; in Taos, 2,036–641; in San Miguel, 1,996–1,387; in Socorro, 595–409; in Mora, 482–173; in Guadalupe, 698–393; and in Grant, 2,416–2,295.[7]

Valencia County, which Chávez thought he could win partly because of his long-held ties to state Senator Tibo Chávez, went for Walker, 2,305–2,013.[8] The state's east side also went for Walker, even though Chávez had befriended several state senators from that conservative region. Walker won in Chaves County, 2,319–1,464; in Curry, 2,597–1,396; and in Eddy, 4,964–3,245.[9]

In Lea County, home of Harold Runnels, a frequent Chávez ally in the senate, Walker won 4,950–1,577.[10] In Luna County, home of I. M Smalley, another Chávez ally in the senate, Walker won 790–618.[11]

Chávez carried Los Alamos, home of Sterling Black and Harold Agnew, by more than two to one.[12] Doña Ana County, where many felt threatened by Chávez's push for a medical science school at UNM and which was embarrassed by Chávez's successful fight to reverse discriminatory practices at what would become New Mexico State University, went for Walker by 96 votes out of more than 6,400 cast.[13]

His defeat in Doña Ana might have been his biggest disappointment among counties, Chávez said. "Attorney Dan Sosa had become a powerhouse in Las Cruces, and he went into the preprimary convention with votes for Calvin Horn," said Chávez. "Dan's parents had come from the Mora area. He and I were very active Young Democrats together after World War II, and I had hoped that he would get his people to shift their support to me after Calvin withdrew, but he didn't."

Such disappointments aside, Chávez was confident that he could have won the 1964 Democrat congressional race, a contest that was pivotal in his political career, if U.S. Senators Anderson and Montoya had remained neutral. "If they had just kept their hands off, if they had left the race to me and Johnny Walker alone, I would have won hands down."

Chávez, indeed, displayed commanding strength in Santa Fe County during the 1964 primary that had not been evident in his previous races.[14] As reflected in the vote totals, he also ran impressively in other key counties, including Bernalillo and northern Democratic bastions.[15]

Defeated in the primary, Chávez watched Walker beat Republican Jack Redman by ten thousand votes in that year's November general election.[16] Morris beat Republican Mike Sims by more than seventy-four thousand votes.[17] Montoya defeated Mechem in the U.S. Senate race by nearly thirty thousand votes.[18]

Mulcock was not certain what might have been needed for Chávez to win the 1964 congressional primary race against Walker. He confidently predicted, though, that if Chávez had won in 1964, New Mexico Democrats would have held on to their control of congressional seats in 1968 instead of losing them both following the forced division of New Mexico into two U.S. House districts for the first time. That was when Anderson, Montoya, and other Democrats in control drew congressional boundaries so that Walker would run from the state's southern district and Tom Morris would run from the north, concluding it was the best approach for keeping Walker in Congress.

"If Fabián had won in '64, he would have run from the northern district in 1968, and Morris would have run from the south," said Mulcock, who went to work for Anderson after Walker's defeat in 1968.

"With Fabián in the north and Morris in the south, Fabián Chávez would still be in Congress; Tom Morris would still be in Congress," Mulcock said nearly forty years after the fateful 1968 election. "There would have been no Manual Luján, no Ed Foreman, no Mud Runnels, no Joe Skeen, no Steve Pearce," he said, referring to New Mexicans who have served in Congress since 1968.

The Democrats' drawing of congressional boundaries for 1968 in a manner to protect Walker "was a watershed event in New Mexico politics," Mulcock said.

Indeed, election of Republicans Manuel Luján Jr. and Ed Foreman in 1968 ended New Mexico Democrats' dominance of the state's U.S. House seats dating back to 1930, when Republican Albert G. Simms served in Congress.

Mulcock said that following the 1964 primary against Chávez, Walker made it clear to other party leaders that he did not want to run in a district that would be dominated by Bernalillo County. "Walker would absolutely freeze when he thought of Bernalillo County," Mulcock said. "After 1964, he'd start sweating if he came to campaign in Albuquerque because the 'grass rooters' that had supported Chávez had intimidated him so."

As 1964 concluded, Walker prepared to join Morris in the U.S. House. Montoya moved over from the House to the U.S. Senate. Chávez, allied closely with Gov. Jack Campbell, was out of the state legislature and struggling to determine where he would fit into plans of New Mexico Democrats. The party's most prominent leaders themselves were uncertain what was to become of this complex firebrand who had been embraced enthusiastically by the emerging liberal "grass rooters" as they signaled that they intended to be factors in setting the state's course.

Chávez and the "grass rooters," though, came to learn within months after the 1964 preprimary convention that they would have to pursue their goals without Henry Kiker Jr. Kiker and his wife were killed in an auto accident in Albuquerque, and with the deaths went considerable promise for the Democrats' developing liberal wing in New Mexico.

CHAPTER FIFTEEN

The Governor's Office within Grasp, then Desperation

T. E. "Gene" Lusk of Carlsbad had been out of state government for six years and in 1966 was looking to get back in—in a big way. Son of Georgia Lusk, the first woman to represent New Mexico in Congress, he wanted to be governor. He had defeated former Gov. John Burroughs for the Democratic nomination by more than twenty-eight thousand votes and was paired for the general election with the man who in 1961 succeeded him as senate majority leader, Fabián Chávez Jr.[1]

"It was an interesting pairing because I felt there was a strong rivalry between Fabián and Gene Lusk," said Richard Folmar, the administrator at the Legislative Council Service who worked closely with Chávez on liquor reform proposals. "When Gene spoke, people listened. The first time Gene came in to make a request to me he was very authoritarian. I thought, here's a guy you don't cross."

Lusk and Chávez were matched against the Republican gubernatorial ticket of David Cargo, a two-term state representative from Albuquerque, and E. Lee Francis, who had served in the state house from Valencia County.

Even though he was just a second fiddle in the 1966 campaign, Chávez ran into familiar opposition in the Democratic Party's primary race. "Joe Montoya's fingerprints were all over," Chávez said. "His group got Jack Jones to file for lieutenant governor. Jones owned a Ford dealership in Albuquerque. Every Montoyista that I knew supported Jack Jones. Joe Montoya got Robert McKinney at my hometown paper, the *New Mexican*, to endorse Jones with the argument that New Mexico needed someone who had proven himself to be successful in business. Joe Montoya had made that argument on the stump elsewhere.

"I countered by saying that if to be successful in politics you must first prove to everybody that you are a successful businessman by opening insurance companies and shopping centers, then Senator Montoya is right because I've devoted my time to serving the public. I was referring to Joe Montoya, who owned a shopping center in Santa Fe, and Clinton Anderson, who owned an insurance company in Albuquerque. Both of them built up their businesses while politicians. Their businesses didn't make them successful politicians.

"The *New Mexican* ran its editorial, and I countered with a full-page ad. The paper had written many stories and editorial praises of the work that I had done while taking on the liquor dealers, court reform, capital building construction in Santa Fe. I had copies of all those clippings, and I arranged them within the ad. Down at the bottom I used a term that I stole from a popular gasoline commercial: 'It's performance that counts.' I thought that was a devilishly cute way to respond to their claim that you couldn't get anything done in politics unless you had first been successful in business."

Chávez easily beat Jones in the May primary, 76,609–47,386.[2]

Cargo barely defeated Albuquerque investment broker Clifford Hawley 17,836–16,588 in the Republican primary.[3] Francis was unopposed in the primary.[4]

Francis was little known, but Cargo had begun making a name for himself several years earlier while pressing for a remapping of state legislative districts to promote better representation and improve the chances of minorities getting elected. He also had received attention, like Chávez, for standing up to Pancho Padilla during the much-publicized incident at La Fonda at the end of the liquor reform battle in 1963.

After two consecutive terms, Jack Campbell was leaving as governor. His reviews were mixed, but Democrats still enjoyed an advantage of approximately two to one in voter registration over Republicans statewide.[5] Edwin Mechem, the only New Mexico Republican who had proven himself capable of repeatedly winning a high-profile statewide race in decades, had now been out of office for two years.

The smart money, at least initially, was on the Democrats in the 1966 governor's race, and when it came to money, Democrats had most of it. Cargo said Lusk probably outspent him by more than three to one.

Cargo not only lacked money; as a maverick far more liberal than the established leaders of his party, he was short on support from the state GOP powers.

Still, Cargo had other support that translated into votes on election day. "I had pressed for legislative reapportionment during my first term in the house and that led to the election of minorities who until then couldn't get their foot in the door," Cargo said. "Down in the valley of Albuquerque, Hispanics couldn't win when they had to run at large. All that changed when they could run in their own districts. There wasn't one of them that could have been elected if it hadn't been for me.

"In that 1966 race against Lusk and Fabián, I had all the Hispanic legislators on my side, except one: Ed Delgado of Santa Fe. These were Democrats, but some of them were helping me pretty openly."

Chávez disputed the assertion. In fact, he disputed much of what Cargo said about support he purportedly received behind the scenes from prominent Democrats beginning with the 1966 race for governor and in some cases, carrying over to his reelection bid in 1968. Among prominent political names in dispute: Bruce King, Emilio Naranjo, Filo Sedillo, Edward López, Matias Chacón, Albert Amador, Donaldo "Tiny" Martínez, George Baca, Fermín Pacheco, and S. Q. "Chano" Merino.

Other parties not customarily mentioned in political discussions also figured into Cargo's assertions. "The Catholic Church helped me. Archbishop James Peter Davis and I were very, very close friends. I had a fundraiser at the Hilton in Albuquerque, and the archbishop gave the invocation and the closing prayer. They couldn't formally endorse me, but I got support from the church." If so, it was the same church Chávez believes informally sided with his opponent in his 1960 campaign for the state senate. In addition, according to Cargo, an extension of the group that had helped Chávez's father upset established political leaders in Mora County decades earlier helped Cargo in both of his races for governor. "Los Hermanos Penitentes were big supporters of mine. I'd go to all the moradas and campaign," Cargo said.

Disputes over supporters aside, the Democratic Party in New Mexico undeniably lacked the punch in 1966 that might have been expected based on the party's voter numbers and electoral history. There was an "antiadministration backlash" at both the state and national levels, wrote *Albuquerque Journal* reporter John McMillion. Furthermore, the Democratic gubernatorial campaign that year was "one of the most disorganized in recent history," he wrote.

One prominent Democrat who abandoned his party's top candidates in 1966, according to Cargo, was liquor wholesale giant George Maloof. "George and I used to work out together at the YMCA on First and Central in Albuquerque. He called me into his office one day and said, 'You know, I'm a hard-line Democrat, but I gotta tell you I don't think much of this

Gene Lusk. I can't support him, and I don't support Fabián, either.' He said, 'I'm not going to announce publicly that I'm supporting you, but I'm going to help you out.' Then all of a sudden he calls in his secretary and told her to get all of his regional managers on the speaker phone. Once everyone was connected, George said, 'I've got Dave Cargo in my office. I'm not endorsing him, but when he comes around to your plants, make sure he

~ **FIGURE 21.** ~
Fabián Chávez Jr. (left) with U.S. Senator Edward Kennedy and T. E. "Gene" Lusk during the 1966 New Mexico gubernatorial campaign. Courtesy Fabián Chávez Jr.

The Governor's Office within Grasp, then Desperation ~

gets introduced to all your salesmen. I'm not endorsing him, but I'm voting for him.'"

Cargo said Maloof contributed five hundred dollars to his 1966 campaign.

If Lusk failed to excite Maloof, he had similar problems beyond New Mexico's conservative east side. The Democratic ticket won in Colfax, Curry, Eddy, and Lea counties but battled for splits elsewhere in the state.[6] Lusk and Chávez narrowly won Doña Ana and McKinley counties but lost in Chaves, Lincoln, and Los Alamos counties.[7] Chávez's home base of Santa Fe County went for the Democratic ticket but only by four hundred votes out of more than sixteen thousand recorded.[8]

The big blow for Lusk and Chávez came in Bernalillo County, where the Republican ticket won 50,274–29,431.[9] Bernalillo County is what had kept Chávez's hopes alive in the 1964 primary congressional race. Two years later, though, the county ensured victory for Cargo and Francis in the governor's race that ended in a final statewide tally of 134,625–125,587.[10] Cargo asked that he be sworn into office by Justice David Chávez, the Democrat Fabián Chávez Jr. had enthusiastically supported since the 1940s. "I wanted him to do it because Senator Dennis Chávez and his family had supported me so strongly when I was in the legislature," Cargo said.

Cargo relished his victory in Bernalillo County. "In those days, the liberal grassrooter Democrats, who were all Anglos and up in the heights, were constantly fighting with people in the valley," Cargo said. "You might not think so, but I did fine with Democrats in the valley. They'd have their precinct conventions, and I'd be their speaker."

Chávez had little trouble explaining the Bernalillo County vote of 1966. "The race that year was between the two gubernatorial candidates," Chávez said. "What's a lieutenant governor except someone who is using the position so that he can go on and run for something else? I say that, because I wasn't surprised we lost so badly in Bernalillo County. I wasn't really one of the candidates that people were choosing from. Their choices were Lusk and Cargo."

Lusk came out of the gate in 1966 by angering some of his party's most notable leaders. "Gene came out and publicly attacked people like Harold 'Fats' Leonard, Paul Case, Victor Salazar, and Tom Montoya," Chávez said. "They were recognized political powerhouses, and Gene's plan was to run against them. What happened is that it put these influential men and all the people who followed them to work against Gene like you wouldn't believe."

Cargo recalled that Lusk's controversial approach included labeling men, like those Chávez mentioned, as "the four horsemen of the apocalypse." He kept expanding the list and alternating names to include people like Charlie Davis, Alonzo González, and even John Burroughs, Cargo said.

Veteran Albuquerque television newsman Dick Knipfing said Lusk's approach to the 1966 campaign was not surprising. "Gene was a reformer kind of guy. And he was able to rely on that reputation beginning with the primary that year when he took on John Burroughs, who had the reputation of being an insider kind of guy," Knipfing said.

Maralyn Budke, the longtime legislative aide who had worked for Cargo during his first term, said Salazar, Leonard, and Case, who was an established legislative lobbyist, acted as powerful Democratic insiders to handpick Burroughs as the party's candidate for governor when he was elected in 1958. "Word got around that Paul Case, Victor Salazar, and Fats Leonard sat down and said we need someone who is tall, distinguished looking, gray haired, and a pipe smoker. They looked around and said John Burroughs is our guy," Budke said.

Lusk in 1966 had little trouble getting past Burroughs, the Portales peanut farmer who owned several radio stations. Extraordinary divisions within the Democratic Party led to much of the support that Cargo received from outside the GOP, however, even if Chávez disagreed about some of the names Cargo claimed. Democrats had used the spoils system well, but the outgoing governor also had stirred resentment, Cargo said.

"Jack Campbell had been governor for two terms, and the Democrats had all their county chairmen, all the politicos, on the state payroll," Cargo said. "But Jack didn't get along very well at all with many Hispanics. That included people like Emilio Naranjo in Española, Filo Sedillo in Los Lunas, George Baca in Socorro. Campbell used to bait some of these guys, and some of them didn't like Campbell worth a damn so when I came around, they'd round up votes for me in improbable places." Cargo also had other help while plucking support from within the Democratic Party, particularly among Hispanics. Married to a charismatic Hispanic woman from Belén, Cargo often was greeted with warm welcomes in central and northern New Mexico.

Cargo was able to wrap such support around a simple strategy that proved difficult to beat. "You have to give David Cargo credit because he ran a very smart campaign," Chávez said. "He cultivated this 'Lonesome Dave' image. Gene couldn't buy the publicity that Cargo got for free with that 'Lonesome Dave' thing.

"I'll always remember Cargo walking across a field and crossing a fence to go shake hands with some guy who was working alone in the middle of another field in the distance. The cameras were there, and the image went out around the state for everyone to see."

Chávez said he and Lusk spent very little time together in the 1966 race. "Our relationship was a little strained," Chávez said. "Once in a while we'd be together in a very large gathering if that's what the party wanted us to do. Otherwise, they would split us up. I'd be up in the north talking in English and Spanish while Gene would be working the southern part of the state."

Chávez said he might have had ten thousand dollars to spend on his race for lieutenant governor besides what the Democratic Party contributed to the ticket. "When it came to the media, I did most of my campaigning on the radio. We didn't have to worry much about expensive TV then. TV ads really hadn't stepped forward yet as a prominent force. I was a radio guy, having worked at KTRC in Santa Fe, so I cut spots in English and Spanish. I remember getting help from Ivan Head at rival KVSF. He liked me, so he coached me; he helped me a lot with pronunciation and enunciation so that my Spanish didn't cross over to English."

One time—a critical time—when Lusk and Chávez were both expected to be in the same hall, Lusk nearly did not make it. "Gene was scheduled to debate Cargo at the old Hilton Hotel in downtown Albuquerque, and I was there to watch the debate. All of a sudden, it turned out that Gene got delayed, and we didn't know if he was going to make it or not. I said, 'I'll debate Cargo.' The Republican chairman was M. B. 'Sonny' Johns, a prominent businessman and founder of the popular Bull Ring bar and restaurant in Santa Fe. Sonny Johns said to my offer to debate Cargo, 'Hell you will!'

"Gene finally came in, and Cargo laid into him immediately, criticizing him for several of his votes while in the legislature, including the fact that he had voted against the minimum wage act. Gene spent all his time trying to defend his votes, and that's not the way you debate a guy like Cargo. You have to know going in what he has done or has not done. If he hits, you counterpunch. You never get caught trying to explain yourself. Gene was a lawyer, so I thought he would have been a better debater. You could feel the worm turning against us that day."

Cargo might well have felt fortunate to have had Lusk, not Chávez, as his debate opponent. Cargo had developed respect for Chávez's speaking skills and his ability to get votes that Lusk could not. "That was just the second election since the governor and lieutenant governor candidates were paired to run as a team," Cargo said. "If that election had been run under the old rules where lieutenant governors ran separately, Fabián would have easily beaten Lee Francis. I know Fabián would have been elected lieutenant governor handily under the old system."

Chávez would have smiled upon returning to the state senate as its presiding officer, but he had yet to hit forty-five and, for the long term, still had his eyes set higher than lieutenant governor.

◆ **FIGURE 22.** ◆

Gov. David F. Cargo (center) greets well-wishers following his 1967 inauguration.
At left is the state police chief, Joe Black. Courtesy David F. Cargo.

"I ran for lieutenant governor just to keep my political profile up," Chávez said.

Chávez's profile was plenty high two years later when he told Democrats he wanted to take Cargo on head to head. Although he was the sitting governor, Cargo was seen by many as an anomaly, an incumbent who would have trouble winning a second term. Chávez was not alone in wanting to take advantage of the situation. Five other big-name Democrats filed for the 1968 primary race, hoping for the chance to unseat Cargo.

Chávez had worked alongside most of them and respected them all: former Lt. Gov. Mack Easley of Hobbs; the house speaker, Bruce King, of Stanley; former house speaker Calvin Horn; state Rep. Bobby Mayfield of Mesilla Park; and the former assistant attorney general, Harry Stowers Jr.

"We all had excellent backgrounds, and we considered Cargo to be vulnerable," Chávez said. "We figured Cargo didn't win in 1966; Lusk lost. So we thought it would be easy to knock him off."

Chávez, whose primary political goal was Congress, had watched intently as Democratic Party leaders leading up to 1968 had drawn the north-south boundary for the state's two new U.S. House districts. Having narrowly lost the 1964 congressional primary to E. S. Johnny Walker, Chávez had figured that Walker, whose home at the time was in Santa Fe, would be positioned to run from the state's new northern congressional district in 1968. Chávez was prepared to challenge him in that year's primary if he were. When party chiefs and Walker agreed that he would move to Las Cruces to run from the state's new southern district instead, Chávez opted against challenging ten-year incumbent Tom Morris in the northern district.

Although figuring prominently in speculation about the 1968 Democratic gubernatorial primary, Chávez was the last to announce his candidacy. When he did, he was the lone Hispanic in the crowded field. That, along with his record of appealing to Anglo voters, immediately propelled him to the front of the field. "Insiders see Chavez as politically strong enough to pull as many 'Anglo' votes as any of the five who have announced," wrote Jim Boyer, *Albuquerque Tribune* political editor. "And they see his 'edge' as a huge pile of Spanish-American votes that the five 'Anglo' candidates could not corner."

It all had the state's Democratic Party establishment worried, wrote Paul Wieck in the *Albuquerque Journal*. "It's the kind of thing none of the party's leaders are going to be talking about, publicly," Wieck wrote. "But there are already whispers in Washington 2,000 miles away, of the danger Chavez poses to the party establishment and open discussion of what might be done about it."

Columnist Fred Buckles wrote, "U.S. Sen. Joseph M. Montoya, who bosses state Democratic affairs, does not look with favor on Chavez's candidacy."

One option for the Democratic establishment, wrote Wieck, would be to get at least two more Hispanics—controlled by party bosses—to get into the race; another would be to talk some of the Anglos out of the race.

Lost amid the Anglo candidates or not, Mayfield on filing day sought to stand out from the crowd. A bit of a maverick, like Chávez, press accounts said Mayfield walked into the secretary of state's office and paid his $1,050 filing fee in $1 bills. "I just want to show you that as chairman of the House Taxation and Revenue Committee for six years, I know the value of every dollar," he said for reporters' ears.

Chávez admired the flair of the Doña Ana County lawmaker who just a few years earlier had courageously helped him to secure funding for a basic medical sciences school at the University of New Mexico and propel what both men consider to have been a golden era of legislative accomplishments through the mid-1960s.

If Chávez started out as the favorite in the 1968 Democratic guber-natorial race, he built on his support throughout the contest, playing on his independence as well as on his experience and his willingness to take on entrenched interests. "Experience, accomplishment, courage," became his tag. While working against some of his party's biggest leaders, Chávez turned more than occasionally to the line, "It's people who elect people."

From the start, Chávez said he was beginning his efforts "without cam-paign funds, present or pledged." He promised to stay in the race "even if I have to hitchhike across the state" to meet with voters, the *New Mexican* reported.

As Chávez sought to gain political mileage from his independence and experience, there were already questions about whether New Mexico vot-ers might be tiring of his presence following his 1964 and 1966 statewide races ending in defeat. "One big drawback Chavez has is he's played the same tune for so many years that to those who know him well he is begin-ning to sound a bit like a broken record," wrote the *Albuquerque Journal's* John McMillion.

Despite such opinions, Chávez's record of accomplishments was not as well known in some quarters as he would have liked. "I was campaign-ing on the east side one day when this man stepped up and spit on my face. Others immediately stepped in to separate us if it became necessary. It wasn't. I asked the man, 'What is it that makes you do something like that to me?' He said he didn't like me because I voted against the minimum wage. Somebody had turned things around for him. He didn't know that I had promoted an increase in the minimum wage three times, that I was a champion of the minimum wage. I explained the whole thing to him and later even mailed him a copy of the latest bill. He became a disciple for me after that."

Pancho Padilla, who surprisingly threw his support behind Chávez in his 1964 primary race for Congress, backed Horn in the Democrats' 1968 gubernatorial primary.

"That race involved a bunch of heavyweights, and we ran a very clean campaign," Chávez said. "Odis Echols was master of ceremonies at a rally in Clovis, and I remember saying how lucky we all were to have such dedi-cated, qualified people running for governor. When I was done speaking about my opponents' impressive backgrounds, I'd simply ask people to remember what I had fought for and what I would continue to fight for.

"I'd speak about the need for better highways and how we needed to improve the distribution of funds at the primary and secondary school lev-els. Poorer school districts still weren't getting as much money from the state as richer districts. Because of good staff work, I was able to talk a lot about local issues as I went around the state. But when it was all over, I don't think we candidates were separated by our stands on the issues. I think people just voted for the person that they liked best, and that might have helped me because I was remembered for my David-and-Goliath battles while in the legislature. People looked at my record and saw little Fabián versus the giants."

Giant returns developed for Chávez when primary votes were counted August 27, 1968. Showing the kind of dominance he had never displayed before, Chávez tallied 41,348 votes.[11] Next came King with 24,658 votes; Horn, 24,376; Easley, 21,436; Mayfield, 19,528; and Stowers, 2,543.[12]

Among five candidates in the Democratic race for lieutenant governor, Albuquerque state Senator Michael Alarid narrowly defeated Albuquerque attorney David Kelsey, 31,764–29,584.[13]

"It not only marked the first time in fifty years that there had been a viable Hispanic at the head of the Democratic ticket, it was the first time that two Hispanics made up the ticket," said James "Bud" Mulcock, the former aide to E. S. Johnny Walker and Clinton Anderson.

In the gubernatorial primary, King had publicly predicted that he would easily beat Chávez in Santa Fe County, where they both lived, but Chávez prevailed, 4,042–3,067.[14] Chávez also won convincingly in other northern counties like Rio Arriba, San Miguel, Taos, Los Alamos, Sandoval, and Guadalupe.[15] He was strongest in Bernalillo County, where he collected 14,216 votes.[16] King got closest to Chávez there with 7,568 votes.[17] Chávez came in third to Mayfield and Easley in Chaves County.[18] He was second to Mayfield in Doña Ana County.[19] In central New Mexico, Socorro, Valencia, and McKinley counties joined Bernalillo County in backing Chávez.[20] On the far east side, Chávez went winless, though he got within a hundred votes of Easley in Eddy County.[21] He was trounced in Lea and Curry counties.[22]

King said he got as close in that race as he expected. "We had five Anglos and one Hispanic. I knew when we started that probably the best I would do would be to come in second. Old Fabián was a great legislator and a well-respected statesman. He had a lot of friends and a lot of respect. I don't think any of us ever said a disparaging word about any of the other candidates. After the primary, I guess all of us helped him. I sure did."

Mescalero Apache Pres. Wendell Chino saw success ahead for Chávez. "I am looking forward to working with you during your first term as governor," Chino wrote in a telegram dated August 28, 1968. There were other well-wishers. Clovis senator W. H. Duckworth, a Republican, wrote in an August 29 telegram, "Let me again confirm what I have told you on many occasions: If New Mexico is going to have a Mexican governor, you are my number one choice." Author Paul Horgan wrote in a short note dated

September 26 on letterhead of the Lord Baltimore Hotel in Baltimore, Maryland, "All congratulations—and here's hoping you win."

Mayfield, citing time he spent working alongside Chávez in the legislature, said he concluded Chávez would be a strong general election candidate. "I think back to when Jack Campbell was governor. Jack was aware that some of our state agencies were being denied funding because of the conservative, real conservative, people in control. John Mershon was chairman of the House Appropriations Committee, and he was *the* power as far as money was concerned. He just did not want to part with money. I was chairman of the Taxation and Revenue Committee and a member of the Appropriations Committee, so Campbell and I had several meetings to see if I could agree with him for funding some of these state agencies and institutions. Jack asked me if I could put together a majority in the Appropriations Committee to override John Mershon's iron hand.

"I was able to do it. We got money for institutions of higher learning, including ten million for their first capital outlay fund. And we helped places like the School for the Deaf in Santa Fe, the School for the Blind in Alamogordo, and for what in those days was called the insane asylum in Las Vegas. Conditions there were deplorable, deplorable. When the appropriations bill got out of the house, Fabián took care of it when it arrived in the senate. We passed sizeable increases in state government that were sorely needed."

Chávez rode that kind of reputation into the 1968 general election campaign. He also, however, had to overcome harmful conditions that had developed during the very hours the primary election was concluding and the fall campaign was beginning. "The national Democratic convention was scheduled for Chicago in late August that year, so our state's primary election was scheduled for the same period, August 27," Chávez said. "I was nominated in New Mexico's primary election on the same night that the riots associated with the party's national convention broke out.

"Not only was my nomination overshadowed by national news reports coming out of Chicago, I had only two months to campaign before the general election. David Cargo, as the sitting governor, enjoyed the advantages of incumbency and had been campaigning for reelection throughout his first term.

"It's also important to remember that Democrat Hubert Humphrey came out of that Chicago convention as a crippled nominee largely because of his past support of the Vietnam War and because of the tremendous negative publicity associated with the national convention."

Cargo turned to the legions of Democratic Party members who had supported him in 1966, including George Maloof, who helped Cargo openly in

꘏ **FIGURE 23.** ꘏

Fabián Chávez Jr. (left) campaigns with Robert F. Kennedy in 1968 just weeks
before Kennedy was assassinated in Los Angeles. Courtesy Fabián Chávez Jr.

1968. "George Maloof organized a fund-raiser in Albuquerque for Cargo in
his race against me," Chávez said. "But by then, two of the other big wholesalers, Richard Zanotti and Louis Hymel, had gotten beyond our differences
over liquor reform and not only supported me but contributed to my campaign. The liquor industry was not as organized against me. They were all
split up at that time."

Beyond Maloof, Cargo retained other help from within the Democratic
Party but not as much as he had enjoyed when he upset Lusk two years
earlier. In heavily Democratic San Miguel County, Cargo claimed to have
the support of the county's party leaders in 1968, including that of emerging boss Donaldo "Tiny" Martínez, even though it was Chávez who was
praised in a letter of endorsement from Martínez a week before the primary election.

In his letter dated August 20, 1968, Martínez wrote in Spanish and spoke
of Chávez's experience, intelligence, and knowledge of the state's needs. He

also said Chávez had the best chance of winning Bernalillo County as well as the majority of the state's Hispanic voters.

Martínez's letter, going out just before the primary election, might have been intended only to influence the crowded Democratic Party race for governor. It could have been meant to help ensure that Democrats nominated someone acceptable to Martínez and his followers just in case Cargo faltered in the general election. "I don't doubt that Tiny supported Fabián in the primary," Cargo said. "A lot of people liked Fabián, but a lot of people switched to me in the general election. I was at a meeting in Mama Lucy's restaurant in Las Vegas during the campaign for the general election where Mama Lucy and Tiny both spoke for me."

Chávez remained convinced that he had Martínez's support throughout. One critical example of how Chávez rode support in the 1968 primary that later went for Cargo was evident, however, in Silver City. "Going back to 1966 we told David Cargo that we couldn't support him because we didn't support Republicans," said S. Q. "Chano" Merino, who was president

⚞ **FIGURE 24.** ⚟

Fabián Chávez Jr. (left) campaigns with Hubert H. Humphrey in 1968. Courtesy Fabián Chávez Jr. MILO Photographer; Recorder no. 2188–71. Santa Fe, NM.

The Governor's Office within Grasp, then Desperation ☞ 225

of Local 890 of the United Steel Workers of America in Silver City at the time. "But then in 1967 workers of the copper industry went on strike in New Mexico and surrounding states. We shut down the copper industry, but our workers were hurting.

"I called Governor Cargo and said we needed help. He said, 'I'll be right there.' He came down to the union hall, and he declared Grant County a disaster area. Our members became eligible for commodities and other help. And of all the governors in states where we were on strike, Cargo was the only one who opposed President Johnson when he wanted to invoke a cooling off period through Taft-Hartley.

"Fabián Chávez was a very close friend of mine, and he was a labor kind of guy," Merino said. "He had always supported labor in the legislature, but I told him we were going to support David Cargo [in 1968] because of what he did for us during the strike. He said he understood, but he asked that we support him during the primary. We did, but then in the general election we endorsed Cargo and got money for him from our international steel workers union."

Without question, lines of support in politics can get crossed and entangled. In that atmosphere, King said Cargo had a knack for claiming support where little or none existed. "He came up to the ranch to visit one day during the [general election] campaign, and he put up Cargo signs on posts all the way up to the house," King said. "I don't think the signs stayed up too good. Anyway, I visited with him and gave him a cup of coffee."

Cargo recalled having a meal and a pleasant conversation, not just coffee, with King that day. He also speculated that he won at least a little favor with King.

Cargo, no doubt, had a way of making life interesting. "Dave would go up to the Indian reservations and put up signs and then go out and get the press and tell them, 'The Indians are all behind me.' Dave did those kinds of things, but he was also a better politician than we sometimes thought," King said.

Maybe so, but there were those who considered Chávez to be far better prepared to serve as governor. "Dave Cargo couldn't carry Fabián's briefcase when it came to knowing state government, its structure, its operations, its functions," Mayfield said.

Cargo, himself, acknowledged feeling more than a bit lost when he was first elected governor and said he promptly turned to a government insider who was a widely respected authority on finances. "I asked Franklin Jones to come in and help. He said, 'You know, I'm a Democrat, and I didn't vote for you.' I said, 'That's okay. I don't know a thing about being governor.'"

It was different with Chávez. Ever since he was a young man, Chávez was determined to make government work for people, King said. "Our dads were very good friends. Fabián always used to say we were the crew of '24. That's the year we were born. He said people elected us because they were good friends of our dads, and now it was up to us to do something."

Richard Folmar, the former administrator with the Legislative Council Service, said Chávez knew enough about systems and people to get things done when others could not. "He could read a legislative body like a book. He would do favors for people. He would not gratuitously embarrass another legislator. A lot of times he backed off just to avoid embarrassing anyone. Outside the Capitol, he really knew the people of this state."

Maurice Trimmer, who was a ranking aide to Gov. Jack Campbell after having worked for years as a reporter for United Press International, said he thought voters had distinct options for governor in the 1968 election. "Compared to Cargo, well, Cargo is a great guy, but Fabián had all this experience and as far as I know there was no black mark on his record other than his encounter with Pancho Padilla—and that wasn't a black mark."

Because of the fatal car wreck in Albuquerque two years earlier, Henry Kiker Jr. was no longer around to help Chávez in Bernalillo County in 1968. Chávez continued leaning on people like Bert and Imogene Lindsay and a relatively new friend, a former military veteran like Chávez who had turned sour on what the military was doing in the 1960s.

"I met Fabián in the early '60s. A group of us organized to oppose the Vietnam War," said Edward Romero, who at the time was a regional manager for a direct-sales company based in California. He would go on to become Bernalillo County Democratic Party chairman, one of New Mexico's most successful businessmen, and U.S. ambassador to Spain. "At the time that we formed the group, it was really considered unpatriotic to oppose the war.

"Those of us who were veterans, well, we thought nobody would question us, especially those of us who had been through wars," said Romero, a veteran of the Korean War. "No one could question our patriotism. Speaking out against the unjust war was a manifestation of our patriotism."

Chávez, with five battle stars from World War II and the recollection of having lied about his age to enlist in the army, felt that his patriotism was beyond reproach.

"Fabián was already majority leader in the senate, and he was making a hell of a mark on the state," Romero said. "He was obviously the shining star in the New Mexico political landscape. He came to our veterans' meetings. I didn't know him well, but I knew about him from various friends."

Romero, like so many others, had been impressed by Chávez's high-profile battles against the JPs and what Romero called "the liquor mafia." Along with the reputation he developed as a successful legislator, Chávez had also added to his political stature while serving along with former

Gov. John Miles as cochair of John F. Kennedy's 1960 U.S. presidential campaign in New Mexico.

"Fabián's position and his capacity to lead were very, very noticeable and very frightening to the entrenched political system at the time," Romero said. He said U.S. Senators Clinton Anderson and Joseph M. Montoya considered Chávez a political threat not only to entrenched political constituencies they purportedly supported but also "in terms of their own political careers.

"So they decided to get rid of him," Romero said. "In those days, the two very prominent benefits of politics were not only your power, but also patronage, the spoils system. I think these two men were very reluctant to share that patronage system or have it disrupted. You talk about control. They controlled the political nature of this state, and they certainly didn't need anybody else with any amount of power, and not only power, but courage. Fabián had courage, and he was very capable of going toe to toe with them on issues that they supported and he didn't.

"I was impressed by all of that."

Chávez and Romero had grown close by the late 1960s, and Chávez asked Romero to work as his treasurer in the campaign against Cargo.

⇜ **FIGURE 25.** ⇝

U.S. Senator Clinton P. Anderson (center) in a meeting with unidentified companions. Courtesy Palace of the Governors (MNM/DCA), negative no. 030433.

⊰ **FIGURE 26.** *⊱*

Joseph M. Montoya (left) casts his ballot in 1964 while running for the U.S. Senate.
Courtesy Palace of the Governors (MNM/DCA), negative no. 030271.

Romero said many Democratic county chairmen and precinct chairmen, those aligned with Anderson and Montoya, opposed Chávez in 1968.
Associates of the two senators cut off political contributions from those
they could influence, he said.

"It was all based on, here is an intruder, a very knowledgeable intruder,
a very savvy intruder that was a threat to their power. They did not want
to share their power base," Romero said of Anderson and Montoya. "All
their people were out there bad-mouthing Fabián. Among voters, he had
everybody's imagination. Those more issue-oriented people were more
impressed with Fabián than with anybody else."

Romero said it was his impression that Anderson and Montoya would
rather share limited power with an isolated Republican than with a member of their own party who might pose a serious, long-term threat. Cargo
did not appear to be nearly as threatening.

Maralyn Budke, who had worked as executive secretary of the state
Legislative Finance Committee for two years before Cargo's first term
as governor in 1967, found herself working for Cargo soon after his first

legislative session as governor. The LFC staff were technically employees of the Legislative Council Service assigned part time to the LFC.

Since its creation, the Council Service was expected by legislators to be politically nonpartisan. Budke, however, who later became allied with conservative Democratic legislators John Mershon and Aubrey Dunn, wrote a letter while LFC executive secretary that was sharply critical of some fiscal findings advanced by influential Rep. Bobby Mayfield and others. She called some of the findings "a comedy of errors."

"It did not endear me to Mayfield, and some folks knew I wasn't going to survive at the LFC once he became chairman," Budke said. "Meanwhile, some people had convinced Cargo that he needed someone to straighten up the governor's office in 1967. It already had become clear after Governor Cargo's first legislative session that there was no organization in his administration. The governor called me up for an interview and said, 'You're a registered Democrat?' I said, 'No, sir.' He said, 'You're an Independent?' I said, 'No, sir.' I said I was a registered Republican. Cargo slammed his hand on the desk and said, 'Oh, my God, the party is going to think I did something right.'"

Budke is widely credited for keeping Cargo's office operations relatively stable amid the governor's largely undisciplined approach to his work. "For all practical purposes, she was assistant governor," Chávez said.

It was not easy, according to Budke. "Man, it was a tough job," she said. "David would tell the press what he was going to do before he would tell the staff. I would come into the office every morning and read the papers to see what our policy position was going to be on something."

Budke said she would go through newspapers each day looking for stories that might upset him. "Later, if he found some small item on Section D, it could set him off."

Budke said *Albuquerque Journal* reporter Wayne Scott told her during the 1968 general election campaign that his paper was considering endorsing Cargo but only if Budke and the finance director, Ed Hartman, agreed to stay on for a second term. "I said no. I would leave the day after the election."

The *Journal* on October 27 endorsed Chávez, citing his work to reform the state's court system and his efforts "in bringing the liquor lobby to its knees." It called Chávez compassionate, a good administrator, and capable of uniting "the three cultures of this state." Cargo, the paper suggested, had spent his first term campaigning for a second. "Gov. David Cargo . . . had his chance, and muffed it."

No matter who scored the victory, Budke knew what she would do after the votes were counted. "The day after the election, I announced my resignation and went back to the LFC, where I was hired as director," she said.

Cargo dismissed the *Journal*'s stand. "The *Journal* had given me a fit. It was vehemently opposed to me," said Cargo, who was thirty-nine at the time. "The *Journal* almost never hired Hispanics in those days and, of course, they thought I was too pro-Hispanic so they really got after me. They thought my wife, Ida Jo, was a member of Reies Tijerina's Alianza. Despite their record, they endorsed a Hispanic because they thought I was worse."

The *Albuquerque Tribune*, the only daily newspaper to endorse Cargo in 1966, endorsed Chávez in 1968 in a front-page editorial that ran even before the *Journal*'s. The *Tribune*'s editorial of September 20 said Cargo "has been quick to jump into situations where he thought he could take advantage of discontent and make political hay." It said Cargo "thrives on trouble" and described Chávez as the candidate "most likely to pull us together in unity, not tear us apart in bickering and bitterness."

Thriving on trouble or not, Cargo did not seem overly concerned about creating it, particularly in his discussions of politics and political allies. Years after his service as governor, Cargo pointed to King's close association with U.S. Senator Clinton Anderson and suggested that King did little if anything to help Chávez in the 1968 race despite their long friendship. "Bruce just didn't support Fabián," said Cargo, who speculated that King quietly backed him. "Well, it kind of looks that way. I think Bruce was kind of favorable," he said.

Cargo beat Chávez, 54–44, in King's Stanley precinct in the 1968 general election.[23] King collected all 71 votes cast in that precinct in the 1968 Democrat primary race for governor.[24] Back in the 1966 Democratic primary race for lieutenant governor, Chávez beat Jack Jones 36–23 in Stanley.[25] Stanley favored Lusk and Chávez over Cargo and Francis 56–44 in the 1966 general election race for governor.[26]

Chávez said he did not know how much help he got from King in Stanley and beyond during the 1968 general election race for governor. Chávez ally Ed Romero said it was easy to read too much from election day numbers recorded in Stanley. After anyone's efforts, people in Stanley might simply have preferred Cargo over Chávez, Romero said. "Bruce paid a lot of attention to Clinton P. Anderson, but Bruce was his own man. I really do not remember and can't say what he did or didn't do when it came to Fabián in 1968," Romero said.

Indeed, one did not have to look far to find evidence of Cargo's popularity. Precincts 3-A and 3-B along Chávez's own Acequia Madre in Santa Fe gave him only modest margins over Cargo in the 1968 general election[27] after having given Chávez substantial victories in that year's Democratic primary.[28] In the general election, Chávez and Alarid beat Cargo and

Francis 253–214 in precinct 3-A.[29] Chávez and Alarid won in precinct 3-B, 303–206.[30] King was Chávez's closest competitor in precincts 3-A and 3-B in that year's Democratic primary. Chávez beat King 112–44 in precinct 3-A; it was 142–45 in precinct 3-B.[31]

"Fabián had a problem with a lot of ranking members of his own party. I think he turned a lot of them off," Cargo said. "Fabián did a lot of show-boating. It was kind of his way of doing things. He was still in the primary, and he kept challenging me to debate him. He kept saying, 'The governor is afraid to debate me.' Finally, I said, 'Number one, he first has to be nominated. Two, if he's so damned anxious to debate, maybe he could get some of our families to debate.' Some reporter asked, 'Are you suggesting that your wives debate?' I said, 'Yeah, my wife will debate his wife in Spanish.' Fabián didn't quite know what to do with that, but I never should have said it. That's one time that I should have kept quiet."

With the remark, Cargo was calling attention to his Hispanic wife and to Chávez's Anglo wife. Chávez remembered it as racist. Others said it was stupid, at least. "I think it was crude. It was a terrible thing to say," said former U.S. Rep. Tom Morris.

⇥ **FIGURE 27.** ⇤
Fabián Chávez Jr. (left) with wife, Coral Jeanne, and brother, Fray Angélico,
during the 1968 governor's campaign. Courtesy Fabián Chávez Jr.
Don W. Eicher & Associates. Albuquerque, NM.

Chávez said more than a few Democrats who were still sour on him as recently as 1966 had changed their opinions by 1968. "By then, the state supreme court had found that I was right in what I argued during the liquor reform battle, and some of the sting from the JP battle was going away," Chávez said. "There's no question that a lot of liquor dealers and old JPs supported Cargo, but some of them had begun coming back to me."

While Cargo enjoyed substantial support from within the Democratic Party, he had to overcome opposition he faced from within his own party. "Rex Mattingly was the state Republican chair at the time, and he thought I was some kind of left-winger. He supported Fabián." Cargo said there were other conservatives who were convinced he was going to run the state into the ground. "The old Republican guard fought me. I think Fabián got some of that vote, that's for sure," he said. Chávez said that along with Mattingly, M. B. "Sonny" Johns turned against Cargo. It was in Johns's Santa Fe home where Cargo was sworn into office for his first term as governor.

Still, Chávez faced bigger hurdles, Cargo said, alluding to the state's Democratic congressional delegation. "When you have both U.S. senators supporting the other candidate, you've got a problem," Cargo said.

"It was kind of an odd-ball exchange," he said of how he and Chávez were able to draw support from ranking members of their opposing political parties and, apparently, from the same people once in a while. "Tom Bolack gave money to my campaign," Chávez said of the former Republican lieutenant governor whom he tutored and protected from partisan assaults on the floor of the state senate.

Cargo, though, claimed to have a deeply rooted friendship with Bolack. "Tom used to say that he was quite fond of Fabián, but Tom and I were very close for many, many years right up until he died. We'd go fishing to places like Costa Rica."

Cargo claimed other big political fish as friends as well, his comments tracking with Ed Romero's evaluation of the 1968 political scene. "I think Clinton Anderson and I got along pretty well. He wasn't particularly fond of Fabián. He really wasn't. He took me to a Rotary Club meeting at the Hilton Hotel in Albuquerque one day and said, 'I've got Governor Cargo here with me, and I think he's going to get reelected.' Everybody just looked.

"Joe Montoya just didn't like Fabián. I never really could figure it out. I suppose some of it had to do with liquor. Joe Montoya was pretty closely tied to the liquor people . . . And those JPs had to be 99 percent Democrats, and a lot of them were Hispanic. Fabián didn't make any friends there. Oddly enough, I favored liquor law reform, too, but the liquor people never voted against me. I had favored changing the justice of the peace system, but they didn't blame me. They were after Fabián, and they didn't care how I voted."

Cargo acknowledged that his relations with Anderson probably were boosted by a large contract Cargo had awarded during his first term to the influential senator's insurance company. "The contract was to provide insurance through the state workers' compensation program for all of the agencies," Cargo said. "I awarded the bid to his company, and Clint called and said, 'You know, you don't have to give it to me. You can give it to any of the top three bidders' . . . Later we had lunch at La Fonda. He asked, 'Are you asking anything in return for it?' I said, 'Not a thing, senator.' He later asked if he could be associated with Manuel Luján Sr.'s insurance company to do some of the servicing because Luján's company was in Santa Fe. So he did."

Although some of Cargo's claims of support from within the Democratic Party are open to dispute, others are acknowledged, even by Chávez. Both Cargo and Chávez agreed that the Santa Fe County Democratic Party chairman and Santa Fe mayor, George Gonzales, backed Cargo. "Johnny Vigil and his people had this meeting of the county central committee on the Sunday prior to the election," Cargo said. "Johnny invited me to come and speak. During the meeting, Victor Salazar and Alonzo Gonzales came in, and they were running the state campaign pretty much for the Democratic Party. They came in with all the money for these Democratic precinct workers. They had stacks of dollar bills so it looked like there were many thousands of dollars on the table. Johnny Vigil had given me a pitch, and Mayor George Gonzales spoke on my behalf, but after I got up and said the things I did, all these people got up kind of mad and started leaving the room. Johnny Vigil had to shout at them, 'Come back, come back. You forgot the money!'

"And then there were the Young Democrats who held their convention in Albuquerque. David Branch had been state chair of the Young Democrats, and he invited me to come speak at the convention. They quietly endorsed me. They didn't say anything in the press, but they quietly endorsed me and worked for me."

Then there was the issue of an all-Hispanic ticket. Two Hispanics on the Democratic ticket cut both ways in terms of public support. "Joe Montoya called it the tortilla ticket," said Cargo. Poll results suggest it helped in the north, where Cargo himself had developed considerable support through frequent visits and more than a little patronage. "Dave Norvell and Bruce King had this news conference and said all you have to do to get a job with Cargo is be from northern New Mexico and be Hispanic," recalled Cargo.

The all-Hispanic ticket hurt Democrats elsewhere. "You know, the east side just wasn't ready for it," said James "Bud" Mulcock.

Such prejudice was not limited to any one region of the state. "Some of the resentment that Fabián came upon [among Hispanics] was because he was married to an Anglo," said Ed Romero.

Cargo came to New Mexico before his thirtieth birthday and promptly looked to settle into the state's Republican Party. "I got a bachelor's degree from the University of Michigan and got a master's degree in public administration," Cargo said. "I then went into the military service during the Korean War and as a result lived in Germany a couple of years. I later went to the University of Michigan Law School. When I came to New Mexico, the only three people that I knew were Dennis Chávez, Ed Mechem, and Harry Robins, who had been the Republican state chairman in New Mexico.

"I'd only been here about six weeks, and I got elected state chair of the Young Republicans. It was at the Hilton Hotel, and there were only seven people at the convention. I looked around the room, and there was nobody else around."

Cargo immediately had a platform from which to begin launching the eminently quotable one-liners and other quips for which he would become known in and out of political circles throughout New Mexico.

"Running against Cargo in 1968 was like running against a stand-up comedian. He liked the one-liners, but you couldn't pin him down on issues," Chávez said. "He was not what I would call a formidable candidate. I was running on the issues, but he wasn't, so how are voters going to be able to get an issue-oriented campaign?"

Cargo said he did not dodge issues but simply used his own attention-grabbing approach while addressing them. One example of that approach came while he and Chávez addressed the issue of taxes in Lovington. Cargo, according to the *Albuquerque Tribune*, accused Democrats of professing their support for low-income residents only to tax them once in office. Referring to Democrat Jack Campbell's first term as governor beginning in 1963, Cargo said, "That old party of the people, God bless them, raised taxes on beer and left it alone on Scotch."

"This brought loud laughter from the throng," reported the *Tribune*'s Jim Boyer.

If Cargo was quick with the quips, however, he, like Chávez, had made a name for himself while addressing serious issues in committee rooms and halls of government. "At times in the past, both Gov. David Cargo and Fabián Chávez stood virtually alone as they persisted in their efforts to bring important functions of state government out of an archaic, status quo situation into the mainstream of current affairs," Associated Press reporter Bill Feather wrote as the 1968 campaign began.

Feather specifically credited Cargo for calling upon the state legislature to reapportion its own districts in the early 1960s and then successfully taking the issue to court when the legislature refused. Cargo's work on reapportionment did not endear him to leaders of his own party, but it did win him favor with minority groups, "particularly the Spanish and Indian citizens of New Mexico who found a new political authority in reapportionment," Feather wrote.

Referring to Chávez's battles against the state's liquor industry and the old JP system, Feather said Chávez "appeared at one time to be tilting with two windmills and blaspheming the sanctity of two holy cows."

Both Cargo and Chávez seemed to enjoy arguing their cases "flamboyantly through newspaper headlines," wrote Sydney Schanberg in the *New York Times*. "Both are articulate and both love a verbal scrap."

Schanberg wrote that the race "turns almost entirely on the personalities and reputations of the two men and on local issues." When addressed amid personal attacks and disputes over each man's record, some of those local issues included road repairs, education funding, college tuition rates, gun control laws, and expansion of gubernatorial terms from two years to four.

Even when sharp differences separated the two candidates on issues, as did their positions on gun control (Chávez favored national regulation over allowing each state to pass its own legislation; Cargo opposed national gun legislation), it was the personal tension and accusations hurled between the two men that caught lasting attention. "Democratic gubernatorial challenger Fabián Chávez and Gov. David Cargo indulged in their own version of a 'barroom brawl' Friday, each accusing the other of representing the liquor industry," the *Albuquerque Journal* reported two weeks before the election.

Chávez spent considerable time working to make Cargo appear reckless. Chávez, Boyer reported, told an assembly in Gallup that Cargo's first two years as governor had left New Mexico "in a state of confusion that is incomparable to any period in the history of the state . . . Gov. Cargo insults legislators and others because he thinks it is cute. Cargo does not have the ability to get along with legislators to get anything done."

Chávez and Cargo engaged in one televised debate during the campaign. "Channel 7 had us on for an hour toward the end of the campaign," Chávez said. "But I don't think that debate won or lost either one of us a single vote. It wasn't like the debate that Cargo had had with Gene Lusk in 1966 when Lusk seemed to be stuck on the defensive."

Chávez often made his way around the state during the 1968 campaign in a Plymouth loaned to him by the same Santa Fe dealership that had loaned a car to his opponent, E. S. Johnny Walker, in the 1964 primary race for Congress. "Tom Old was a partner in the Hancock-Old dealership, and he liked what I did with liquor reform and the JPs. I never asked him if he was Democrat or Republican. I knew he was a very strong supporter of the National Rifle Association."

Incumbency allowed Cargo to get around pretty much at will, and as he did, political newcomer Manuel Luján Jr. at times was not far behind. Son of a former Santa Fe mayor and one-time Republican gubernatorial candidate, Luján had handily defeated five other men in the 1968 GOP primary for the right to challenge Democratic incumbent Tom Morris for the state's new northern district congressional seat. "I was carrying Manuel Luján. I was taking him all over those northern counties," Cargo said.

Although Chávez considered those same northern counties to be his base, he might have lost support there while trying to win favor elsewhere. "Once I won the primary nomination, it was logical to get an Anglo from the east side, where I was going to need some help, to be my campaign chairman. So I asked Penrod Toles, a former state senator from Roswell, to run the campaign."

Toles, who had served one term in the state senate, said years later that Chávez was wise to reach for help in the east side "I think Fabián's reasoning was exactly right. Whether or not it had a big effect, I don't know," he said.

Toles said that less than a hundred thousand dollars was spent on Chávez's campaign against Cargo because that was what Chávez wanted. "It was at the insistence of Fabián himself. His decision was that we weren't going to throw money at the campaign. We had the most economical race for governor ever up to that time."

True to his character, Chávez might well have wanted to be frugal, but his 1968 campaign treasurer, Ed Romero, said the Democratic team found it hard to raise money. "We were selling Coca-Cola bottles. We were having enchilada dinners at a dollar a plate. Big contributions just didn't come in."

Toles was a conservative who came to Chávez's campaign with at least a little baggage. Senator Joseph M. Montoya personally phoned Chávez to express opposition to Toles, according to Chávez. "He asked me to get rid of him," Chávez said. Toles drew other fire as well. "Toles is flagrantly anti-Spanish," Cargo told Jim Boyer of the *Albuquerque Tribune*. "Toles drew up a weird plan for districting Chaves County only to keep the Spanish-Americans out of the Legislature."

Toles said Cargo was wrong in his evaluation and was simply looking to wound the opposition. Still, he acknowledged, ethnicity might have been an important element in the 1968 campaign. "There were two Hispanics on the Democratic ticket for the first time, and some people tried to make something of it in the southern and eastern parts of the state," he said. "The state wanted a change after Cargo's first term, but whether it wanted a change in the way of Chávez and Alarid, I just don't know. Fabián was an excellent candidate, and Mike Alarid was, too. Both were extremely knowledgeable and well spoken. But the uniqueness of two Hispanics on the ticket might have had something to do with how the election turned out in some parts of the state."

Cargo fanned ethnic tensions more than once, at times intentionally injecting his twenty-seven-year-old wife's Hispanic background into discussions, Toles said. "He was accusing me of prejudice and said something like, 'I sure wouldn't want my wife running into Senator Toles in a dark ally.' The next time I saw him he put his arms over his face like he thought I was going to hit him because of what he had said," Toles said.

Remarks with racial overtones were not unusual at all during the campaign. Nor were they left out of news reports. "One reason Mr. Chavez is considered the underdog is the heavily Spanish make-up of his Democratic slate in a state whose population is nearly 70 percent Anglo," Sydney Schanberg wrote in the *New York Times*. "The southeastern corner of the state . . . is regarded as right wing and anti-Spanish . . . and almost invariably votes for a conservative over a liberal and for an Anglo over a Spanish-American."

Cargo years later noted that Democratic U.S. Senator Joseph M. Montoya himself called attention to the ethnic issue in a way that could have fueled anti-Hispanic feelings in regions of the state. "He did it by talking about 'the tortilla ticket,'" Cargo said.

Ed Romero said that particular reference to the Chávez-Alarid team by itself likely did not affect the outcome of the race one way or another. "Fabián didn't lose because of the 'tortilla ticket,' he lost because Joe Montoya didn't support the 'tortilla ticket' and other leaders of the party didn't support the 'tortilla ticket.' The big guys, like Joe Montoya and Clinton P. Anderson, would show up at party functions and talk about the Democratic Party, but all their lieutenants, their right-hand guys, their staff members, their family members would be working against us . . . Clinton Anderson did a lot for New Mexico. Joe Montoya did a lot for New Mexico. But they were concerned about Fabián's continued rise in politics and about diluting their own influence."

Another big-name Democrat also hurt the Chávez-Alarid team in New Mexico, albeit unintentionally. Hubert Humphrey was running for president and was soundly defeated by Republican Richard Nixon in New Mexico.[32] "He dragged other Democrats in the state down," said James "Bud" Mulcock, who was working to get E. S. Johnny Walker reelected to Congress.

"I knew the governor's race was real close going into the election, but I really thought we were going to win," said Toles.

Nixon beat Humphrey by nearly forty thousand votes in New Mexico.[33] Toles and other Democrats with their eyes on election night numbers saw their totals stay well below what they expected.

Cargo and Francis defeated Chávez and Alarid 160,140–157,230.[34] The tiny margin of 2,910 was built as late results came in from Albuquerque's northeast heights, which gave a solid majority to Nixon and other Republicans, Chávez said.

"I lost the election because of Nixon's coattails," Chávez said. "I think it's historically unfair to blame my running mate because he was Hispanic like me. You can't blame my running mate. You can't blame me and say I was a bad campaigner. You can't blame the lack of money. You can't blame the north side, the east side, or anything like that. I lost the governor's race by less than three thousand votes because Hubert Humphrey lost New Mexico by forty thousand votes."

Despite support from the liberal "grassroots" Democrats, Chávez lost Bernalillo County, 50,801–49,570.[35] Cargo was glad for the win in his home county, even though the margin was far below his spread of more than 20,000 votes in his 1966 race against Lusk.[36]

Chávez in 1968 won his home county of Santa Fe, 10,427–8,788.[37]

Doña Ana went for Chávez.[38] Among other counties that went his way were Grant, Hidalgo, McKinley, Otero, Sandoval, Socorro, and Valencia.[39]

Most of New Mexico's eastern counties went for Cargo but not by the large margins that Chávez anticipated when the race began, except maybe in Chaves County, home of Penrod Toles. The county favored Cargo, 8,089–5,385.[40] Cargo won in Curry, 5,291–4,388; in Eddy, 7,589–6,921; in Lea, 7,383–7,114; in Lincoln, 1,641–1,379; and in Quay, 2,158–1,766.[41]

Los Alamos favored Cargo, 3,386–2,856.[42]

Chávez and Cargo fought personal battles in Valencia County, which was home to Cargo's wife as well as to longtime Chávez allies. They did so as well in Mora, where Chávez's parents made their home for years; in San Miguel, where Chávez and Cargo both claimed support from Donaldo "Tiny" Martínez and other Democratic Party bosses; and in Rio Arriba, where Cargo cultivated many friendships despite a well-oiled Democratic machine.

"Cargo says he had support from Filo Sedillo in Valencia County, and he'd refer to his wife a lot in Valencia County because that's where she was from," Chávez said years after the election. "But Filo Sedillo helped organize one of the biggest rallies ever in Los Lunas with me as the main speaker. I knew that Cargo had used his wife, Ida Jo, to try to win Valencia

County when he ran against Lusk, and he succeeded. I spoke at that rally in 1968, and I opened my remarks by saying, 'I wonder what my grandfather, Eugenio Chávez from Jarales, would say if he were alive to see his grandson running for governor of the state of New Mexico.' I knew that scored a lot of points."

Cargo had his own stories, like this one, about battleground counties in his race against Chávez: "Democrats had an office on the plaza in Las Vegas, and there was this sign on the window that said, 'Vote straight Democrat.' There was a smaller sign below it that said, 'Re-elect Gov. Cargo.'"

Chávez claimed Valencia County, 6,336–5,381, and Rio Arriba County, 4,948–3,816.[43] Cargo won San Miguel County, 4,140–4,066, and Mora County, 1,189–1,053.[44]

Cargo said it was not always his stands on policies that led to support that he built during his first term in office. "I entertained all the Democratic Party officials at the Governor's Mansion. Dennis Chávez's widow used to come and stay in the mansion all the time. I remember Lorella Salazar, Joe Montoya's sister, said that in all the years she had been active in politics, she had never been in the Governor's Mansion. Filo Sedillo said, 'I've elected Democratic governors, and I've never been to the mansion.'"

Cargo said he made an open invitation to a party at the mansion once while speaking at a Democratic Party assembly in Santa Fe. "I got up and said, 'Mayor George Gonzales and I are going to put up a bash at the Governor's Mansion tomorrow.' I said, 'Anybody who wants to bring some food, go ahead and bring it. We'll have a little music, and if you want to bring some beer, bring it and we'll provide the ice.' We got a very good turnout."

Indeed, Cargo might have been better than Chávez at connecting one-on-one with rank-and-file voters of both parties, even though it was rank-and-file voters who benefited from much of Chávez's work. Evidence of that perception was seen one day in the early 1980s while Chávez worked hallways of the Capitol as a lobbyist for Gov. Toney Anaya. Nearby, over-looking the Rotunda, an executive assistant to Anaya visited with a Capitol carpenter. As Chávez approached, the carpenter told Anaya's aide in Span-ish, "Here comes Fabián. I bet he'll talk to you, but he'll ignore me com-pletely." Chávez stopped to visit briefly, and the carpenter was right: He was not acknowledged. "That's why Fabián lost to Cargo," the carpenter said later. "Cargo talked to everybody." But even if such conclusions were true, Chávez insisted that too many people overanalyzed his 1968 defeat. "If Hubert Humphrey had been kind enough to lose by thirty thousand votes instead of forty thousand votes, I would have been elected governor that night," Chávez said.

Maralyn Budke lent support to that argument. "Fabián came close to being governor, but he was running against an incumbent in what was a strong year for Republicans," Budke said. She suggested Chávez had what people look for in their governors. "He's smart, quick, articulate, strategic. He plans beyond the end of that large nose of his."

U.S. Reps. Tom Morris and E. S. Johnny Walker both were defeated by upstart Republicans in 1968. "The Democratic Party was in such disarray that year," Morris said. "Too many Democrats in New Mexico at that time were taking care of number one. Fabián worked hard, and he's very bright. He's really a brighter guy than Clinton Anderson and some of the other people."

On many occasions after the 1968 election, Chávez told of walking into a small gathering at La Fonda's bar where Filo Sedillo pointed to Chávez and told others, "Here comes Damn-Near Governor."

Damn-near was not close enough, however, and Chávez was stung especially hard by his defeat to Cargo even though his primary goal in politics was not to serve as governor. "The only reason I ran for lieutenant governor in 1966 and then for governor, frankly, was to have a platform from which to run for the U.S. Senate," he said. "My long-term goal, if things fell just right, was to get to the U.S. Senate like Dennis Chávez. But I knew that on my way to the Senate, I would have been a very good, progressive governor."

Chávez had little time to lick his wounds following the 1968 defeat before he and other politicians began looking at options available in 1970. "All things considered, I probably should have run again for governor," Chávez said. "I had beaten a very strong field of Democrats in the 1968 primary, I ran a strong race in the general election, and there would be no incumbent governor in 1970. Bruce King won the 1970 gubernatorial primary, and I beat Bruce by nearly seventeen thousand votes two years earlier.

"But I allowed myself to be talked out of that race by none other than Clinton Anderson. That was a real big boo-boo on my part. I was in Washington on other business, and Clinton called me into his office. He said this is Manuel Luján's first term so this was the time to get him. He spent a good hour talking with me, trying to convince me that I would make a good congressman and that Manuel had had limited time to build up his constituency. He said raising money would be no problem."

Chávez made no commitments that day in Washington, and Anderson felt pressed to make his case further, but this time with Chávez's wife, Coral Jeanne. On U.S. Senate letterhead, Anderson wrote to Coral Jeanne Chávez on February 6, 1970, and explained why he had encouraged her husband to run for Congress that year. "In the first place, I think Fabian could do a good job in serving the people of New Mexico . . . I have watched him for a period of years, and I think he would do a very good job in Congress."

Anderson in his letter also addressed the fact that Chávez would not have to run against a Democratic incumbent to get to Congress. "He could run against a sitting Congressman not of his own party and that is quite different from a contest for the nomination in his own party."

New Mexico's senior member of Congress then told of benefits that accompany work in Washington. "The Congressional pension is the most liberal that I know. It may not attract him or you; but after a long period of time here in Washington, I have seen the value of it and I urge you to consider that feature as well in making a decision.

"I am not trying to tell Fabian what he should or should not do. I only suggest that my years in Washington have persuaded me that the House of Representatives is a great institution, has a fine history and offers an excellent future to anyone making it a career."

The envelope carried a ten-cent U.S. airmail stamp.

Chávez was not certain he was up for the campaign that Anderson suggested. "Manuel Luján and I were friends. We went to St. Michael's College together. Our fathers were old friends," Chávez said. "I also had to consider that I had run in the three previous statewide elections staring in 1964. I was limited in the amount of time that I could campaign because I had to work to make a living for the family. Santa Fe Cable Vision was in the process of constructing its system, and I was working as its general manager."

The pull of politics proved to be too much for Chávez to ignore. "I asked Coral Jeanne what she thought, and she said she would support me in whatever I decided. I decided to run against Manuel because I thought that with Clinton Anderson behind me, I'd be able to raise all the money I needed. It didn't turn out that way, though. I didn't get any money from Anderson or any of his sources. When Joe Montoya showed up, it was only to get in the way.

"I remember AFL-CIO's political arm was going to contribute ten thousand dollars to my campaign because I had been a longtime advocate for labor. Joe Montoya told them, 'Let me handle the money. I can handle it better for him than he can for himself.' I don't know where Joe used that money. I didn't see any promotions for me. I felt like Clinton Anderson had made an empty promise to me.

"I was so disgusted. I knew I was beat early on, but I campaigned as best I could to maintain some kind of political dignity. I'd tell people that Manuel Luján was a Republican and that he votes for the rich people, he's against the minimum wage, he's not a strong advocate for civil rights, all that stuff. I'd give them the progressive piece versus the conservative wherever I went, but I knew I was beat.

"Manuel, meanwhile, had done a very good job of communicating with voters in his first two years in office. One of his best gimmicks was to mail out a questionnaire and ask voters to list their priorities. People were impressed that their congressman wanted to know what they felt. Everywhere I'd go, I'd run into people who would say, 'Manuel is such a nice guy. Why are you running against him?'

"Why did I run against Manuel and not for governor again in 1970? I guess that was another boo-boo on my part."

Chávez said his brother, Cuate, was convinced that Anderson and others deliberately set Chávez up to lose in the 1970 election. "I think Cuate had the best explanation for what happened. He said they induced me to run for Congress and then abandoned me, figuring that if I lost in a high-profile race again, they'd be rid of me. It's hard to accept but it sort of makes sense."

Luján said he got no contributions from Anderson or anyone in his camp. "No, of course not," he said.

Chávez lost to Luján, 91,187–64,598.[45] Luján's margin was substantially larger than what he had mounted two years earlier when he surprised Tom Morris, 88,517–78,117.[46] Chávez lost to Luján in Bernalillo County by more than 20,000 votes, Santa Fe County by nearly 2,000.[47]

In that year's Democratic gubernatorial primary, which Chávez briefly considered entering, Bruce King beat his closest Democratic primary opponent, Jack Daniels of Hobbs, 62,718–47,523.[48] King then went on to defeat Pete Domenici of Albuquerque, 148,835–134,640, in the general election for what would be King's first of three nonconsecutive terms as governor.[49]

Chávez sat out political elections until 1982, when King was finishing the second of his terms as governor. "I hadn't given serious thought to another race until very close friends of mine in organized labor convinced me that Toney Anaya, the Democratic front-runner in the party's 1982 primary, was not going to be successful."

A Santa Fe lawyer, Anaya had been a very high profile attorney general from 1975 through 1978 and in 1978 ran a credible race against Domenici, who by then was seeking a second term in the U.S. Senate.

"Toney was the front-runner from the beginning in that 1982 governor's primary. The other guys were all archconservatives," Chávez said.

The other guys were Aubrey Dunn, a former state senator from Alamogordo, and Les Houston, a state senator from Albuquerque.

"My friends in labor convinced me that stuff about Toney was going to come out during the campaign, wounding him badly and maybe forcing him to get out of the race. That would leave me with the only real chance of winning statewide, so I got in, still confident that I was better prepared than most people to be governor."

Chávez was thus stunned in March at the party's reinstated preprimary convention, where both he and Houston failed to get the 20 percent of votes required to be placed on the party's primary ballot. News reports said Chávez fell thirty-seven votes short. His first major disappointment in the race came before the convention, when labor endorsed Anaya. "[Chávez] took it for granted that some labor people as individuals might still support him at the convention," wrote columnist Fred McCaffrey. "But the bosses of the AFL-CIO in New Mexico insisted on total discipline at the convention . . . Hence there was no movement toward old Fab no matter what his record shows about his affection for labor causes." Offering an explanation, McCaffrey said labor likely saw Anaya as a winner and Chávez as "a has-been."

Chávez and Houston both went on to collect the necessary number of signatures on nominating petitions to be placed on the June primary ballot, but Anaya proved to be unstoppable. "The negative stuff that supposedly was going to come out on Toney was all rumor so fortunately he never had to deal with it," Chávez said.

Anaya was confident at the time that outgoing Gov. Bruce King, Dunn, and his supporters talked Chávez into running in that year's primary. "Senator Dunn was the favorite of the old-line establishment Democrats with whom I had always been on the outs," Anaya said years later. "That crowd assumed that Senator Dunn's supposed stature in the state senate for so many years would automatically translate into statewide stature that would make him the odds-on favorite. When my strength continued to increase and it was clear to them that I was a serious challenge to their plans to elect Senator Dunn, I firmly believed they convinced Fabián to run on the faulty notion that he would 'divide' the Hispanic vote and deny me the nomination.

"I was so confident—possibly too cocky—that when the Democratic nominating convention was convened and it was obvious that Fabián would not have sufficient votes to get on the ballot, I asked the delegates committed to me to make sure that enough of them voted for Fabián to assure him a place on the ballot, as I wanted to beat anyone and anything that the 'establishment' wanted to throw at me."

Apparently not enough of Anaya's delegates got the message because Chávez left the convention with insufficient votes and in pursuit of more petition signatures. Chávez was incensed when Anaya during the campaign publicly expressed his belief that Chávez was put forward to divide Hispanic voters. He dealt with his anger by jokingly accusing Houston of sponsoring Anaya simply to take votes away from Chávez.

"In some ways, Toney duplicated what I had done when I first ran for governor in 1968," Chávez said of Anaya's strength that year. "I took on the liquor interests and the JPs, who were solid supporters of our Democratic Party structure. Toney, as attorney general, took on some prominent people in and out of the party to prove that he was for good, honest public service. Both of us got attention statewide because of those movements. Both of us made our marks as reformers."

Even as he prepared in mid-April 1982 to file additional petitions to get on the primary ballot, Chávez neither looked nor sounded optimistic about his chances. Chávez met with a handful of supporters for lunch in a quiet corner of The Bull Ring in Santa Fe before filing petitions later in the day. The conversation was low; the faces were long. It looked like a political last supper.

Chávez and his associates were discussing the uphill battle they would face in collecting campaign funds, given Chávez's standing after the preprimary convention. Even then, though, Chávez was hoping for a break that might go his way. A federal court was reviewing challenges to the legislature's reapportionment of the state following the 1980 census, and Chávez was hoping it all would push back New Mexico's primary election from June to August. Extra time to campaign would give voters a chance to see the differences between him and the other candidates, he thought. Before April was over, however, news reports announced that only state legislative races could be delayed; the court ruled that candidates in all other races would have to face the voters in the regularly scheduled June 1 primary. Anaya easily won the primary, collecting 101,077 votes.[50] Dunn was second with 60,866; Chávez was third with 11,874; and Houston finished with 3,673.[51]

Anaya went on to defeat Republican John Irick in the November general election, 215,840–191,626.[52]

"Halfway through the primary campaign I met in Albuquerque with Martin Chávez and other supporters," said Fabián Chávez Jr. "I told them, 'Fellows, we don't have a chance to win, but let's lose with dignity; let's do the best we can with what we've got.' When the race was over, I immediately sent Toney a telegram and told him, 'I gave it my best shot. You won. How can I help you?'"

Chávez had run his last political race.

CHAPTER SIXTEEN

From Roundhouse to White House, Chávez Shines as Aide

Unable to secure the governor's office for himself, Fabián Chávez Jr. was no stranger to helping those who had.

Jack Campbell during his second term as governor from 1965 to 1966 turned often to Chávez for help. "I remember returning from a trip to Durango, Mexico, and walking into Jack's office. Ernestine Evans, who was one of his aides, was there, and she told Campbell, 'Have you seen all the good publicity that Fabián has been getting for you?' Campbell said, 'Why do you think I send him out as my representative?'

"And that's what I was: his official representative on trips where requests were made for his presence. Mack Easley was Campbell's lieutenant governor, and he'd represent the governor sometimes, but I remember asking Campbell why he didn't send Mack more often. He said Mack was very busy practicing law down in Hobbs.

"Sending me to Mexico was a natural because I was bilingual. For the same reason, Jack asked me to be one of the principal participants at the first Southwest border governors' meeting that he had organized in Santa Fe."

Soon after Bruce King was elected governor in 1970, Chávez was called in to help Lt. Gov. Roberto Mondragón prepare for presiding over the state senate. Much as he had tutored Republican Tom Bolack a decade earlier, Chávez taught Mondragón the formalities and the tricks that go along with keeping senate sessions on track.

King had his own eyes on Chávez, too. "The first thing I did when I got elected was appoint Fabián cabinet secretary for tourism because he had helped me a lot," King said.

Chávez said the appointment for him was a natural fit. "I had grown up in Santa Fe so I was always thinking about the impacts of tourism. I was bilingual, and I had this lifelong love affair with New Mexico, so promoting it was almost something I could do in my sleep."

There was something else that made King want Chávez in his cabinet: his knowledge of the legislature and legislative processes. "While serving on the cabinet, I became one of Bruce's three chief legislative lobbyists, along with Roy Davidson, a former legislator from Ratón, and Franklin Jones, who was a recognized authority on finances and one hell of a tax collector when he directed the Department of Taxation and Revenue in the Cargo administration. Franklin Jones was 99 percent effective when it came to collecting taxes. He wasn't 100 percent effective because he failed in his attempt to collect taxes on people who worked from cigar boxes, not cash registers, while selling things like tamales at the Santa Fe Fiesta. And he couldn't collect taxes on jockeys at the State Fair who threatened to strike if Jones kept after them."

Chávez described Jones as "a close and trusted friend." Chávez soon found himself working against both Jones and Davidson on an issue that would impact the state for generations, however. The issue involved the proposed purchase of approximately 500,000 acres of prime forest land in northeastern New Mexico known then as Vermejo Park. The property was owned by a Texas man named W. J. Gourley. Gourley had accumulated 492,000 acres near New Mexico's northern border and was aware of the land's value to the state. He asked that after he died his wife offer it to New Mexico for $26 million.

"The owner had hoped that the state would buy the property when he died, and that's what his widow conveyed to us," Chávez said. "People on the state's Board of Economic Development encouraged me to try to get the land. Ray Powell, who was on the board and was very close to Bruce, was among those promoting the purchase."

Chávez helped craft legislation to buy the property. Introduced in the state house of representatives, the measure was sponsored by the chamber's ranking members. Opposition was rooted in beliefs like those of John Mershon, a fiscal conservative from Cloudcroft who chaired the house appropriations committee with an iron hand.

Maralyn Budke was director of the Legislative Finance Committee at the time and knew Mershon well. "He didn't want to shell out that kind of money for the purchase, and he wanted the property to stay on the tax rolls," Budke said.

King said he wanted the state to purchase the acreage and that he gave Chávez the green light to pursue it. "I thought it would make an ideal state park and recreational area," King wrote years later.[1] Chávez encountered resistance, however, from King's two other lobbyists, Jones and Davidson, who worked against the proposed purchase alongside others like organized cattle growers and New Mexico's farm bureau.

Chávez was never convinced that King, a rancher, truly supported the effort. "If he supported it, he simply could have directed Jones and Davidson to back off," Chávez said. He said he came to learn that the King family was actually trying to get into a position to buy the property for itself after it had been offered to the state. Chávez's assertion was supported later by a source close to the issue during the writing of this book.

Chávez helped organize an impressive presentation for the legislation as it was being considered in the house. The house passed the bill over Mershon's objections, and the presentation made in the house also secured a convert in the senate.

"Senator Morrow from Colfax County at first was opposed to the purchase, but he listened to the presentation in the house, and he became a disciple for the legislation," Chávez said.

Once in the senate, the bill was assigned to the Senate Finance Committee, which was chaired by Alamogordo's Aubrey Dunn, a fiscal conservative like Mershon. Also like Mershon, Dunn was known for maintaining strict control over his committee.

"I knew Aubrey very well, and in a strange sort of way he was very political," said Jerry Apodaca, who served in the state legislature before being elected governor in 1974. "He gave the appearance of not being political, but when it came to his ideas, he was very political, and he could get away with it. If you were from Rio Arriba County, for example, you were automatically considered to be political, and it carried a negative connotation with the media and others. Aubrey could work around that kind of thing and still get things his way."

Budke also had watched Dunn work in ways that would have heaped scorn upon others. "As committee chair, he'd hold onto legislation that he favored and then in one motion he'd pass eighty bills on the last day of the session. It was absolutely unconstitutional."

Budke apparently was unaware of the struggle that pitted Chávez against Jones and Davidson while all three worked for King. She said, though, that Jones was a natural ally for Mershon and Dunn on the issue. "I could see Franklin in that role. The love of his life was the purity of the tax system and that included keeping property on the tax roll and not having it in public ownership."

Chávez remembered a somewhat contentious hearing in the Senate Finance Committee where Dunn aggressively questioned Mrs. Gourley. "Aubrey was unbending, and he asked her, 'If this is such a good deal for the state, why aren't private interests lined up to buy the property?' Mrs. Gourley said several parties had, in fact, offered to buy it, but she wanted first to try to carry out her husband's wishes."

Chávez said it was a clever legislative move by Dunn that ended up killing the attempt to have the state buy the property. "Aubrey had a real firm control of the Senate Finance Committee because the first thing that he would do was take care of the requests that came from his committee members so they were like his puppets after that. Toward the end of the legislative session that year, the house of representatives passed a special bill on education appropriating $10 million more for the schools without saying specifically where it was to go. Aubrey hated that kind of thing.

"When the bill was sent to the senate, it was immediately assigned to the Senate Finance Committee, where it was placed into the huge stack of bills that were awaiting recommendations of the committee. Aubrey, true to form, made sure that his committee members were satisfied with whatever legislation they had brought to the panel. Then he brings out this $10-million education bill and says, 'This and every other bill under it in this stack will remain in the committee and die here. You guys in the committee have to pledge to fight any effort to try to bring up any of these bills.' One of the bills in that stack was the Vermejo Park bill.

"I had to find a way to beat that maneuver from my position outside the senate. So I go to my good friend, Tibo Chávez, who is now majority leader. I told Tibo that I didn't want a motion to blast the bill out of Senate Finance because that would fail. I asked him to call a committee of the whole senate for a hearing on the Vermejo Park bill. I had already sold Tibo on the merits of the bill. It was an opportunity that the state would never have again to buy nearly half a million acres. I had assembled a wonderful presentation for the bill when it was in the house of representatives, and I knew that once the senate saw the same presentation, they would pass the bill.

"Meanwhile, Senator Morrow was madder than hell at Aubrey Dunn for burying the bill in the stack that would never come out of the committee room. Morrow got so worked up about it that without consulting me or Tibo or anybody else, he moved to blast the bill out of committee before the plan that I had worked out with Tibo got a chance to unfold. John Morrow's motion was killed. In his enthusiasm, he didn't realize that he would kill the bill by moving to have it blasted out of committee.

"I walked over to The Bull Ring down the street, sat down in a booth by myself, ordered a double Scotch and water, and cried. It was the only time, the only time, that I cried after having lost a piece of legislation."

Vermejo Park Corp., a subsidiary of Pennzoil, bought the property in 1973.[2] "Pennzoil had a gathering at Santa Fe's Hilton Hotel, and the president of the company told me that he'd be lying if he said he was sad that I had lost in my attempt to have the state buy the property, but he said he admired what he called my noble efforts," Chávez said. "He also said publicly that it was his intention to make sure that the land was protected and maintained in the same pristine condition that it was in when the Gourleys had it."

Pennzoil explored the area for fossil fuel deposits during the following decade and authorized livestock grazing and timber harvesting.[3] In 1982, Pennzoil donated 101,794 acres of its original purchase to the U.S. Forest Service and walked away with a $20-million tax credit.[4] Shell Oil bought Pennzoil in 2002.

"A $20-million tax credit gave new meaning to the term 'donation,'" Chávez said. "For $26 million, the state could have owned almost five times more than what was 'donated' at great cost to the government."

The property that was exchanged for a federal tax credit was at the center of a congressional dispute more than two decades later. U.S. Rep. Tom Udall, a New Mexico Democrat, sponsored legislation to protect the 101,794 acres of what became known as Valle Vidal from energy and mineral development. Passed in the U.S. House, the measure was pushed in the Senate by New Mexico's Democrat Jeff Bingaman. Republican Pete Domenici of New Mexico withheld his support for months but once he extended it, the measure was adopted by the Republican-controlled Senate, and Pres. George W. Bush signed it into law during the final weeks of 2006.

Chávez's other work as state tourism director helped set in motion the new waves of popularity among travelers that began sweeping into Santa Fe and other parts of New Mexico in the late 1970s. "Santa Fe and various other regions of the state had tremendous potential for tourism development, but there was little coordination between those communities and the state Tourism Department," Chávez said. "I got money from the legislature to begin a more thorough coordination of advertising and promotions in communities like Santa Fe, Taos, Albuquerque, Española, Socorro. We used state money to match funds available in local communities, and at times when there were no matching funds, we made state money available anyway.

"Santa Fe was an easy draw so we used it as a magnet. While you're in Santa Fe, we said, you can also visit this attraction or that attraction without having to travel very far. Taos with all its art, history, and beautiful scenery also lent itself to successful promotions. Between Santa Fe and Taos, of course, there were the weaving shops and Indian pueblos that as a very young boy I myself had used as destination points while serving as an unofficial tour guide for visitors who were wandering around Santa Fe's Plaza looking for somewhere else to go.

"In southern New Mexico, we promoted Carlsbad Caverns and White Sands as two of the greatest natural attractions in the world, which happened to be located within a couple of hours of each other."

Michael Cerletti, who worked as New Mexico's tourism boss in the 1990s and again a decade later, said Chávez's work contributed to the decades-long boom in New Mexico's popularity among travelers. "Santa Fe, especially, in the late 1970s started becoming an in spot, and it went up from there," Cerletti said. "I think we can give Fabián significant credit. In these kinds of things, it can take several years before you see the fruits of your labor. I think Fabián was a great spokesman for the industry, and his efforts went a long way."

While Chávez aggressively promoted New Mexico around the country, he also placed more emphasis on encouraging residents of the state to spend their travel dollars close to home. "We started getting them to recognize that they didn't have to leave New Mexico to experience great historical, cultural, and scenic treasures," Chávez said. "My theme for New Mexico became: Heaven is right next door."

Jerry Apodaca succeeded King as governor in 1975 and promptly began looking for ways to streamline state government. He was not at all convinced that the economic development office was effective and considered disbanding it. "I was in the process of forming the state's first cabinet," Apodaca said. "There were 114 agencies that answered to the governor's office. It took me four years, but I converted those agencies to twelve major departments. It was during that process that Fabián came to see me and asked to be named secretary of the Department of Economic Development. He wasn't at all bashful about asking for what he wanted. He had been director of tourism and assured me he could be successful in economic development."

Chávez said Apodaca did not require much convincing. "I asked him to give me a chance to make it work." Chávez, however, encountered obstacles that had long blocked successful major development in most of the state's communities. "I worked with bigger communities to try to get small industries into our outlying communities. The economic development group in Albuquerque, for example, worked hand in hand with us to attract industry to places like Mountainair, Las Vegas, Taos. We developed economic profiles for communities of a thousand or more. When industry expressed an interest, we had a package of things and places to show them. Invariably, they would tell us of their needs, things like access to railroads, airports, main highways.

"It was pretty difficult getting industry anywhere but to the center of the Rio Grande corridor. With tourism, you can use a shotgun approach; you can attract people by promoting various sites at once. When it comes to industry, you're talking about shooting a rifle. Industry has specific needs, and you have to meet them all in one site to be successful. Their desire for what you might call social ambience always was high on the list. Las Vegas, for example, has I-25, the railroad, Highlands University, Luna Technical-Vocational School. It used to be New Mexico's biggest community, and it's situated close to both the Great Plains and the Rocky Mountains. Many of us love it, but it isn't developed in the way that many in industry would like to see. It's usually not what they're looking for so they look elsewhere.

"Then there are problems like what happened to us in Las Vegas once. We had a package put together and had assembled a welcoming team for one recruit, but then somebody shot up a PNM electrical transformer right when the group was coming in. Not everyone in the community was eager for development, at least not back then. We lost the recruit, who couldn't help but notice the publicity that came from the vandalism."

Successes were far fewer than Chávez would have liked. "Because of Albuquerque's proximity, you can do things with Los Lunas and Belén. Las Cruces has grown, but industry can be discouraged from coming in because the major airport is in El Paso, forty-five miles away. If it weren't for oil and gas up in the Farmington area, it would still be apple country. Simply, the private sector selects where it goes, we don't decide. Companies are investors. They're not going to put millions of dollars into many of our communities. For some of them, I can see only a constant struggle."

Apodaca considered Chávez to be an asset to his administration despite the obstacles in his path. "He served me very well. He was a good outside person. He always communicated to the general public very well. And he was a good inside person because he knew politics very well," Apodaca said. "He was an articulate communicator. He was able to communicate the message very well. And he was very loyal."

The breadth of Chávez's loyalty was evident one day when Chávez and Apodaca were in a state plane returning to the capital from a business recruiting trip. "We were playing gin on the plane, and we were getting close to landing in Santa Fe," Apodaca said. "I told the pilot to circle around for a while to give me enough time to beat Fabián."

Chávez recalled a little more to the story. "Jerry could be very explosive," Chávez said. "We had been playing cards for a while, and it seemed I couldn't lose. I must have seen that Jerry was getting ready to blow up, so I said, 'Governor, life is full of turns in the road. I'm sure things will turn in your favor pretty soon.' Jerry said something a little saltier than, 'Damn the blasted curves in the road. Shut up and play cards.'"

Apodaca ended up winning before the plane landed, as Chávez had struggled to ensure.

Chávez worked as New Mexico's chief economic developer for two years. Soon after Jimmy Carter was elected U.S. president in 1976, Chávez was encouraged to apply for a position in the new federal administration.

"I was very involved at that time with friends in the Carter administration, and I was able to provide input and recommendations to the administration," said Ed Romero, who was on his way to becoming one of New Mexico's most successful businessmen and one of the nation's wealthiest Hispanics. "I was one of those that recommended Fabián for a job in the administration. He was one of those who stood out. Fabián was more than a masterful politician. He was an intelligent, savvy, get-it-done type of guy."

Romero's influence helped when it came time to ensure that Chávez got the attention needed for him to personally make his pitch for a post in the federal administration. The groundwork had already been laid, apparently, by the man Chávez hired to succeed him as state director of tourism. "I hired Bill Kondradt when I became secretary of the state's Economic Development Department," Chávez said. "Kondradt was attending a national meeting in Washington, and he saw an article in the *Washington Post* that said Jimmy Carter was going to appoint Hispanics to various positions in recognition of the support they gave him during the election.

"Kondradt sent my name in without me knowing anything about it. Then, one day I got a notice from Carter's transition team that said I had been recommended for the position of assistant secretary of commerce for tourism. It came with a lengthy application. I called Bill in and said, 'Here. You sent my name in; you fill out the application.' I said to myself, 'This is a joke. How are they going to choose me way out here in New Mexico?' But Bill did such a good job of filling out the application that I was called in for an interview."

Chávez said that approximately forty people from around the country had applied for the position. A dozen were invited for interviews. "It was the most unusual way of interviewing twelve people that I had ever seen," Chávez said. "We all were asked to sit around this long mahogany table and we were all interviewed at the same time. I decided I wasn't going to say anything unless asked. I wanted to listen to others and then try to come up with something different that would set me apart. Everybody talked about advertising and promotions. I took a different approach. I spoke about the economic development that is associated with tourism.

"I pointed to the Bridge Marriott viewed from the Commerce Department building and told of all the jobs that were created to build that large hotel. I told of all the money that went into purchasing material for the building and of the hundreds of people who were then employed to keep the hotel going. I said there was already an infrastructure out there of hotels, airlines, and travel agents who promoted travel to the United States. The Commerce Department, I said, must coordinate all that, but I said I looked beyond the attraction of people; I looked more to the creation of jobs. I said I wanted to work with states around the country to get their leaders thinking in terms of economic development when they considered tourism. That reduced us down to three applicants. One was a lady with a master's degree in business administration who had worked from New York as a vice president for a major television network on travel and tourism. The other was a major investor in hotels along the Atlantic coast who also was a major contributor to the Democratic Party."

Chávez was the only Hispanic among the finalists but did not like his chances unless he somehow could get an opportunity to talk directly with the commerce secretary, Juanita Kreps. He turned to a fellow New Mexican for help. "Tim Kraft was appointments secretary for Jimmy Carter, and he happened to be a close friend of Ed Romero. I asked Tim to get me an appointment with Secretary Kreps."

Kraft recalled the incident. "Fabián asked to meet with a 'decision-maker.' I said, 'That would be Juanita Kreps.' Fabián said, 'Just get me in the same room with her, Tim.' I did, and he sold himself. Anyone surprised?"

Kreps ended up interviewing all three finalists.

Chávez's pitch for economic development resonated at a time when about 8 percent of the nation's workers were unemployed.[5] Carter, while campaigning for president, had promised to create more jobs by increasing federal spending and encouraging business expansion.[6]

"I was flying TWA on my way back to New Mexico via Chicago, and when we stopped in Chicago, there was a message waiting for me," Chávez said. "The message said I was to call the governor's office in Santa Fe right away. I called, and Jerry Apodaca tells me, 'Fabián, I just got a call from Washington. You've been chosen to be assistant secretary of commerce.' And so it was. It happened more as an accident than by design. Bill Kondradt had submitted my name sort of as half a joke."

Not everyone in Washington was laughing, at least initially. Senator Daniel Inouye, a Hawaii Democrat who reviewed Chávez's nomination by Carter, had somebody else in mind for the position. "His chief aide told me the senator thought I lacked necessary experience and that I got the appointment simply because I was Hispanic," Chávez said. "People from the AFL-CIO went to see the senator and told him I was one of their boys. That took care of it."

As promised during his interview in Washington, Chávez worked with states to encourage tourism as an economic development tool. He pressed for promoting specific attractions in individual states to international travelers as well as to residents elsewhere in the United States. "It was much like what we had done in New Mexico. I'd speak all over the country, and I'd tell tourism promoters, 'Visitors come to your state, they leave their money, and the only thing they take with them is a smile.'"

There was also work associated with the World Tourism Congress and the millions of dollars the country spent annually through advertising firms in Europe, Asia, and the Americas. "The World Tourism Congress was divided into European, Asian, and Western Hemispheric groups so I did a lot of work with countries between North and South America," Chávez said. "Meetings of Western Hemispheric nations often were held in smaller countries, and it was one such meeting that had us in Havana, Cuba, in 1978. Before leaving, I was called by the State Department and told to visit with its South American desk. They told me they had received information from their American Cuban interest section, which operated out of the Swiss embassy in Havana, that it was possible that I would get to meet with President Fidel Castro because of my surname and my Hispanic background. I was advised as to what I could and could not talk about with Castro if I had an audience with him.

"I was told that if the subject of improved relations with the United States came up, I was to say that it was very possible, providing that the Cuban government addressed two major problems. One was that Cuba had to stop being a surrogate for the Soviet Union in sending troops to assist in revolts in other countries. The second was that there had to be some kind of settlement for reparations for property confiscated from American interests as a result of the Cuban revolution in 1959.

"The Carter administration in my estimation wanted to improve relations with Cuba. For example, there was a desire to start regular airline flights directly from the U.S. into Cuba rather than just the limited charter flights that were going in. We could also assist in the development of facilities in Cuba to make it more attractive to visitors from around the world.

~❦ **FIGURE 28.** ❧~
Fabián Chávez Jr. (right) visits with Cyrus Vance, secretary of state,
which prepared Chávez for a meeting with Cuban Pres.
Fidel Castro in 1978. Courtesy Fabián Chávez Jr.

It was my impression that the Carter administration felt we could open windows to let some fresh air of freedom flow across Cuba."

Chávez said the Cubans were prepared for him. "They knew everything about me. I found that they even had a bottle of Johnny Walker Red Label Scotch, my customary drink, waiting in my suite. I was chauffeured around Havana by Cuba's so-called tourism director. I saw all the things they wanted me to see, and when we'd get down to walk, I'd talk to the people in Spanish, and it was easy to see that Castro had vast public support.

"About noon of the day that I was supposed to catch my flight out of Havana, my escort told me that arrangements were being made for me to meet with President Castro. My plane was to leave at 9 p.m., and I was told to make myself available to meet with the president between 4 and 6."

Chávez was picked up at his hotel around 6 p.m. and driven to Castro's compound. "The chief presidential aide escorted me into Castro's main office," Chávez said. "Castro got up from behind his desk and walked toward me. He extended his big right hand for what was a firm handshake. His first words were, 'Bienvenido, señor secretario.' I replied, 'Me da gusto en conocerlo.'

"Our entire conversation was in Spanish, and while we were still standing, he complimented me on my Spanish. He asked if I learned it in school. I said it started with my parents and grandparents and that I later refined it in school. That's when something happened to loosen the conversation. Castro said, 'You speak Spanish very well but with a Mexican accent.' I said, 'Thank you, Mr. President. You speak beautiful Spanish, too, and with a Caribbean accent.'"

Chávez said Castro at least pretended to be intrigued. "He said, 'Yeah? What is the difference?' I told Castro, 'In Spanish, one says: Buenos días. ¿Cómo está usted? With a Caribbean accent, it sounds like this: Bueno día. ¿Cómo etá uted?' I left out eses and spoke very rapidly.

"Castro broke out laughing and said, '¡Bien dicho!'

"I could see he was a charmer," Chávez said. "And on that day, at least, I sensed I might be able to hold my own with him. It's as if through our first few minutes of feeling one another out, we reached this unexpressed agreement for what would follow: You don't bullshit me, and I won't bullshit you."

It was after that initial exchange that Castro asked Chávez to sit with him on a couch. The meeting that was supposed to last fifteen minutes went on for more than two hours. "Castro started the conversation by saying, 'First, I want you to know that I admire President Carter very much because he is not afraid to take on the big oil monopolies that you have in the states, and he appears to have a big heart.'

"At one point later, President Castro told me, 'It would be nice if we could improve relations between our two countries. What do you think about that matter, Mr. Secretary? Would your country recognize mine officially?'"

That turned the conversation to delicate matters on which the U.S. State Department had briefed Chávez before his departure. "I expressed the two conditions that had been laid out by the State Department. Then I said that the United States already recognizes socialist countries like Russia, China, Yugoslavia, Poland, and others. It is only logical that we should recognize a socialist country that is only ninety miles from Florida.

"I told him how we could improve travel between our two nations by reestablishing scheduled airline flights. I told him flights were already coming in from Canada and Mexico. Why not from Miami to Havana? I was flying by the seat of my pants here. I wasn't coached on this stuff.

"He told me that Cuba's new constitution does not allow the kind of flights I was proposing, but I got the impression that he felt things could be renegotiated, that problems were not insurmountable.

"I told him Cuba has some of the most beautiful beaches in the world but that they haven't been taken care of. I said he needed experts to come

∾ FIGURE 29. ∾

Fabián Chávez Jr. (right) meets with Mexican Pres. José López Portillo
while serving as assistant secretary for tourism in the
U.S. Commerce Department. Courtesy Fabián Chávez Jr.

in and help with such things. Again, he said foreign assistance of that type
was forbidden.

"I said, 'Perhaps, Mr. President. But I happen to know that we had a
recent delegation from the Socialist Republic of China come to Washington,
DC, to meet with me and representatives of major tourism organizations
that could go to China and assist them in expanding their tourism projects.'
I told him the meeting ended with a written agreement, and he asked if I
could make a copy of it available to him."

Chávez called it a stimulating meeting and could not help but think
of the briefings he had gotten from the State Department prior to earlier hemispheric meetings in Miami, when he was instructed not to talk

about opening relations with Cuba. "I followed those instructions when in Miami, but it didn't make any sense to me. I couldn't understand why we were forcing all the people of Cuba to starve just to satisfy some pissed off Cubans in Miami."

Chávez's visit with Castro ended amicably, but no changes in foreign policy came from it. Chávez resigned from the Commerce Department a few months later, largely because he missed his home two thousand miles away.

Best wishes to Fabian Chavez
Jimmy Carter

~ **FIGURE 30.** ~
Fabián Chávez Jr. (right) meets with Pres. Jimmy Carter while serving as an assistant secretary in the U.S. Commerce Department. Courtesy Fabián Chávez Jr. Official Photograph, The White House, Washington. No. 10AG7912370–10.

"We were sorry to see Fabián voluntarily leave a little early," Kraft said. "I think he and Coral Jeanne missed New Mexico."

Ed Romero recalled sitting at a table with Commerce Secretary Kreps at a dinner after Chávez had submitted his resignation. "The administration knew it had a jewel in Fabián," Romero said. "He was doing a hell of a job. I introduced myself to the secretary and told her I was a friend of Fabián's. Her face lit up when I mentioned his name. She went on to tell me what a great man he was and how it was one of the best appointments the president had made."

Carter himself offered his own words of appreciation in a letter dated March 15, 1979. He specifically thanked Chávez for "your contributions to a tourism agreement with Mexico; the successful negotiation of increased air routes with Mexico and other countries; your exploration of new countries as sources of tourism to the United States; and the development of a tourism bill of rights."

CHAPTER SEVENTEEN

A Final Stop to Take on Giants

Good Friday 1988 arrived in northern New Mexico like so many others. Thousands of pilgrims were walking from all directions to the Santuario de Chimayó, the small Roman Catholic shrine of old adobes and timber where people for generations have deposited pleas for help and prayers of thanks.

The state corporation commissioner, Eric Serna, would be among pilgrims that day. The two other men who sat on the regulatory panel knew it and picked the day to tend to an important matter of business before them.

Vicente Jasso, longtime state insurance superintendent, had retired. The vacancy gave the corporation commission an opportunity for a plum appointment. More than a few politicians as well as prominent members of the insurance industry maneuvered behind the scenes in hopes of influencing the commission.

Commissioners lacked unanimity as they looked at possible successors to Jasso. Amid the jockeying, Comms. John Elliott and Jerome Block turned to a very familiar figure in state government, Fabián Chávez Jr.

"They deliberately appointed me on Good Friday because they knew that Eric and his wife would be walking to the *santuario*," Chávez said. Serna, alone, could not have blocked the appointment, but he was certain to have fanned concerns at the meeting among those who favored other candidates and those who wanted a broader search.

Block said neither he nor Elliott was concerned that the meeting would get out of hand. "We just wanted to keep a low profile on a slow news day," he said. By "a slow news day," Block meant that many of the area's reporters would be covering the pilgrimage to the santuario, and others wouldn't be terribly driven to dig up news around the capital on a day that they customarily had used as a sort of respite.

Both close to former Gov. Bruce King, Chávez and Serna had an uneasy relationship. Tension between the two men had probably taken root a decade earlier while Serna worked in Washington as a young aide to U.S. Senator Joseph M. Montoya, long one of Chávez's principal political rivals.

Chávez possessed one of the most-recognized names in Santa Fe, but he had not held an elected public position since 1964. Though all failed, his five political campaigns since then accorded him a prominence that few others could claim. So did his storied service in the state legislature and his work as an aide to four governors. Still, his appointment as insurance superintendent was not greeted warmly beyond his closest circle of friends.

"Most of the insurance agents around the state were very, very upset," said Edward Luján, whose family had owned an insurance company in Santa Fe and Albuquerque for decades. Luján also was a leader of the state Republican Party and brother of U.S. Rep. Manuel Luján, whom Chávez challenged unsuccessfully for Congress in 1970.

"People were upset not because they didn't like Fabián," Luján said. "Most knew him by reputation but felt at the time that he wasn't in the insurance business and didn't know much about the business itself. A lot of them were angling for other people within the industry to become superintendent. All of a sudden Fabián is appointed. Many of the agents felt he got it because of his political connections and feared we were going to get a superintendent who knew nothing but politics."

James Koch, who had been in the insurance business for more than twenty years, agreed. "Everyone was suspect of Fabián," he said. Along with Edward Luján, Koch was among the state's most influential independent insurance agents of the time.

Chávez could not help but be aware of the sentiment against his appointment. Much of it was expressed openly. "There were a lot of squawks," he said. "I was the first to admit that I knew nothing about insurance. That's why I immediately hired Ted Knight to be my deputy. Ted was a lawyer with decades of experience in insurance, both as a company employee and government regulator. He had the knowledge and experience that I lacked."

Luján was among those who promptly rose to Chávez's defense. "I knew Fabián. I thought he was going to do a super, super job. Most of the agents asked me why. I said there were a number of reasons. For one, this was likely going to be Fabián's last stop in his career, and being a politician, he would want to leave a legacy. Two, he's an extremely bright man, and as far

It could have been a contest for the biggest nose, says Fabián Chávez Jr.
(right) while meeting with former U.S. House Speaker
Thomas "Tip" O'Neill. Courtesy Fabián Chávez Jr.

as insurance is concerned, he'll pick it up very, very quickly. He doesn't need
to know the intricacies of each policy. That's why he has lawyers and staff
members. And thirdly, Fabián knows his way around the Roundhouse."

Chávez went to work quickly. In fact, Elliott and Block appointed Chávez
largely because he knew the insurance department's needs well. "I had been
lobbying prior to my appointment, and one of my clients happened to be
the corporation commission," Chávez said. "John Elliott and Jerome Block
asked me to get more money for the insurance department. I was successful
in getting money to hire actuaries, rate analysts, financial examiners. Elliott
was interested in doing something about the insurance department because
he didn't think it was functioning as it should.

"Suddenly, with money it hadn't had before, the insurance department
was in a position to truly make its presence known. The two commissioners told me, 'Now that you got us the money, why don't you come and run
the department?'"

As quickly as he set out to work, Chávez began winning converts. "We
had a couple of hearings, and Fabián immediately showed his fairness

to everybody," Luján said. "It's a three-fold constituency that you have in insurance: the companies, the agents, and the public. Fabián showed his fairness in dealing with everyone. You might not have liked his rulings, but you knew they were fair.

"Among those who were upset when Fabián was appointed, I'd say 100 percent were behind him after a couple of years. Because of his knowledge of the legislature, he was able to bring money to the department along with new rules and regulations that were very beneficial to the industry and the consumer. He was the first to hire in-house attorneys rather than use assistant attorneys general. He put together an actuary office that would predict things that companies look at for their rating system. He boosted the department's administrative offices to the point where we were all getting good service."

Block said increased reliance on actuaries reflected the growth and professionalism that Chávez brought to the insurance department. "Back in the olden days, companies used to file for rate increases, and if they weren't acted upon within a certain number of days they were automatically approved," Block said. "Companies would come in with boxes and boxes full of information, and we didn't have actuaries to actually study what they brought. Suddenly, with actuaries we were in a position to scrutinize rate increase filings before they'd go into effect."

Chávez, in fact, had helped get a law passed two years before his appointment as insurance superintendent that prevented an insurer from increasing premiums before receiving approval from the department.

David Cox was the first property and casualty actuary Chávez hired in 1988 to help begin putting the state's insurance department on more solid footing. "Fabián became an agent of change for the department of insurance," said Cox, who arrived in New Mexico from Dallas, Texas. "He took on issues of workers' compensation insurance, corrupt insurers and politicians, public protection, staffing, title insurance, and the politics of insurance."

The law Chávez had helped secure to keep companies from raising rates without action from the insurance department, alone, did not keep premiums from soaring.

"Enforcement of this law . . . was part of the reason Fabián had become superintendent," said Jerry Fickes, a Kansas City resident Chávez hired in 1988 to review all requests for rate increases from health insurance companies. "Fabián felt that an insurer should be able to seek adequate premium based upon past experience that would cover future expected claims, allowing only a prudent amount to cover expenses. The new premium could not pay the company back for any past losses. Those were history. Not all insurance companies agreed with this."

There was a bigger problem the state and insurance companies had to address. The state had been slow to act on rate increase requests, often meaning that what was eventually approved was no longer adequate to cover a company's needs. Companies tended to request rate increases larger than what they needed at the time, anticipating that by the time the state responded, they could justify whatever was approved, Fickes said.

Chávez required that rate increase requests be reviewed more quickly. The backlog was eliminated within his first year on the job. Chávez also directed his staff to work with the National Association of Insurance Commissioners to help standardize from state to state the expected loss ratios and expense margins for all types of health insurance.

"New Mexico became the leader and not the follower in establishing health insurance model laws and regulations," Fickes said.

The period when Chávez stepped in as New Mexico insurance superintendent was marked by turmoil nationwide, according to Fickes. "In 1988, insurance companies were being bought and sold right and left. They were also going out of business at a record rate . . . Also, health insurance costs were rising so rapidly that individuals were dropping their insurance coverage. Medicare supplements were not regulated consistently, and increases in premiums were causing seniors to give up their insurance."

Fickes, with thirty-nine years of experience that included time spent as director of several life and health insurance companies, said Chávez hired him because "I knew where all the bones were buried" amid the unfolding conditions of the industry.

"Fabián wanted to help the people living in New Mexico while at the same time encourage growth in the insurance industry within the state," Fickes said. He told of a situation that he thought showed how Chávez approached his work. It came as Blue Cross Blue Shield of New Mexico, one of the largest health insurers in the state, filed for a rate increase on almost all its health insurance business. The company's financial statements supported the requested rate increases but also reflected something else. "The company would be insolvent within the year," Fickes said.

Chávez called company administrators to his office and sought to work out the serious problems. "Fabián, technically, should have ordered an immediate financial examination and based upon the results declared the company insolvent. The problem with that was the insurance department did not at the time have an internal examination section. Also, the company insured over eighty thousand individuals in New Mexico."

Those people would have become uninsured if Chávez had declared the company insolvent. Many likely would not have qualified for another policy. Chávez could have required another company to acquire all the risks, but that carrier would be able to set new premiums that thousands might have found unaffordable. Instead, Chávez gave the company thirty days to correct its financial weakness.

"Fabián felt it was more important to keep eighty thousand-plus people insured than to invoke his authority to close the company," Fickes said. "The company's counterpart in another state inserted enough funds to make the New Mexico company solvent again."

Chávez later established an examination division that reviewed financial statements of all companies every three years and worked with companies when problems were found. The division also reviewed reports about companies other states submitted to help keep problems discovered elsewhere from being deposited in New Mexico.

Preventing fraud by companies and agents required more than cursory reviews, Fickes said. Problems often were caused by overzealous agents and even by people who masqueraded as agents or insurers. "Their income from such ventures was initially large until they had to pay claims. Then they rapidly ran out of money, leaving clients' claims unpaid."

Whenever possible, companies were held accountable for misrepresentations by their agents. "In the first year that Fabián was superintendent, the New Mexico insurance department returned over $2 million to New Mexicans for such misrepresentations," Fickes said. "In addition, many thousands of dollars in fines were paid to the state."

With so many companies around the country failing at the time, Fickes said, Chávez was very cautious about allowing new insurers in New Mexico. He said that not one company engaged in life, health, and annuity insurance and admitted to New Mexico during Chávez's seven years as superintendent failed financially. He said failures were occurring every month before Chávez's arrival.

Repeatedly, Chávez "stood tall" and showed the insurance community that "in New Mexico, it must be done right," Fickes said. He said the message was delivered loud and clear to managers of the New Mexico Life and Health Insurance Guaranty Fund midway through Chávez's tenure. The fund is administered by directors insurance companies select and subject to approval of the state superintendent. Directors in New Mexico at the time included representatives from some of the largest carriers in the nation, all of whom were attorneys.

The fund is designed to cover policyholders in life, health, and annuities in cases where insurers become insolvent. The number of claimants resulting from such insolvencies had mounted by the time Chávez was hired. New cases also arose involving companies that had been admitted to New Mexico before Chávez arrived, according to Fickes. "For months, letters and telephone calls kept coming to the department of insurance from doctors, banks, hospitals, and policyholders or contract owners," Fickes said. "Their claims were not being handled.

"This is when Fabián had his finest hour. He picked up the telephone and called the Prudential vice president who served as chairman of the Life and Health Guaranty Fund in New Mexico and informed him that as superintendent, he was removing him and all of the other directors from the board. They had not performed and were no longer acceptable to him. He was going to appoint a new board."

Sitting board members at first asserted that Chávez lacked authority to remove them but then agreed to a meeting in Atlanta, where Chávez would be the following week. "At that meeting, Fabián gave them an ultimatum that they would start to pay claims immediately and include interest payments for the delay. He also insisted that they reorganize so that the board included financial and administrative personnel, not just attorneys. He gave them ninety days to create a plan of operation acceptable to the department of insurance, to create an executive committee, and meet with the department of insurance monthly until the claims were current. They could agree immediately or as their last act as directors, disagree.

"Fabián won this battle, and many thousands of New Mexicans benefited from the results."

In another high-profile case, Chávez shut down Meadowlark Insurance Company from operating in New Mexico after it was found to have defrauded policyholders and their claimants. The company originally operated out of Wyoming but on the heels of legal problems began selling insurance out of New Mexico. Chávez aggressively opposed the company and went to the legislature to close it down. Two people associated with the company were later sent to federal prison.

In another case, though, Chávez did not start off aboard the same white horse. The case involved the man whom Chávez succeeded as insurance superintendent, Vicente Jasso. Jasso, after leaving his state post, was hired to help get a license in New Mexico for National Auto Mutual Insurance Co., which operated out of Houston. The company took premiums from high-risk taxi and trucking interests and diverted funds needed to pay claims. "At the time of licensing, there were serious concerns about the people forming the company," said David Cox. "I think Fabián wanted to do a favor for Vicente Jasso and may not at the time have realized the danger to the policyholders . . . Once the fraud became evident, Fabián shut the company down." The insurance department successfully sued the company's founder, but many claims of injured people were not paid in full, according to Cox. Some claims are still being paid.

Licensure of the company was a rare misstep by Chávez, he said.

Cox said the sound judgment and courage more commonly associated with Chávez were evident while Chávez battled an entrenched title insurance sector. "When Fabián saw that title agents and insurers were making too much money, he ordered rate reductions or otherwise limited profits," Cox said. "The title industry fought back, hiring [house speaker] Raymond Sánchez's law firm to represent them. They contributed heavily to New Mexico politicians.

"Fabián fought hard, and he exposed the title insurance industry in the press and made it difficult for politicians to support them."

Cox said the two superintendents who followed Chávez, Chris Krahling and Don Letherer, "continued the battle but did not have Fabián's ability to use the press or sway corporation commissioners" in efforts to bring title insurance rates down.

In truth, Chávez's efforts to reduce title insurance rates were not nearly as successful as he—or most New Mexicans—would have liked. Years after Chávez left as insurance superintendent, rates remained grossly excessive, said Victor Marshall, a former Republican state senator and Albuquerque attorney who represented interests looking to lower those rates. Companies in other insurance sectors pay out sixty cents to eighty cents for every dollar they collect in premiums, Marshall said in 2006. Companies selling title insurance pay about five cents on the dollar. "About seventy-eight cents of that dollar goes to the local title insurance companies as commission," Marshall said.

"Fabián was aware of the problem and tried to fix it. He knew what a rip-off it was," he said. Marshall said, though, that local title insurance agents enjoy great political clout.

State law designates the New Mexico insurance superintendent solely responsible for setting title insurance rates, but the superintendent must work within previously established guidelines. "I wanted to change the law as much as the next guy, but apart from the extraordinary profits, we lacked the information that would be needed to build a solid case that would lead to massive revisions," Chávez said. "It was kind of like the situation I faced while trying to reform our liquor laws in the 1960s." As in the liquor battle, Chávez acknowledged, politics figured into the issue.

"Still, I can honestly say that as insurance superintendent, I never allowed myself to be influenced by anyone in politics while making a decision," Chávez said. "I would have liked to make major changes in title insurance, but a lot of my time was taken up while working with others to get major changes in workers' compensation insurance. That's an area where many, many New Mexicans are affected, far more than in title insurance, so I had to set priorities for the time that I had as superintendent."

Workers' compensation insurance had indeed become a major headache in New Mexico before Chávez's appointment as superintendent. "In 1987, Supt. of Insurance Vicente Jasso's approval of a 24-percent rate increase for workers' compensation insurance shocked the state's employers," Cox said. Before that, in 1985, the insurance industry filed for a 37-percent rate increase, but it was disapproved. The state legislature froze rates from July 1985 to July 1987, but three months after the freeze was lifted, the huge increase approved by Jasso signaled trouble ahead, according to Cox.

Even after Jasso's action, insurers still considered workers' compensation rates to be inadequate. In addition, Cox said, the legislature continued to expand benefits under workers' compensation while insurance rates were not allowed to increase accordingly. "Insurers were abandoning the market to the Assigned Risk Pool."

Chávez said the Assigned Risk Pool was not the answer for mushrooming problems. "It was a dumping ground for employers that would not be insured by your regular insurance companies. And it was mostly small businesses that were being tossed into the pool because they weren't considered to be cost-effective," Chávez said.

Luján said that about 90 percent of New Mexico's companies were in the Assigned Risk Pool. "Everybody was suing for more benefits. Nobody would settle a claim without a lawsuit, especially your fairly large claims. Most insurance companies just decided to leave that particular kind of coverage. Everything was going into assigned risk."

In October 1988, the insurance industry filed for a 44.8-percent rate increase for assigned risks and a 15.6-percent increase for other employers. Chávez denied the request. Meanwhile, employers applied political pressure for reforms.

The industry in September 1989 petitioned for a 64.3-percent rate increase for assigned risk and a 51.8-percent rate increase for others. Citing technical problems with the request, Chávez denied it, but the industry returned within months, asking to increase the assigned risk rate by 39.3 percent, according to Cox.

"These were intense times," Cox said. "For many businesses—construction, manufacturing, mining, oil, ski basins, hospitals, moving, and hauling—workers' compensation premiums are second only to salaries and benefits in importance. High workers' compensation premiums caused New Mexico industries to be uncompetitive. Wages were being squeezed.

Because Fabián could not continue to keep rates low, pressure for a political solution was mounting."

In fact, as Cox sees it, Chávez forced legislative action. "He did it by threatening to approve a devastating workers' compensation rate increase," Cox said.

In the 1990 legislative session, the house speaker, Raymond Sánchez, assembled a committee to consider workers' compensation reform. As an Albuquerque lawyer, Sánchez had drawn income from years of disputes rooted in workers' compensation claims. Interestingly, to pursue reform, he turned to another Albuquerque lawyer, Martin Chávez, who had collected even more from those disputes.

Sánchez named Chávez chairman of the workers' compensation reform committee. A first-term state senator, Martin Chávez is a distant cousin of Fabián Chávez Jr. and son of Lorenzo Chávez, whom Fabián Chávez Jr. consulted with frequently on labor issues while serving as a state legislator. Martin Chávez was the only lawyer to sit on the panel that for the most part included influential representatives of both business and labor. James Koch, who was close to Sánchez and had encouraged him to appoint the committee, was the only insurance person on the panel.

"Fabián was not a member of the committee. He was an advisor to the committee that worked all that summer." Koch said. "Fabián brought a strong, professional presence. If we had had a weak superintendent, things would not have worked out."

Cox said Chávez assertively pointed to needs and problems but avoided taking sides as competing interests jockeyed for favorable treatment. "Fabián pushed for equitable benefits, efficient dispute resolution, and a structure that promotes workplace safety," Cox said.

Another central part of the reforms was the cap of ten thousand dollars that was placed on fees that could be charged by attorneys brought into workers' comp disputes. "Raymond and Marty used to get business from such disputes, but they didn't oppose the cap," Koch said.

As insurance superintendent, Chávez joined others to ensure that reforms included creation of the New Mexico Mutual Casualty Company, a state-sponsored insurance company that would specialize in meeting the needs of small businesses that previously had been banished to the Assigned Risk Pool. "I thought that by creating this company, we could involve independent agents from around the state, develop a new pool of insurers, and provide cheaper workers' compensation coverage," Chávez said. "Jamie Koch came to me and said he thought it was a great idea. Jamie was very, very influential among independent insurers, so I thought that with his support we could really make this thing work. The big insurance companies had said that covering small businesses was not cost-effective. We showed not only that it could be done, but done at reasonable rates, too. A $10-million loan was secured from the State Investment Council to create the company.

"To succeed at the legislative level, we needed the private sector, the insurance industry, and the executive branch of government to sign on to the mission," Chávez said. "All three came through. Involvement of the executive branch was reflected in the $10-million loan that Governor Bruce King was instrumental in securing."

Reforms also called for the governor to appoint additional members to the state's workers' compensation administration to further expedite resolution of insurance claims. "It used to take months and sometimes years to settle some of these claims. By expanding the workers' comp administration, we were able to settle them in a very short period of time."

Creation of the state-sponsored company, changes to the workers' comp law, and expansion of the workers' compensation administration all came about in a five-day special session of the legislature in September 1990.[1]

Edward Luján said the reforms represented a complete turnaround. "Reform didn't hurt the consumer; it didn't hurt the insurance companies. It was win-win. All of a sudden companies started coming back. Reforms that were passed still serve as a model to all other states. It was a monumental change. It's bigger than most people realize."

Luján referred to business owners when he spoke of consumers, the people who buy insurance for their workers. The workers also did very well in reform. Under the old system, settlement of claims could take years, but settlements were expedited under new legislation, and legal red tape was reduced.

Sánchez, like Fabián Chávez Jr., said the cooperation among parties was extraordinary and responsible for the success. "The greatest accomplishment was bringing business and labor together to produce a bill that kept everyone in the ball game and working together," Sánchez said. Getting lawyers, physicians, and insurance company representatives to cooperate as advisers was also helpful, he said. "Putting all that together was really enjoyable."

Martin Chávez said that as chair of the committee Sánchez impaneled, he worked to keep advisers at arm's length even while collecting information from them. "Doctors, lawyers, insurance companies: They had all been getting their fingers into the pie," Martin Chávez said of the years leading up to reform. He acknowledged that he was among lawyers who had been in the mix prior to reform, which included a cap on what lawyers could charge in workers' compensation cases. "I cut my own throat. I was the one who wrote the law that led to many lawyers leaving the field. They wouldn't talk to me anymore."

A key part of the reform, Martin Chávez said, was "designing a system that for the most part didn't require lawyers to come in" as often. "People on the committee came to agree that we're all New Mexicans. We all wanted what's best for the state. The message was simple: If workers' comp rates are too high, businesses fail. If businesses fail, there's no work for those who need jobs."

Fabián Chávez Jr. contributed to securing cooperation, said Martin Chávez. "Fabián was a critical player. He has extraordinary people skills."

Also in 1990, major change worked its way into health care insurance accorded for the first time to thousands of retired state government employees. Working closely with the state house majority whip, Ben Luján of Nambé, Chávez pressed for adoption of the New Mexico Retiree Health Care Act.[2] In the senate, Republican stalwart Billy McKibben of Hobbs carried the legislation. The intent was to create for state government workers

⇥ FIGURE 32. ⇤
Fabián Chávez Jr. (right) visits with Pres. Bill Clinton.
Chávez continued to be a respected authority in New Mexico politics
as the new millennium approached. Photo by LeRoy N. Sanchez.
Courtesy Fabián Chávez Jr. LeRoy N. Sanchez, Photographer. Santa Fe, NM.

a retiree health care program similar to what public educators already had access to.

There was enough support for the idea that the first bill introduced in the legislature was passed by both the house and the senate and sent to Gov. Garrey Carruthers for his signature midway through session, said Chávez. The measure was flawed, though. "There were a number of problems with the bill, including the fact that it wasn't properly funded," Chávez said. "Jerry Fickes told me the proposed bill would be a disaster before we knew it, so I went to Maralyn Budke and told her the bill wouldn't work. Maralyn Budke was, for all intents and purposes, assistant governor, much as she had been for David Cargo. I asked that the bill be vetoed by the governor. Then I got people together in the legislature, including Ben Luján, and we came back with a bill that was workable."

Once in place, state workers had the option of joining the new health care program as part of their retirement package that already included other benefits from the Public Employees Retirement Association. The state insurance superintendent or his designee serves on the board of directors and has total oversight authority.

Luján said creation of the program was a response to increasing difficulties in choices forced upon retirees. "Many had to choose between health care or making ends meet for other basic necessities," Luján said. "With the increasing health care costs, far too many retirees were struggling. I felt that for all the years of hard work, dedication, contributions in their service to the citizens and the state of New Mexico, this was no way to spend their retirement."

McKibben said the program has met all expectations. "I'm very pleased that I can put that one in the accomplishments column," he said. "So many requests come in, and there's no way the legislature can fund them all. But when you set priorities, if health care is not at the top, what would be? Fabián realized that, and he worked hard to get it done."

More than fifteen years after its creation, Luján said the program was meeting expectations. "In this day of increasing costs and complexity, it has been well run and well controlled to provide the maximum support to our retirees," he said.

The same could not be said, however, for the company created to help small businesses secure workers' compensation insurance. "There were some scandals among ranking administrators of the New Mexico Mutual Casualty Company," Chávez said. "Four of them had arranged to secure substantial golden parachutes for themselves as well as other major monetary enhancement. I had been gone from the state insurance department for about a decade and in 2003, I asked Gov. Bill Richardson to appoint me to the company's board to help clean up the operation and to ensure that we recruited top-notch administrators." All but one of the administrators who had become embroiled in controversy had already left; the last one was on his way out as the search began for a new president.

"We contracted with a search firm and attracted some very qualified people," Chávez said. "We went through the whole process and after months came down to the top three. We were about a week away from a selection when we got word that Governor Richardson wanted us to hire Chris Krahling, someone who wasn't even among the final ten on our list. Until that call, it was apparent that we were going to be unanimous in our selection of Robert Kellogg, a man from Michigan who already had been successful as president of one or two companies. This guy really stood out.

"Chris succeeded me as state superintendent of insurance, and he became a good friend of mine. I like Chris. I had supported him for another position in our company's administration but not as president. Chris had very good contacts with independent insurance agents, but he didn't have the experience needed to serve as president of our company.

"I told others on the board that we should stick with what our search process had produced. I said I would resign from the board if we departed from the process we agreed to follow. Prior to all that, Chris had withdrawn his name from consideration, and after we had reached the three finalists, he asked that we put his name back among the candidates. Three or four days before we were to select a candidate from the finalists, a special meeting of the board was called solely to interview Chris."

Bill García of Santa Fe, well regarded in business and government circles, was board chairman. He sided with Chávez in backing Kellogg, but after the board's vote was hung at four to four, García said he sent the board home for the night. He changed his vote the following day, and Krahling was hired. "Bill talked Bob Kellogg into coming in as chief operating officer, but I resigned, as I said I would. If there's an upside to what transpired, it's that Kellogg, in my estimation, has been the one running the company."

García said the team, led by Krahling, has worked well. "Chris has proven to be extremely effective, and the company is strong."

It was not the way Chávez had hoped to end his reform-minded efforts in insurance, begun in 1988 when he became the state's superintendent overseeing the industry. Carruthers recalled Chávez as "a pretty sophisticated operator" in his work as state superintendent. "The only time we saw the superintendent of insurance was on budgetary issues or occasionally when he would ask me to support or veto a bill," Carruthers said. "I never thought of him as being intrusive. I never thought of him as asking for anything that was out of the ordinary or unusual. Fabián always stayed in touch. He pretty much kept you up-to-date. There were never any surprises from the department of insurance."

Paula Tackett, as director of the Legislative Council Service, said she and her staff worked with Chávez in crafting legislation for his various missions. "Fabián is so smart. He mostly knew what he wanted. I think there is some staff that would say, 'God, could he stop talking so I could get the work done.' But with Fabián, you could also say, 'I'd love to work with you on this, but could we do it later because I'm very busy right now?'"

Tackett suggested she did not put Chávez off often. "I always liked working with Fabián because he always loved taking on the big guys and winning."

James Koch said Chávez's work as insurance superintendent shone brighter than all his other accomplishments. "Of all the other things he's done, that's what he did the best," Koch said. "He was very thorough, very fair. Surprisingly, there was no politics. He brought a professionalism to that office that hadn't been there before."

Fickes has worked with commissioners, superintendents, or directors of insurance in many states since the 1960s. "There were some very good ones . . . but none of them was a Fabián Chávez," he said. "Fabián's time helped people from coast to coast, even people who never met or heard of him."

Chávez's reputation in 2007 led to a proposal to name a planned new PERA building after him. Chávez, who served on the PERA board of directors from 1999 through 2003, suggested otherwise. The building should be named after the employees who contribute to the association's $13-billion retirement fund, he said. In the process, he warned the association to beware of groups that might be out to gain control of the board and its substantial pension fund. He referred specifically to the large labor union, AFSCME, which helped him win a seat on the PERA board and was contributing increasing sums to get people elected to the board. AFSCME denied it was doing anything out of line.

Tackett said Chávez's willingness to jump into the big fights did not surprise her. "I think it's in his family blood," she said. "I would think most politicians are happy to get publicity when they can, but I really think Fabián just likes to take on the giants. Maybe he likes the reputation of being a giantkiller because he has done it over and again. Politicians are known to talk a bit. But I've said that if Fabián has done just half of what he says, it's ten times more than the rest of us will do in a lifetime."

Conclusion

If this man named Fabián had shown himself to be undeterred by life's biggest challenges through most of the twentieth century, he found himself five years into the new millennium up against perhaps his most demanding test ever. The person dearest to him was at his side. In fact, it was she for whom he battled.

Coral Jeanne Chávez would not have expected it to be any other way.

"She was a Kansas flower who blossomed after being transplanted in New Mexico," Fabián was fond of saying.

Coral Jeanne was enamored of her husband, proud of his many accomplishments. "As a legislator, Fabián was so interested in helping other people and trying to pass legislation that would help people in a positive way," she said as work on this book began. "It was wonderful to watch him convince others about what needed to be done. He would take things that nobody else would try to pass in the legislature. I think it had a lot to do with his upbringing, his parents, and his experiences in the war.

"His family had such a big influence on him before and after the war. He was brought up to be honest and sincere and to fight for the rights of other people."

Coral Jeanne also was understanding about her husband's shortfalls, particularly his failed attempts to win election to Congress and the governor's office. "I think that some people in the government at that time were jealous of Fabián and felt threatened by him because he was so honest and straightforward. That's how I felt about it then, and I still do."

Watching Fabián respond to failure fueled Coral Jeanne's admiration. "He was disappointed, but he didn't fall apart or quit doing the things that he thought were necessary. He bounced back like a rubber ball," said the woman who did not like large political gatherings and was cool toward Washington. "He really didn't require much counseling or hand-holding on my part. He wasn't bitter or mean or anything like that. He took it like a man, and we went on with our lives. We kept doing things together, which is what you do when you love somebody a lot."

Fabián said it was Coral Jeanne, more than anyone or anything, who kept him going during high times and low. "She was always so beautiful, so classy; one of God's great creations. I was always so proud to have her on my arm, and I always felt like I had to do my very best just to keep up with her. I never wanted to disappoint her."

Their lives had become unalterably entwined as reflected in evidence big and small. Coral Jeanne, for example, kept some of her most treasured jewelry in the carefully crafted hardwood cigar box that once had been packed with Fidel Castro's favored smokes and that the Cuban leader had given to Fabián following their extraordinary meeting in Havana.

Coral Jeanne had grown seriously ill in 2005 and for the most part had confined herself to the condominium little more than a stone's throw from the Governor's Mansion in Santa Fe's eastern foothills that she and her husband had picked as their final home.

Fabián was with her most of the time, and when he'd leave briefly, he turned to his cell phone for frequent checks. "I was a free spirit and a self-appointed playboy as a young man," Fabián said. "Then I was introduced to Coral Jeanne, and everything changed for me. She became my compass, and she gave me purpose. How could I not be at her side when the trials of old age started visiting both of us?"

On a Sunday in October 2006, Fabián was tending to one of Coral Jeanne's customary morning pleasures. "I had just taken tea and 'crumpets' to her bedside," he said. "We playfully called them crumpets, but they really were just her favorite Danishes that I would cut into small slices. She was in the bathroom, and I heard her start to make her way out, so I moved toward the door. She looked faint, and, suddenly, she collapsed toward me. I caught her and almost immediately realized that my darling wife had died in my arms."

The profound love affair that began on a hardwood dance floor at El Nido early in 1949 had ended in almost-storybook fashion just weeks after both man and wife had turned eighty-two. A family friend, Franciscan Father Crespin Butz, presided over Coral Jeanne's funeral Mass and Monsignor Jerome Martínez gave the homily. It was in the grand Cathedral Basilica of St. Francis off Santa Fe's Plaza from which church leaders fifty-two years earlier had steadfastly refused marriage to the "Kansas flower" and her adoring companion, whose family's devotion to the church was a prominent part of everyday life.

Fabián was a high school dropout who returned from World War II to earn a GED while boarding at an aunt's house near Highlands University. He was a great thinker, and his plan was to become a lawyer. Limited finances and the lure of politics pressed him to cut college courses short, before getting a bachelor's, much less a law degree.

"I don't think a college degree is evidence of smarts, especially in Fabián's early days," said longtime state legislative aide Paula Tackett. "There were members of the legislature then who maybe had no more than an eighth-grade education: farmers, ranchers, store owners. Fabián is smart . . . Smaaaaaart!"

For Richard Folmar, the ranking legislative aide who worked with Fabián on liquor reform, there were few with Fabián's knowledge. "He knew this state backwards and forwards. He knew the legislature backwards and forwards. He knew the people. God, he would have been a good governor."

Others of diverse backgrounds and reputations agreed. "Fabián is almost a symbol of public service to those of us who have been around for more than three or four decades. He's always ready to serve," said former Republican Gov. Garrey Carruthers. "In a kidding way I say there, if not for me, goes the greatest hustler in the world. Fabián has a charming way about him. He always had that big smile and that great handshake. I think he is the epitome of the friendly New Mexican.

"I would guess his adversaries thought of him as someone who would listen to their views even if he didn't accept all of them. That's the mark of a good political leader: someone who can listen to people and get the job done . . . He's just a stylish guy."

Manny Aragón recalls that one of his first political acts was, out of family loyalty, to oppose Fabián in the 1968 primary race for governor. Aragón, the Albuquerque South Valley Democrat who spent many of his thirty years in the state senate as one of the chamber's leaders, was twenty years old when he was pulled into the kind of political strategizing that would color his own future. "My dad and a lot of the politicians he worked with were opposing Fabián at the time, and they set up a deal to support Bruce King," Aragón said.

"I was getting a haircut, and my uncle Benny, who was in the legislature, came in and told my dad they should reestablish the Young Democrats of Bernalillo County for the sole purpose of endorsing King. For lack of anybody else, they said, 'Let's get Manny to do it.' My only mission was to get elected president of the county's Young Democrats and then endorse Bruce King.

"It was funny because my dad and uncle had tremendous respect for Fabián, but it was the justice of the peace thing that they didn't like. There were a lot of people in the JP system who were very helpful in what we were doing to beat Fabián. Fabián never disrespected my dad. He didn't hold any grudges. It's strange because I came from a family of old-time politics. Me being raised as an ordinary citizen, grudges were a part of life. Fabián knew my dad and uncle were in the opposition, but he always continued to reach out.

"Fabián saw that I was supporting King, and he said, 'Bruce King is a good guy. If you're going to support someone, do your best, don't worry about it. Don't tell someone that you're supporting him and then don't work for him.' What did it matter to Fabián? I was twenty and couldn't even vote. It just showed what always impressed me about Fabián: He was a high-level, classy kind of politician."

Much of state government beginning in the late 1960s has been run out of buildings that were constructed or remodeled under legislation Fabián was instrumental in getting passed. "We constructed the Roundhouse; the state library, which later became an annex to the Roundhouse. We remodeled the Bataan Memorial Building. We provided money to buy the Lamy Building and to purchase the property where the PERA Building was constructed in 1965."

Purchasing property to be obtained later by the Public Employees Retirement Association brushed Fabián up against many old, familiar names. Among them was that of Doña Tules, the prominent and controversial gambling hall proprietor of Santa Fe's 1800s whose funeral procession, led by Archbishop Lamy, was punctuated by a local priest some thought to have been her lover.

The property for generations had served as the city's main Roman Catholic cemetery until Rosario Cemetery was opened across town in 1865. The abandoned, neglected cemetery is the one Fabián had crossed innumerable times as a boy because it stood between his childhood home and just about everything else that figured into his young life. "Before the PERA Building went up, the church desanctified the property, recovered whatever bones still existed, and then reburied them in a common grave at Rosario," Fabián said.

Fabián's ultimate political goal was to serve in Congress—first the House, then the Senate. If he had won in his first attempt to get there in 1964, he likely would have stayed in Washington for as long as voters wanted. Governors' races would have been left for others. "The one factor that would have changed that would have been my darling wife," he said. "She didn't particularly care for Washington, especially in the humid heat from July through September. If serving in Washington in any way would have jeopardized my relationship with Coral Jeanne, I would not have stayed in Congress."

It is an unambiguous statement of love from a man who acknowledged that he had displayed an abundance of interest in women as a young man. It is also a statement that might put into perspective some of his conduct later in life. Fabián was engaging and genuine as a public speaker but "acted differently around women, especially if they were attractive," said David Cox, who, with considerable admiration, served Fabián as an insurance actuary late in his career. "He made compliments and acted overchivalrous," Cox said. Embarrassing at times, he said the conduct was "probably a product of [Fabián's] generation and culture."

Enmeshed in an arena characterized by flirtation and dalliance, Fabián said he enjoyed his wife's trust. "I never would have done anything to hurt her. God never made a more wonderful person," he said.

Early in his political career, Fabián, while campaigning, came upon a storekeeper in Mora County who pointed to wooden cabinets and identified them as handiwork of Fabián's father. Fabián said he never forgot that he was carrying his family's name wherever he went. As a delinquent kid, Fabián often was admonished not to embarrass his brother. He came to recognize that to mean his brother, Angélico, the priest.

Respect, in truth, flowed in multiple directions within the Chávez family. Fabián's brother, Cuate, became a trusted political confidant and took to his grave disdain for at least some of Fabián's opponents. The longtime Santa Fe municipal judge helped organize Democrats for Schmitt in 1976 when entrenched Democratic powerbroker Joseph M. Montoya was dislodged from the U.S. Senate by Republican moonwalker Harrison "Jack" Schmitt.

It was the Senate seat Fabián had hoped would be his one day.

As Fabián battled to recover from his wife's death, he began giving away memorabilia accumulated over the years: small cards from his first legislative race; campaign buttons from his 1968 campaign for governor; an impressive silver and turquoise paperweight whose design he selected for New Mexico's golden anniversary; a watercolor of the White House; a lapel pin with Jimmy Carter's signature and still in its original packaging; the cigar box Fidel Castro had given him. Donated years earlier to the College of Santa Fe were copies of the Great Books and the *Federalist Papers* that Fabián had bought in the 1960s at the suggestion of Jack Campbell.

It is as if this remarkably driven man of great pride had suddenly lost his need to impress, perhaps even had shed some of his desire to reminisce about certain events in his life that to him curiously no longer seemed as important.

They were important, though. "With just a few others, Fabián is in that category of being bigger than the rest of us who have been in public service," said Garrey Carruthers.

Another former governor, Jerry Apodaca, said Fabián is one of the few people in New Mexico who came to be known from one corner to the other by his first name alone. Evidence of that is visible in the quotations throughout this book. This author refers to him in these last few pages only by that name as a subtle acknowledgement of Apodaca's assertion.

Fabián.

A friend counseled him against giving away too much following Coral Jeanne's death. "Sadly, she's gone," the friend said, "but you likely still have several good years left. Don't be hasty to withdraw."

The advice must have resonated for Fabián. Coral Jeanne herself said one could never count her husband out on the things that matter in people's lives. It's what made him Fabián.

NOTES

Chapter 1

1. Fray Angélico Chávez and Thomas E. Chávez, *Wake for a Fat Vicar* (Albuquerque: LPD Press, 2004), 47.
2. Ibid, 48.
3. Ibid, 47.
4. Ibid, 49.
5. Ibid, 109–10.
6. Ibid, 110.
7. Ibid, 110.
8. Richard W. Etulain, ed., *New Mexican Lives: Profiles and Historical Stories* (Albuquerque: University of New Mexico Press, 2002), 126.
9. Ibid, 126.
10. Tony Hillerman, ed., *The Spell of New Mexico* (Albuquerque: University of New Mexico Press, 1976), 64.
11. Dan Murphy, *New Mexico: The Distant Land* (Northridge, CA: Windsor Publications, 1985), 120.
12. Paul Horgan, *The Centuries of Santa Fe* (New York: Dutton, 1956), 272.
13. Ibid, 272.
14. Ibid, 272.
15. Fray Angélico Chávez, *Chavez, A Distinctive American Clan of New Mexico* (Santa Fe: William Gannon, 1989), 3–5.
16. Ibid, 41–54.
17. Robert J. Tórrez, "A Cuarto Centennial History of New Mexico," in *New Mexico Blue Book, 1997–1998* (Santa Fe: Office of the Secretary of State, 1997), 32.
18. Ibid, 33.
19. Ibid, 33.
20. Chávez, *Chavez*, xii.

Chapter 2

1. *Wikipedia*, s.v. "Pomona, California," http://www.cipomona.ca.us/ (accessed August 26, 2005).
2. Ibid.
3. Ibid.
4. Ibid.
5. Ibid.

Chapter 3

1. Lorrena E. Keenan, *A Brief History of Springer, New Mexico*, http://www.nenewmexico.com (accessed September 11, 2005).
2. Ibid.
3. Ibid.
4. Ibid.
5. Ibid.
6. Ibid.
7. Ibid.
8. Ibid.
9. Anselmo Arellano, written remarks for delivery at Springer's 125th founding anniversary, August 2004.
10. Ibid.
11. Ibid.
12. Ibid.
13. Ibid.
14. Ibid.
15. Ibid.
16. Records of historian Anselmo Arellano.
17. Ibid.

Chapter 4

1. The Detroit News, *War in Headlines, 1939–1945* (Detroit: Michigan Book Binding Co., n.d.), 1, 4, 5.
2. Ibid, 8, 9, 10, 13.
3. Records of Fabián Chávez Jr.
4. The Detroit News, *War in Headlines*, 91.
5. Ibid.
6. Ibid.
7. Ibid.
8. Ibid, 92.
9. Ibid, 92.
10. Ibid, 93.
11. Ibid, 48.
12. Ibid, 93.
13. Ibid, 93.
14. Ibid, 94.
15. Records of Otis Martin and J. C. Slade, 153rd Field Artillery Battalion.

16. Hillerman, *The Spell of New Mexico*, 84–86.

17. Horgan, *The Centuries of Santa Fe*, 327.

Chapter 5

1. Warren A. Beck, *New Mexico: A History of Four Centuries* (Norman: University of Oklahoma Press, 1962), 219–21.

2. Ibid, 222.

3. María E. Montoya, "Dennis Chavez and the Making of Modern New Mexico," in *New Mexico Lives: Profiles and Historical Stories*, ed. Richard W. Etulain (Albuquerque: University of New Mexico Press, 2002), 246.

4. Ibid, 246.

5. Ibid, 247.

6. *New Mexico Blue Book, 1997–1998* (Santa Fe: Office of the Secretary of State, 1997), 102.

7. Arthur Thomas Hannett, *Sagebrush Lawyer* (New York: Pageant Press, 1964), 192.

8. Ibid, 192.

9. Ibid, 194–95.

10. Ibid, 195–96.

11. Ibid, 195.

12. *New Mexico Blue Book, 1997–1998*, 102.

13. Montoya, "Dennis Chavez and the Making of Modern New Mexico," 242, 247.

14. Ibid, 242.

15. Ibid, 242.

16. Ibid, 243.

Chapter 7

1. New Mexico Secretary of State, Official Results of 1948 Democratic Primary Election, New Mexico State Capitol North, Santa Fe, New Mexico, June 23, 1948, 517.

2. Ibid, 458.

3. Ibid, 493.

4. Ibid, 493.

5. Ibid, 458, 493, 517.

6. New Mexico Secretary of State, Official Results of 1950 Democratic Primary Election, New Mexico State Capitol North, Santa Fe, New Mexico, June 6, 1950, 274, 275.

7. Ibid.

8. Ibid.

9. Ibid.

10. New Mexico Secretary of State, Official Results of 1950 General Election, New Mexico State Capitol North, Santa Fe, New Mexico, November 7, 1950, 97, 98.

11. Ibid.

12. New Mexico Secretary of State, Official Results of 1950 Democratic Primary Election, New Mexico State Capitol North, Santa Fe, New Mexico, June 6, 1950, 121.

13. New Mexico Secretary of State, Official Results of 1950 General Election, New Mexico State Capitol North, Santa Fe, New Mexico, November 7, 1950, 1.

14. From the records of Fabián Chávez Jr.
15. Nevada Legislative Council, "Assembly History, Nevada Legislature at Carson City" (Carson City, 1965), 6.
16. New Mexico Secretary of State, Official Results of 1952 Democratic Primary Election, New Mexico State Capitol North, Santa Fe, New Mexico, May 6, 1952, 401, 402.
17. New Mexico Secretary of State, Official Results of 1952 Republican Primary Election, New Mexico State Capitol North, Santa Fe, New Mexico, May 6, 1952, 401, 402.
18. New Mexico Secretary of State, Official Results of 1952 General Election, New Mexico State Capitol North, November 4, 1952, 178, 179.
19. Ibid.
20. Ibid.
21. Ibid.
22. Ibid.
23. Ibid.
24. Ibid, 2.
25. New Mexico Secretary of State, Official Results of 1956 Democratic Primary Election, New Mexico State Capitol North, Santa Fe, New Mexico, May 5, 1956, 70.
26. Ibid.
27. Ibid.
28. Ibid.
29. Ibid.
30. Ibid.
31. Ibid.
32. Ibid.
33. New Mexico Secretary of State, Official Results of 1956 General Election, New Mexico State Capitol North, Santa Fe, New Mexico, November 6, 1956, 109.
34. Ibid.
35. *New Mexico Blue Book, 1997–1998*, 69.
36. Ibid.

Chapter 8

1. New Mexico Secretary of State, Official Results of 1946 General Election, New Mexico State Capitol North, Santa Fe, New Mexico, November 5, 1946, n.p.
2. Ibid, n.p.
3. New Mexico Secretary of State, Official Results of 1946 Democratic Primary Election, New Mexico State Capitol North, Santa Fe, New Mexico, June 4, 1946, n.p.
4. New Mexico Secretary of State, Official Results of 1948 Democratic Primary Election, New Mexico State Capitol North, Santa Fe, New Mexico, June 23, 1948, 236.
5. Ibid, 238.
6. Ibid, 237.
7. New Mexico Secretary of State, Official Results of 1948 General Election, New Mexico State Capitol North, Santa Fe, New Mexico, November 2, 1948, n.p.

8. New Mexico Secretary of State, Official Results of 1950 Democratic Primary Election, New Mexico State Capitol North, Santa Fe, New Mexico, June 6, 1950, 121.

9. Ibid, 121.

10. New Mexico Legislative Council Service, New Mexico State Capitol, Opening Day Roster, Journal of the House of Representatives, New Mexico Legislature (Santa Fe, 1947), 2.

11. *World Book Encyclopedia*, 75th ed., s.v. "Korean War."

12. New Mexico Secretary of State, Official Results of 1950 General Election, New Mexico State Capitol North, Santa Fe, New Mexico, November 7, 1950, 1.

13. Ibid.

14. New Mexico Secretary of State, Official Results of 1952 Democratic Primary Election, New Mexico State Capitol North, Santa Fe, New Mexico, May 6, 1952, 236.

15. New Mexico Secretary of State, Official Results of 1952 General Election, New Mexico State Capitol North, Santa Fe, New Mexico, November 4, 1952, 2.

16. Ibid, 401, 402.

17. New Mexico Secretary of State, Official Results of 1954 General Election, New Mexico State Capitol North, Santa Fe, New Mexico, November 2, 1954, 1.

18. Ibid.

19. New Mexico Secretary of State, Official Results of 1956 General Election, New Mexico State Capitol North, Santa Fe, New Mexico, November 6, 1956, 11.

20. Ibid, 11.

21. Ibid, 109.

22. New Mexico Secretary of State, Official Results of 1958 General Election, New Mexico State Capitol North, Santa Fe, New Mexico, November 20, 1958, 77.

23. New Mexico Secretary of State, Official Results of 1960 General Election, New Mexico State Capitol North, Santa Fe, New Mexico, November 8, 1960, 1.

24. *New Mexico Blue Book, 1997–1998*, 105–6.

25. Ibid, 106.

Chapter 9

1. New Mexico Legislative Council Service, New Mexico State Capitol, Journal of the House of Representatives (Santa Fe, 1959), 42.

2. *World Book Encyclopedia*, 75th ed., s.v. "Brown v. Board of Education of Topeka."

3. New Mexico Legislative Council Service, New Mexico State Capitol, Journal of the House of Representatives (Santa Fe, 1955), 78–79.

4. Record of New Mexico State Majority Leaders compiled by Fabián Chávez Jr., 1961, Fabián Chávez Jr. Papers, Santa Fe, New Mexico.

Chapter 10

1. U.S. Bureau of the Census, *U.S. Census, 1960* (Washington, DC: U.S. Bureau of the Census, 1960), http://www.census.gov/population/censusdata/urpop0090.txt.

2. New Mexico Legislative Council Service, New Mexico State Capitol, Senate Reapportionment Act (Santa Fe, 1966), n.p.

3. *World Book Encyclopedia*, 75th ed., s.v. "Baker v. Carr."

4. Ibid.

5. New Mexico Secretary of State, Official Results of 1966 General Election, New Mexico State Capitol North, Santa Fe, New Mexico, November 23, 1966, n.p.

6. *New Mexico Blue Book, 1997–1998*, 106.

7. Ibid.

8. New Mexico Secretary of State, Official Results of 1958 General Election, New Mexico State Capitol North, Santa Fe, New Mexico, November 20, 1958, 77.

9. *El Senador*, videotape (Albuquerque: University of New Mexico Center for Regional Studies, 2000).

10. Ibid.

11. Ibid.

12. Ibid.

13. Ibid.

14. New Mexico Secretary of State, Official Results of 1962 General Election, New Mexico State Capitol North, Santa Fe, New Mexico, November 6, 1962, n.p.

15. New Mexico Secretary of State, Official Results of 1964 General Election, New Mexico State Capitol North, Santa Fe, New Mexico, November 3, 1964, n.p.

16. *New Mexico Blue Book, 1997–1998*, 69.

17. Ibid, 106.

18. New Mexico Secretary of State, Official Results of 1982 General Election, New Mexico State Capitol North, Santa Fe, New Mexico, November 23, 1982, n.p.

19. New Mexico Secretary of State, Official Results of 1968 Democratic Primary Election, New Mexico State Capitol North, Santa Fe, New Mexico, September 17, 1968, n.p.

20. Ibid.

21. Ibid.

22. Ibid.

23. New Mexico Secretary of State, Official Results of 1968 Republican Primary Election, New Mexico State Capitol North, Santa Fe, New Mexico, September 17, 1968, n.p.

24. Ibid.

25. New Mexico Secretary of State, Official Results of 1968 General Election, New Mexico State Capitol North, Santa Fe, New Mexico, November 8, 1968, n.p.

26. Ibid.

Chapter 11

1. New Mexico Legislative Council Service, New Mexico State Capitol, Journal of the Senate (Santa Fe, 2002), 2.

2. Jake W. Spidle Jr., *Doctors of Medicine in New Mexico* (Albuquerque: University of New Mexico Press, 1986), 291.

3. Ibid, 290–91.

4. Ibid, 312.

5. Ibid, 283–87.

6. Ibid, 283–87.

7. Ibid, 283–87.

8. Ibid, 311.

9. Ibid, 312.

10. Ibid, 312.

11. Ibid, 313.

12. Ibid, 316.

13. Ibid, 323.

14. Ibid, 324.

15. Ibid, 318.

16. Ibid, 325.

Chapter 12

1. State Judicial System Study Committee, *The Courts in New Mexico, January 1961* (Santa Fe: New Mexico Legislative Council Service, 1961), 10.

2. Ibid, 15.

3. Ibid, 32.

4. Ibid, 1.

5. Ibid, 1.

6. Ibid, 1.

7. Ibid, 6.

8. Ibid, 5.

9. Ibid, 5.

10. Ibid, 7.

11. Ibid, 5, 6.

12. Ibid, 8.

13. Ibid, 9.

14. Ibid, 11.

15. Ibid, 14.

16. Ibid, 15, 16.

17. Ibid, 18.

18. Ibid, 18.

19. Ibid, 19.

20. Ibid, 34.

21. Ibid, 35.

22. Ibid, 36.

23. Ibid, 36.

24. Ibid, 36.

25. Ibid, 36.

26. New Mexico Legislative Council Service, New Mexico State Capitol, Laws of the State of New Mexico passed by the first regular session of the Twenty-seventh Legislature (Santa Fe, 1965), 2:1534–36.

27. Ibid, 2:1527–28.

28. Thomas A. Donnelly and Pamela B. Minzner, "History of the New Mexico Court of Appeals," *New Mexico Law Review* 22, no. 3 (1992): 596–97.

29. New Mexico Legislative Council Service, New Mexico State Capitol, Laws of the State of New Mexico passed by the first session and the special session of the Twenty-eighth Legislature (Santa Fe, 1967), 1622–24.

30. New Mexico Secretary of State, Official Results of 1965 Special Election, New Mexico State Capitol North, Santa Fe, New Mexico, October 11, 1965, n.p.

31. New Mexico Secretary of State, Official Results of 1966 General Election, New Mexico State Capitol North, Santa Fe, New Mexico, November 23, 1966, n.p.

32. Donnelly and Minzner, "History of the New Mexico Court of Appeals," 603.

33. Ibid, 604.

Chapter 13

1. New Mexico Statutes, 46–9–11.
2. Ibid.
3. Ibid.
4. Richard Folmar, State Restrictions on Local Government Liquor License Fees, the 1962 Liquor Price Survey and Other Memoranda Prepared for the New Mexico Legislature (Santa Fe: New Mexico Legislative Council Service, 1964), 67.
5. *Drink, Inc. v. Babcock*, 77 N.M. 277, 421 P.2d 798 (S. Ct. 1966).

Chapter 14

1. New Mexico Secretary of State, Official Results of 1958 Democratic Primary Election, New Mexico State Capitol North, Santa Fe, New Mexico, May 13, 1958, 1.
2. New Mexico Secretary of State, Official Results of 1964 Democratic Primary Election, New Mexico State Capitol North, Santa Fe, New Mexico, May 5, 1964, 1.
3. Ibid.
4. Ibid.
5. Ibid.
6. Ibid.
7. Ibid.
8. Ibid.
9. Ibid.
10. Ibid.
11. Ibid.
12. Ibid.
13. Ibid.
14. Ibid.
15. Ibid.
16. New Mexico Secretary of State, Official Results of 1964 General Election, New Mexico State Capitol North, Santa Fe, New Mexico, November 3, 1964, n.p.
17. Ibid.
18. Ibid.

Chapter 15

1. New Mexico Secretary of State, Official Results of 1966 Democratic Primary Election, New Mexico State Capitol North, Santa Fe, New Mexico, May 3, 1966, n.p.
2. Ibid.
3. New Mexico Secretary of State, Official Results of 1966 Republican Primary Election, New Mexico State Capitol North, Santa Fe, New Mexico, May 24, 1966, 2.
4. Ibid.
5. *New Mexico Blue Book, 1965–1966* (Santa Fe: Office of the Secretary of State, 1965), 116.
6. New Mexico Secretary of State, Official Results of 1966 General Election, New Mexico State Capitol North, Santa Fe, New Mexico, November 23, 1966, n.p.
7. Ibid.
8. Ibid.
9. Ibid.

10. Ibid.

11. New Mexico Secretary of State, Official Results of 1968 Democratic Primary Election, New Mexico State Capitol North, Santa Fe, New Mexico, September 17, 1968, 1.

12. Ibid.

13. Ibid.

14. Ibid.

15. Ibid.

16. Ibid.

17. Ibid.

18. Ibid.

19. Ibid.

20. Ibid.

21. Ibid.

22. Ibid.

23. New Mexico Secretary of State, Official Results of 1968 General Election, New Mexico State Capitol North, Santa Fe, New Mexico, November 8, 1968, n.p.

24. New Mexico Secretary of State, Official Results of 1968 Democratic Primary Election, New Mexico State Capitol North, Santa Fe, New Mexico, September 17, 1968, n.p.

25. New Mexico Secretary of State, Official Results of 1966 Democratic Primary Election, New Mexico State Capitol North, Santa Fe, New Mexico, May 3, 1966, 1.

26. New Mexico Secretary of State, Official Results of 1966 General Election, New Mexico State Capitol North, Santa Fe, New Mexico, November 23, 1966, n.p.

27. New Mexico Secretary of State, Official Results of 1968 General Election, New Mexico State Capitol North, Santa Fe, New Mexico, November 8, 1968, n.p.

28. New Mexico Secretary of State, Official Results of 1968 Democratic Primary Election, New Mexico State Capitol North, Santa Fe, New Mexico, September 17, 1968, 1.

29. New Mexico Secretary of State, Official Results of 1968 General Election, New Mexico State Capitol North, Santa Fe, New Mexico, November 8, 1968, 1.

30. Ibid.

31. New Mexico Secretary of State, Official Results of 1968 Democratic Primary Election, New Mexico State Capitol North, Santa Fe, New Mexico, September 17, 1968, 1.

32. New Mexico Secretary of State, Official Results of 1968 General Election, New Mexico State Capitol North, Santa Fe, New Mexico, November 8, 1968, n.p.

33. Ibid.

34. Ibid.

35. Ibid.

36. New Mexico Secretary of State, Official Results of 1966 General Election, New Mexico State Capitol North, Santa Fe, New Mexico, November 23, 1966, n.p.

37. New Mexico Secretary of State, Official Results of 1968 General Election, New Mexico State Capitol North, Santa Fe, New Mexico, November 8, 1968, n.p.

38. Ibid.

39. Ibid.

40. Ibid.

41. Ibid.

42. Ibid.

43. Ibid.

44. Ibid.

45. New Mexico Secretary of State, Official Results of 1970 General Election, New Mexico State Capitol North, Santa Fe, New Mexico, November 18, 1970, 1.

46. New Mexico Secretary of State, Official Results of 1968 General Election, New Mexico State Capitol North, Santa Fe, New Mexico, November 8, 1968, n.p.

47. New Mexico Secretary of State, Official Results of 1970 General Election, New Mexico State Capitol North, Santa Fe, New Mexico, November 18, 1970, 1.

48. New Mexico Secretary of State, Official Results of 1970 Democratic Primary Election, New Mexico State Capitol North, Santa Fe, New Mexico, June 18, 1970, 1.

49. New Mexico Secretary of State, Official Results of 1970 General Election, New Mexico State Capitol North, Santa Fe, New Mexico, November 18, 1970, 1.

50. New Mexico Secretary of State, Official Results of 1982 Democratic Primary Election, New Mexico State Capitol North, Santa Fe, New Mexico, June 22, 1982, n.p.

51. Ibid.

52. New Mexico Secretary of State, Official Returns of 1982 General Election, New Mexico State Capitol North, Santa Fe, New Mexico, November 23, 1982, n.p.

Chapter 16

1. Bruce King, *Cowboy in the Roundhouse*, as told to Charles Poling (Santa Fe: Sunstone Press, 1998), 148.

2. "Vermejo Park Corp.," U.S. Rep. Tom Udall Papers, Washington, DC.

3. Ibid.

4. Ibid.

5. *World Book Encyclopedia*, 75th ed., s.v. "The 1976 Election."

6. Ibid.

Chapter 17

1. New Mexico Legislative Council Service, Laws of the State of New Mexico passed by the second session of the Thirty-ninth Legislature (Santa Fe, 1990), 33–63.

2. Ibid, 13–169.

BIBLIOGRAPHY

Beck, Warren A. *New Mexico: A History of Four Centuries*. Norman: University of Oklahoma Press, 1962.

Chávez, Fray Angélico. *Chavez, A Distinctive American Clan of New Mexico*. Santa Fe: William Gannon, 1989.

———, and Thomas E. Chávez. *Wake for a Fat Vicar*. Albuquerque: LPD Press, 2004.

Chávez, Fabián, Jr. Papers. Santa Fe, New Mexico.

The Detroit News. *War in Headlines, 1939–1945*. Detroit: Michigan Book Binding Co., n.d.

Donnelly, Thomas A., and Pamela B. Minzner. "History of the New Mexico Court of Appeals." *New Mexico Law Review* 22, no. 3 (1992): 596–97, 603, 604.

El Senador. Videotape. Albuquerque: University of New Mexico Center for Regional Studies, 2000.

Etulain, Richard W., ed. *New Mexican Lives: Profiles and Historical Stories*. Albuquerque: University of New Mexico Press, 2002.

Ferguson, Harvey. *The Spell of New Mexico*. Albuquerque: University of New Mexico Press, 1976.

Folmar, Richard. *State Restrictions on Local Government Liquor License Fees, the 1962 Liquor Price Survey and Other Memoranda Prepared for the New Mexico Legislature*. Santa Fe: New Mexico Legislative Council Service, 1964.

Hannett, Arthur Thomas. *Sagebrush Lawyer*. New York: Pageant Press, 1964.

Hillerman, Tony, ed. *The Spell of New Mexico*. Albuquerque: University of New Mexico Press, 1976.

Horgan, Paul. *The Centuries of Santa Fe*. New York: Dutton, 1956.

Keenan, Lorrena E. *A Brief History of Springer, New Mexico*. http://www.nenewmexico.com (accessed September 11, 2005).

King, Bruce. *Cowboy in the Roundhouse*. As told to Charles Poling. Santa Fe: Sunstone Press, 1998.

Montoya, María E. "Dennis Chavez and the Making of Modern New Mexico." In *New Mexican Lives: Profiles and Historical Stories*, edited by Richard W. Etulain, 242–64. Albuquerque: University of New Mexico Press, 2002.

Murphy, Dan. *New Mexico: The Distant Land*. Northridge, CA: Windsor Publications, 1985.

Nevada Legislative Council. "Assembly History, Nevada Legislature at Carson City." Carson City, 1965.

New Mexico Blue Book, 1965–1966. Santa Fe: Office of the Secretary of State, 1965.

New Mexico Blue Book, 1997–1998. Santa Fe: Office of the Secretary of State, 1997.

New Mexico Legislative Council Service, New Mexico State Capitol. Journal of the House of Representatives. Santa Fe, 1955, 1959.

————. Journal of the Senate. Santa Fe, 2002.

————. Laws of the State of New Mexico passed by the first regular session of the Twenty-seventh Legislature. Vol. 2. Santa Fe, 1965.

————. Laws of the State of New Mexico passed by the first session and the special session of the Twenty-eighth Legislature. Santa Fe, 1967.

————. Laws of the State of New Mexico passed by the second session of the Thirty-ninth Legislature. Santa Fe, 1990.

————. Laws of the State of New Mexico passed by the second special session of the Thirty-ninth Legislature. Santa Fe, 1990.

————. Opening Day Roster, Journal of the House of Representatives, New Mexico Legislature. Santa Fe, 1947.

————. Senate Reapportionment Act. Santa Fe, 1966.

New Mexico Secretary of State. Official Results of 1946 Democratic Primary Election. New Mexico State Capitol North. Santa Fe, New Mexico, June 4, 1946.

————. Official Results of 1946 General Election, New Mexico State Capitol North. Santa Fe, New Mexico, November 5, 1946.

————. Official Results of 1948 Democratic Primary Election, New Mexico State Capitol North. Santa Fe, New Mexico, June 23, 1948.

————. Official Results of 1948 General Election, New Mexico State Capitol North. Santa Fe, New Mexico, November 2, 1948.

————. Official Results of 1950 Democratic Primary Election, New Mexico State Capitol North. Santa Fe, New Mexico, June 6, 1950.

————. Official Results of 1950 General Election, New Mexico State Capitol North. Santa Fe, New Mexico, November 7, 1950.

————. Official Results of 1952 Democratic Primary Election, New Mexico State Capitol North. Santa Fe, New Mexico, May 6, 1952.

————. Official Results of 1952 General Election, New Mexico State Capitol North. Santa Fe, New Mexico, November 4, 1952.

————. Official Results of 1952 Republican Primary Election, New Mexico State Capitol North. Santa Fe, New Mexico, May 6, 1952.

————. Official Results of 1954 General Election, New Mexico State Capitol North. Santa Fe, New Mexico, November 2, 1954.

————. Official Results of 1956 Democratic Primary Election, New Mexico State Capitol North. Santa Fe, New Mexico, May 5, 1956.

————. Official Results of 1956 General Election, New Mexico State Capitol North. Santa Fe, New Mexico, November 6, 1956.

————. Official Results of 1958 Democratic Primary Election, New Mexico State Capitol North. Santa Fe, New Mexico, May 13, 1958.

————. Official Results of 1958 General Election, New Mexico State Capitol North. Santa Fe, New Mexico, November 20, 1958.

————. Official Results of 1960 General Election, New Mexico State Capitol North. Santa Fe, New Mexico, November 8, 1960.

————. Official Results of 1962 General Election, New Mexico State Capitol North. Santa Fe, New Mexico, November 6, 1962.

————. Official Results of 1964 Democratic Primary Election, New Mexico State Capitol North, Santa Fe, New Mexico, May 5, 1964.

————. Official Results of 1964 General Election, New Mexico State Capitol North. Santa Fe, New Mexico, November 3, 1964.

————. Official Results of 1965 Special Election, New Mexico State Capitol North. Santa Fe, New Mexico, October 11, 1965.

————. Official Results of 1966 Democratic Primary Election, New Mexico State Capitol North. Santa Fe, New Mexico, May 3, 1966.

————. Official Results of 1966 General Election, New Mexico State Capitol North. Santa Fe, New Mexico, November 23, 1966.

————. Official Results of 1966 Republican Primary Election, New Mexico State Capitol North, Santa Fe, New Mexico, May 24, 1966.

————. Official Results of 1968 Democratic Primary Election, New Mexico State Capitol North. Santa Fe, New Mexico, September 17, 1968.

————. Official Results of 1968 General Election, New Mexico State Capitol North. Santa Fe, New Mexico, November 8, 1968.

————. Official Results of 1968 Republican Primary Election, New Mexico State Capitol North. Santa Fe, New Mexico, September 17, 1968.

————. Official Results of 1970 Democratic Primary Election, New Mexico State Capitol North. Santa Fe, New Mexico, June 18, 1970.

————. Official Results of 1970 General Election, New Mexico State Capitol North. Santa Fe, New Mexico, November 18, 1970.

————. Official Results of 1982 Democratic Primary Election, New Mexico State Capitol North. Santa Fe, New Mexico, June 22, 1982.

————. Official Results of 1982 General Election, New Mexico State Capitol North. Santa Fe, New Mexico, November 23, 1982.

Richardson, Bill. *Between Worlds*. With Michael Ruby. New York: G. P. Putnam's Sons, 2005.

Spidle, Jake W., Jr. *Doctors of Medicine in New Mexico*. Albuquerque: University of New Mexico Press, 1986.

State Judicial System Study Committee. *The Courts in New Mexico, January 1961*. Santa Fe: New Mexico Legislative Council Service, 1961.

Tórrez, Robert J. "A Cuarto Centennial History of New Mexico." In *New Mexico Blue Book, 1997–1998*. Santa Fe: Office of the Secretary of State, 1997.

Udall, U.S. Rep. Tom. Papers. Washington, DC.

U.S. Bureau of the Census. *U.S. Census, 1960*. Washington, DC: U.S. Bureau of the Census, 1960. http://www.census.gov/population/censusdata/urpop0090.txt.

INDEX